THE BULLNOSE AND FLATNOSE MORRIS

Lytton P. Jarman and Robin I. Barraclough

Illustrated
by
Helen L. Stirling, Bray Webb
and Des Measures

DAVID & CHARLES

NEWTON ABBOT · LONDON · NORTH POMFRET (Vt) · VANCOUVER

Dedicated to the late JOHN POLLITT

ISBN 0 7153 6665 3
Library of Congress Catalog Card Number 75–42598

Printed in Great Britain
by Redwood Burn Limited   Trowbridge and Esher
for David & Charles (Publishers) Limited
Brunel House   Newton Abbot   Devon

Published in the United States of America
by David & Charles Inc
North Pomfret   Vermont 05053   USA

Published in Canada
by Douglas David & Charles Limited
1875 Welch Street   North Vancouver   BC

Acknowledgements

One of the pleasures of preparing this book was to find such friendly co-operation from so many people. Of the numerous members of the British Motor Corporation who helped us we must single out for special thanks Peter Burdon, Cecil Cousins, H. F. O. Evans, Wilson McComb, K. C. Revis, M.B.E., Brian Turner, John Thornley, G. A. Willis and Dennis Lowe of the Photographic Department, who provided the majority of the photographs. Other photographs were supplied by Alan Chew, Miss M. G. Chiesman, M.B.E., Norman Findlay, Herbert Art Gallery & Museum, Coventry, John Holyoak, Jack Milne, Gunnar Poppe, Rex Probert, A.R.P.S., Norman Routledge, David Walker and from the author's collection. The beautiful line drawings were the result of hours of hard work by Miss Helen Stirling and Bray Webb.

For much of the information on early Morris cars we are indebted to members of the Bullnose Morris Club and in particular to Dick Barton, Ken Grainger, John Holyoak, Margaret Thomas and Jim Wallace. Information was also unstintingly supplied by Mrs Dorothy Fernihough, G. N. Georgano, the late Sam Gilchrist, Lord Montagu of Beaulieu, Michael Sedgwick, W. Solloway, the late C. P. Wedmore, and the Austin historian, Bob Wyatt. Above all we must thank Dennis Field, the historian of the Veteran Car Club of Great Britain, who most trustingly lent us the unique notes of the late John Pollitt. For the loan of other invaluable literature we must thank Kenneth Ball of Autobooks Ltd., Mrs G. Ahern, John Stanford, Bob Wyatt, Alan Mould and Douglas Irvine, who gave us access to his private library. The details we had of White and Poppe were negligible until we talked to John Dennis, Norman Findlay, S. J. Humphries, the late Gunnar Poppe and Jack Milne, who is a mine of information.

We are most grateful to the editors of *Autocar*, *Motor* and *Motor Sport*, Norman Routledge, Bob Knox and Raymond Gray for permitting us to follow the principle of "don't copy, quote".

Margaret English guided us on the basics of writing and any grammatical howlers are evidence of occasions when we ignored her advice. Finally we must say how lucky we are to have William Boddy, of *Motor Sport* fame, as editor of this motoring series. We freely admit that whenever we require information about Brooklands we find it necessary to consult his masterpiece *A History of Brooklands Motor Course*.

Notes and Acknowledgements to the Second Edition

We are lucky to deal with David & Charles. They were prepared to reprint *The Bullnose Morris* without amendment. However, as an alternative, they were willing to go to the expense of allowing us to add a completely new section on Flatnoses but to keep typesetting costs down to a reasonable level they asked us to avoid numerous minor changes. This was ideal. It gave us an excuse to leave the chapter on M.G.'s unchanged instead of modifying it in the light of the new facts presented by F. Wilson McComb in his *The Story of the M.G. Sports Car*. Despite Michael Sedgwick's review of the first edition we can use the same excuse for retaining the notation $80 \times 90 \times 4$ for a W & P engine instead of laboriously spelling out that it is a four cylinder unit of 80 mm bore and 90 mm stroke. We would like to have incorporated all the useful comments that Eric Longworth of the Bullnose Morris Club made on the technical side but we had to restrict ourselves to the more important ones. We also received helpful comments from Arthur Peeling of the Morris Register, Ann Comery and Lena Hardy.

We were glad to be able to add a section on Flatnoses and quite deliberately we have not even attempted to make it uniform with the remainder of the book. Fortunately we wrote this chapter after the publication of Sir Miles (now Lord) Thomas's autobiography *Out on a Wing*. This is one of three volumes which should be on the bookshelf of every vintage Morris enthusiast. The other two are Wilson McComb's M.G. book and *The Life of Lord Nuffield* by Andrews and Brunner. The latter is unlikely to be rivalled for its wealth of authoritive detail of the business, commercial and financial side of the Morris empire. We hope that this leaves space on the shelf for this work!

We thoroughly enjoyed extending the scope to Flatnoses and we are indebted to Basil Briggs, Hon Secretary of the Bullnose Morris Club and Harry Edwards, Historian of the Morris Register for correcting the proofs. Basil is well qualified for the task, for his Flatnose has been in the family since the late 'twenties. Harry is a true enthusiast who is always willing to share his prodigious knowledge and he saved us from making some serious errors.

We were fortunate indeed that Des Measures was responsible for the additional illustrations to this edition and it is obvious that he combines artistic talent with an enthusiasm for old cars. The knowledgeable Sedgwick/Marshall combine of Midhurst were always most helpful. Is there a worthwhile vintage motoring book which does not contain an acknowledgement to them?

We asked for photographs from members of the Bullnose Morris Club and the Morris Register and our only regret is that we could not print all of them. Prince Marshall kindly provided the two splendid plates 29 and 50 from the files of *Old Motor*.

The list of surviving Bullnoses in the first edition is hopelessly out of date. Most generously Margaret Goding was prepared to let us use her up-to-date and fully revised list of surviving Bullnoses and Flatnoses. However, the cars have survived in such numbers that the list is now a very long one and it would have taken up much of the space available for the new material. We decided against using it in favour of other material solely because it is available already from the Bullnose Morris Club.

Contents

CONTENTS

List of Plates

11

following
page

1

Two wheels, three wheels and then four

"When I last visited the Morris-Oxford works I had to bear the brunt of its designer's wrath for stating in these pages that my radiator was somewhat prone to steam, and that I had ladled water into it out of road puddles with the aid of a sou'wester."

From The Light Car *of the 12th October,* 1915.

William Richard Morris in 1893, when fifteen-and-a-half, was taken on by Mr Parker, a leading cycle agent in St. Giles, Oxford, to learn the trade under the foreman, Mr Dupper. After nine months Morris asked for his wages to be increased from five to six shillings per week, but the request was refused. Morris felt this a poor reflection on his true value and left to set up on his own repairing bicycles in the shed at the back of his father's house in James Street, Cowley St. John. Morris then turned to bicycle assembly, but the significance of this step must not be exaggerated. At this time most cycle agents assembled machines of their own in addition to carrying out repair work and retailing factory built bicycles. Small assemblers were so numerous that firms of the size of B.S.A., Chater-Lea and Albert Eadie produced standardised components on a large scale to meet their needs and the locally produced machine flourished because it usually had a small price advantage over the factory built bicycle, due to the lower overheads. One item which distinguished the numerous local makes from one another was the badge, which in the case of the Cowley St. John machines was a cycle wheel in gilt with the words "THE MORRIS" underneath it.

The first bicycle Morris built in about 1894 was to the order of the local vicar, who being a tall man specified a 28 in. frame and fortunately this machine, although modified, is preserved at Cowley. That the local vicar rode a Morris was a fine testimony to the excellence of the make but even better publicity were Morris's racing successes and sometimes he was seen in action as far afield as Herne Hill. In one or two of his earliest races he is reputed to have ridden an Osmond, an expensive machine for which Parker was agent (an Osmond is preserved in the Science Museum), but soon he raced his own machines. Morris differed from most racing cyclists in that his achievements were not confined to one distance or time, and this is shown in the fact that he was once champion of Oxford (County and City), Berkshire and Buckinghamshire for distances varying from one to fifty miles.

48 High Street, Oxford.

Morris had started assembling bicycles at his father's home, and displaying them in the front room of the house or in sunny weather in the garden, but his business had done so well in the safety bicycle boom that he could afford to rent premises at 48 High Street, Oxford, for a bicycle shop and others in Queens Lane as a repair shop.

Morris's interest was turning towards motorcycles and in 1901 he built himself one with a 1¾ h.p. engine which he machined from bought in castings. The result decided Morris on motorcycle manufacture and so that he could produce in reasonable quantities, which his limited capital prevented, he went into partnership with another Oxford cycle dealer, Joseph Cooper.

1. White & Poppe engined De Luxe Morris Oxford, with Hollick and Pratt body, and a Stewart & Ardern lady demonstrator at the wheel.

2. P. A. Poppe, the engine designer, at the wheel of his Standard model W & P Morris Oxford.

The bicycle side of Morris and Cooper continued to be their mainstay, but in the livery stables, 100 Holywell Lane (since renamed Longwall Street), which the partners used as a bicycle repair depot, they built two motorcycles for exhibition at the 1902 Stanley Show. The motorcycles were only completed in time by repeatedly burning the midnight oil, but their good reception had made the effort worth while. Morris was sufficiently encouraged to want to place an immediate order for three more engines, but Cooper was not as confident about the future of the motorcycle and this divergence of views led to the dissolution of the partnership. Morris was once again short of capital after repaying Cooper, which made a proposition he received all the more irresistible.

An Oxford undergraduate, who had inherited a large sum of money, was eager to join the motor trade and turned to an Oxford business man, F. G. Barton, for advice. Barton was also attracted by the motor trade, but advised the undergraduate that success of any venture would depend on having an experienced technical man and the best in Oxford was Morris. Barton proposed that he, the student and Morris should form a three man partnership which would trade as the Oxford Automobile and Cycle Agency and put the Morris motorcycle into production. Barton, for his part, would contribute his cycle business with head office and showrooms at 16 George Street, Oxford, and branches at Bicester and Abingdon and in consideration of this would be general manager and responsible for sales. The undergraduate would invest in the business, but be a sleeping partner and Morris would also invest in the business and hold the post of works manager. Morris liked the proposition, which promised a bright future for his motorcycle.

The Morris motorcycle employed a 2¾ h.p. M.M.C. (de Dion type) single cylinder air cooled engine, which boasted a mechanically operated inlet valve in 1904, and the purchaser was given the option of a Longuemare spray carburettor or the new wick carburettor of Mr Morris's patented design. The steel tube frame, registered design No. 400850, was looped to clear the crankcase and the employment of a countershaft in the transmission was in advance of its time, the primary drive from the Morris clutch being by chain and the secondary drive by vee belt. The clutch was controlled from the handlebars through a Bowden cable, a system now practically universal, but pioneered by Morris.

The Morris motorcycle was available with a forecarriage, and from photographs it looks as though this had independent coil spring suspension. The three wheeler in 1904, complete with apron and lamp brackets, cost £70 with wicker forecarriage, £72 10s. 0d. with cane forecarriage, and £73 with coach-built forecarriage. The forecarriage was upholstered in green or red and the standard finish of black enamel with plated parts could be set off with lining in gold leaf for an extra 15s. and nickel plated rims at an extra 7s. 6d. per pair. The Oxford Automobile and Cycle Agency in their 1904 catalogue claimed that:—

"With the Fore-carriage fitted, the Motor Bicycle may be used in all weathers, as side-slip is impossible. If only required for one rider, the front seat may be detached by simply undoing eight butterfly nuts, thus converting machine into a Tricycle; or the whole of the Fore-carriage may be detached in a few minutes, and the machine used as a Bicycle."

The 1904 catalogue also contains testimonials, which in a few sentences give a vivid impression of motorcycling conditions and what was expected of machines at the turn of the century. For example, on 4th October, 1903 N.H.J. wrote:—

"It may interest you to know that since February I have ridden 3,800 miles on my machine with only one stop of over five minutes on the road (barring punctures)."

Longwall – pre 1910.

What a pity N.H.J. did not say precisely how many times he had tyre trouble, or whether he used the Clincher A Won tyre as recommended by Morris.

F.P.S. seems to have been a less ambitious character. In a letter dated 8th March, 1903 he wrote:—

"I had a fine ride on Friday last, doing about 35 miles, but I started too late to get through to London. The machine was a perfect revelation in the way of motor bikes, taking a really *stiff* hill in thick mud with the throttle half open."

It was scarcely necessary for P.C.Le.G.S. to write because he was in residence at nearby Queen's College, Oxford, but write he did on 18th March, 1903:—

"I am very pleased to say what I think of the 'Morris' motor bicycle I had from you. I have ridden it during this winter in all sorts of weather and I have had no trouble, moreover she is specially good as to side slip and an excellent hill climber. The ideal machine for trailer work and as fast as any sane person can wish for."

The Oxford Automobile and Cycle Agency had satisfied customers, but not enough of them to justify the undergraduate's heavy spending on unwarranted sales promotion, and about a year after its formation the partnership was dissolved, all three losing heavily. It is good to note that Morris and Barton still retained respect and liking for one another and that Barton was appointed manager of the Morris Garages when Morris wanted to leave himself free to concentrate on car assembly. Because of ill health Barton did not hold the post for long but retired to Devon where he led a remarkably active life, founding the Barton Motor Co., who are still Morris distributors today. After the failure of the Oxford Automobile and Cycle Agency Morris found himself practically back where he started with a shop at 48 High Street

Longwall – post 1910.

and repair premises at Longwall, but he had now firmly resolved to remain in sole control. The motor side of the business at Longwall, named "The Oxford Garage", expanded rapidly and in 1908 Morris sold the cycle side of his business at 48 High Street and the rights of his motorcycle to Mr E. Armstead.

Morris was a most successful garage proprietor and in addition to hiring cars and operating a taxi service he had the agency for Douglas, Enfield, Sunbeam and Triumph motorcycles and Arrol-Johnson, Belsize, Humber, Hupmobile, Singer, Standard and Wolseley cars. Expansion was the keynote of his business and the Longwall Street premises were completely rebuilt to provide more space. The alterations were completed in 1910 and although the new building was in no way as palatial as some modern motor emporiums, none the less it was called "The Oxford Motor Palace" by one of the local newspapers. However, the true trading style of this garage was "The Morris Garage", the change in name from "The Oxford Garage" having been made in 1910. More space was still required and in 1910 premises were taken in nearby Cross Street and in 1913 the old Queens Hotel at 36 and 37

Queen Street were taken as showrooms, the name of the business being expanded to "The Morris Garages (W. R. Morris, Proprietor)".

Firms such as Calthorpe, Humber, Rover and Singer were large and famous bicycle manufacturers who turned to making motorcycles and motor cars, at first as a sideline, to keep their factories busy and expand their activities on the collapse of the bicycle boom at the turn of the century. Morris had also built bicycles, but he had only been a small local assembler, and his plans as a motor car manufacturer were different because from the outset he intended to make car assembly his main line of business. In 1910 he started to plan a car to sell in quantity at a reasonable price and in drawing up a basic design he had the big advantage of having studied the merits and faults of rival designs first hand as a garage proprietor. Cyclecars were beginning to catch on, but Morris dismissed the idea of producing them since their low initial cost was obtained at the expense of quality. In his opinion low running costs were as important as low first cost and above all the car had to be unquestionably reliable. To achieve quickly his aim of a high rate of production with the minimum of capital, Morris knew he would have to buy as many components as possible from outside suppliers. If anything, he argued, this would be an advantage because the suppliers were experienced specialists in their own particular field, and this would ensure the reliability and suitability of their products. Furthermore, buying from outside suppliers would not necessarily incur additional expense provided that sufficiently large orders were placed.

At the 1910 Motor Show Morris's discussions on supplies were purely exploratory because he had insufficient capital with which to start serious motor car manufacture; by the following year his discussions on supplies were with the definite object of placing orders, as he had now been provided with the necessary financial backing by the Earl of Macclesfield. At the 1911 Motor Show it was suggested that for the engine/gearbox unit of his proposed light car, the Morris Oxford, he should approach White and Poppe Ltd. A meeting was duly arranged between Morris, Peter August Poppe, the joint managing director of White and Poppe Ltd., and H. W. Cranham, the Northern distributor for White and Poppe Ltd.

Poppe agreed to build Morris an engine/gearbox unit for the Morris Oxford, which gave him an excellent start, for White and Poppe Ltd. were a firm with a fine reputation. Both White and Poppe were skilled engineers who had gone into partnership in 1899, White concentrating on the commercial side and Poppe on the technical side. Under their guidance the sales of W & P carburettors and engines grew steadily and they numbered among their customers such firms as Ariel and Premier for motorcycle engines, Dennis for commerical vehicle engines and Academy, Calthorpe, Climax, Clyde, Dennis, Globe, Heron, Horbick, Horley, Quadrant, Rothwell, Singer, Swift, West, Withers and Siddeley-Deasy for motor car engines. Of these Singer was probably their best customer. White and Poppe Ltd. deserve a book to themselves, and fuller details are given at the end of this chapter.

The well known firm of E. G. Wrigley and Company contracted to supply Morris with the front and rear axles and the steering mechanism for his car and Raworths, the old Oxford coachbuilding firm, agreed to supply bodies. Contracts were also made for smaller components such as wheels from Sankey, tyres from Dunlops and lamps from Powell and Hanmer. It is questionable whether any parts at all of the first Morris Oxford were not bought in.

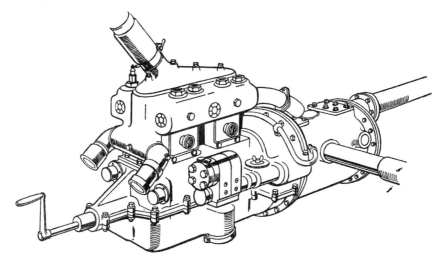

The 1018 c.c. W & P engine fitted to Morris Oxfords from 1913 to 1917.

In August 1912 W.R.M. Motors Ltd. was registered with Morris as managing director and the Earl of Macclesfield, who held £4,000 of preference shares, as president. The prototype Morris Oxford was built at the Longwall Street garage, but for a factory W.R.M. Motors Ltd. acquired the old Military Training College at Temple Cowley, which had formerly been Hursts Grammar School where Morris's father was educated. A major attraction of the old Military Training College was its depressed price due to it having been unoccupied for twenty years.

The Morris Oxford was announced in *The Autocar* in October, 1912. The car had a wheelbase of 7 ft 0 in. with a 40 in. track. The chassis frame was conventional for its time with the front axle suspended on half elliptic leaf springs and the rear axle on three-quarter elliptic leaf springs. The rear axle had a one piece pressed steel casing containing an overhead worm drive of the Wrigley type in which only one tooth of the worm meshed with the wheel. The engine of the first Morris Oxford was a built-in unit with the clutch and gearbox, although at this time engines and gearboxes were often separate and mounted in sub-frames. It was a T-head four cylinder engine of 60 m.m. bore and 90 m.m. stroke and as was common at this time the cylinder head was non detachable, access to the valves being through large valve caps. There was one Bosch sparking plug per cylinder fired by a Bosch ZF 4 magneto, Bosch magnetos having a reputation second to none. The crankshaft was carried on three white metal main bearings, the big-ends also being of white metal. The lubrication system was interesting as there was no oil pump as such. Oil was thrown from the flywheel into a trough, gravity then feeding this oil through galleries to the bearings. The flywheel was quite standard, with no vanes or other means for assisting the oil into the trough, and this proved to be quite satisfactory. The vintage Rhode had a similar lubrication system.

The engine drove through a multi-plate clutch, the description multi-plate being no exaggeration because it had thirty-six alternate steel and bronze plates, to a three-speed gearbox with right-hand gate change. The gears were mounted in a cage and the cage was carried in a cylindrical extension of the clutch housing, this arrangement being strongly reminiscent of the 10/12 Belsize, a make for which Morris was an agent. The drive from the gearbox to the rear axle was by a propeller shaft enclosed in a torque tube via an enclosed metal universal joint. Brakes were on the rear wheels only, there being no transmission brake. The rear brake drums contained four shoes each, the footbrake operating one pair and the handbrake the other pair. The worm and sector steering was fairly straightforward and the only note-able feature was a bad one: the steering draglink was under the axle instead of over the axle. The front axle was of the reversed Elliott type.

The announcement of the car was a trifle premature because none were available and it was impossible to find out if they fulfilled the promises made on paper. The delay in supply was due to the fact that no White & Poppe engine/gearbox units had been made. Many of the foundry trade had been approached to carry out the castings of the White & Poppe cylinder block but it was a complicated design and they shied away from the job. Eventually Willans and Robinson of Rugby, who were famous for their steam engines, agreed to take it on. They were an experienced firm who had, for example, made the three cylinder engine of the English Duryea and cylinder blocks for Forman of Coventry, the proprietary engine manufacturers, but even so the production of the White and Poppe $60 \times 90 \times 4$ cylinder block presented a lot of problems causing delays. The result was that W. R. Morris had no car to exhibit at the 1912 London Motor Show. Undeterred he went to London with blue-prints which he showed to Gordon Stewart of Stewart & Ardern. Stewart was immediately impressed and even though production had not commenced placed a firm order for 400 cars. Morris acknowledged this show of confidence by appointing Stewart & Ardern his sole London distributor.

The delays in the supply of the cylinder block castings continued but this did not prevent a Morris Oxford from being exhibited at the North of England Motor Show at Manchester in February, 1913. The car looked well enough but would not go as the cylinder block was a dummy made of wood. The wooden cylinder block was fitted with brass valve caps, and the water outlet and the inlet pipes were of cast iron. It had no core plugs in the inlet and exhaust manifold or water jackets, and there were no set screws holding the inlet and exhaust tappet guides in the cylinder base. The exhaust outlet elbow was at an incorrect angle and was SOLID, and the sump was made of wood. The wooden block became known as "the wooden horse of Holbrook Lane" because it survived at White & Poppe's Holbrook Lane, Coventry, works until 1931, having been stored as a pattern in error. It was, however, built at the Lockhurst Lane works of White & Poppe.

Although no Morris car had yet taken the road, Stewart and Ardern advertised it in the *Autocar* of 15th February, 1913, and claimed that it was capable of 45–50 m.p.g., which was nothing more than an inspired guess. A sales feature second only to the car's petrol consumption was that the "Morris is the only Light Car which embodies the joint productions of the greatest British experts" or, in other words, is assembled from proprietary parts. This is particularly noteworthy and explains the quick acceptance of the car. Many manufacturers who used proprietary parts tried to disguise the matter, but Morris advertised the fact. The suppliers of the Morris parts were of excellent repute and therefore the public at once accepted the car. If Morris had pretended that he made his own parts, the public would probably have waited for at least a year for the faults to be eliminated from the design before purchasing. In quoting the specification Stewart and Ardern claimed that the Morris at £175 was "absolutely ready for the road", whereas in fact a Morris was not ready for the road until the 28th March, 1913.

The first production Morris was made available to Stewart and Ardern and Gordon Stewart travelled to Cowley to collect it. His first journey in the the Morris Oxford was however a brief one. He let in the clutch, travelled a few yards and the universal joint broke. The universal joint was made of cast iron which had been chosen by Poppe because of its excellent wearing properties – far superior to those of bronze. Unfortunately the cast iron used for the manufacture of these universal joints was not of the fine grained type specified by Poppe, but of the "pots and pans" variety. The result was inevitable. Another "pots and pans" variety of universal joint was fitted and this time Gordon Stewart got from Cowley to High Wycombe before it broke. After this Morris insisted that the universal joints were made of bronze. Morris called Poppe a fool – it is easy to be wise after the event – but Poppe was far from a fool, and the good reputation which the Morris

Oxford enjoyed was, to a large extent, due to the excellence of its Poppe designed engine and gearbox.

Once production got under way the Morris Oxford was readily available. The distributor in the South of England was W. H. M. Burgess and in the North, H. W. Cranham. Both these Morris suppliers were also White & Poppe's distributors, the sole London distributor, as has been explained, still being Stewart and Ardern. Although the distribution of the W & P engined Morris Oxford was confined to these three concerns it was retailed by many others, some of whom have since become Morris distributors. One retailer who never became a distributor was Harrods of Knightsbridge, the famous London store, which advertised the Morris Oxford in *The Cyclecar* of 6th August, 1913, and invited you to inspect it. If the Morris Oxford was not to your taste Harrods could always supply you from stock with a Singer, Invicta, G.W.K., Globe, Alldays, A.C. (four-wheeler), Humberette, Peugeot or Zebra.

The teething troubles of the car which were few were soon ironed out. The first trouble to come to light was the universal joint as has been described and the next concerned the clutch, a thirty-six plate job of alternate steel and bronze plates running in oil. When the oil was cold and thick and "gooey" the clutch refused to free. The design was altered by reducing the number of plates from thirty-six to thirty-four, which helped, but some of the clutches were still reluctant to free. The method adopted by the works rejects department to cure the trouble was to buckle slightly each plate at its centre, so that they pushed apart when the clutch was disengaged. All the cars already delivered had the new design of clutch fitted free of charge. Poppe was delighted with the speed with which his personnel carried out the work, and told Morris with pleasure how the reputation for service of their respective firms had benefited. Morris said in effect "It's all right for Poppe but it nearly bankrupted me!". The steering of the car was odd, most odd, but this was not a thing which could be put right overnight. After about 150 cars had been built, the track was increased from 40 in. to 42 in., which made things easier, but was not the real answer to the steering problem. Forty-three cars were subsequently built (i.e., after chassis No. 244) with the old 40 in. track but all were exported. With the exception of these teething troubles the cars ran splendidly and soon began to get a good reputation which was aided by successes in some of the gentler competitive events.

On the road the most striking feature of the car was the high engine speed and in retrospect an *Autocar* correspondent seven years later described it as "the reviest" small engine sold to the public. The engine was designed to turn at over 3,000 r.p.m., which was a very high figure for those days and moreover it turned at this speed with absolute reliability in spite of having no proper oil pump. For the engine to perform well at these high revolutions it was essential that the recommended grade and make of sparking plug was used. Only a Bosch would do. P. A. Poppe reputedly devised his own method of testing plugs, which was to take a Morris Oxford fitted with the make of plugs under test on to the Kenilworth Road, engage first speed, open the throttle to the full and apply the handbrake to keep the engine revs just below valve bounce speed. Sometimes the plugs blew out altogether, but usually severe detonation set in first. Only the Bosch proved to have the necessary heat conductivity. The one thing about which people generally complained was boiling, or steaming, which is presumably one stage worse. In reply W.R.M. Motors Ltd. emphasised time and again that it was imperative that the correct type of sparking plugs, Bosch, be fitted, otherwise all sorts of engine maladies would ensue. During the war, patriots objected to German goods and so tried various alternative makes. The more expensive and latest type of Lodge racing plug was possibly as good as the Bosch, but other makes were useless. "Runabout" of *The Light Car* in December, 1917, became quite lyrical on the subject of Bosch plugs and the W & P 60 × 90 × 4 engine of the Morris Oxford and thought that "if there was a romance in the petrol engine world it is the singular affection that exists between these plugs and the 60 m.m. White & Poppe engine", but to quote more fully from "Runabout's" interesting column:—

"The other day I ran across an owner who still retains his 1914 Morris Oxford de Luxe. He is one of the few Morris Oxford owners I have met who has never suffered from a steaming radiator, and perhaps this record depends on the fact that his plugs are a certain make with single points. If ever there was a romance in the petrol engine world it is the singular affection that exists between these plugs and the 60 m.m. White and Poppe engine. I never knew it satisfied with any other make, and the owner in question says that his engine always misbehaves if he runs on another make of plug. . . . The Morris Oxford is certainly a car of individuality. When it makes its plugs incandescent it tries to conceal their faults by behaving as if it had some dirt in the jet or float chamber of the carburettor instead of following the ordinary custom of internal combustion engines afflicted by a white-hot wire protruding into the combustion chambers." The make of plug in question is Bosch.

The road test of a 1913 Morris Oxford in *The Cyclecar* of 6th August, 1913, makes interesting reading. The ability of the engine to rev. so impressed the tester that he gave his report the title "3,800 r.p.m. Under Load". To quote:—

"The engine is designed to attain a very high rate of revolution, and does not pull well at low speeds. Therefore, the revolutions must be kept up as high as possible, and all changes down made early. Thus, the change from top to second should be made whenever the speed drops much below 30 m.p.h. on a hill. As over 38 m.p.h. was actually attained in second gear, it will be seen that these changes do not necessitate a low average speed. The second speed has a ratio of $8\frac{1}{4}$ to 1, so at 38 m.p.h. the engine was doing over 3,800 r.p.m. at which speed there was practically no vibration from the engine. On first gear, 13 to 1, it is possible to exceed 20 m.p.h., so it will be seen that the Morris Oxford is a speedy little machine."

The suspension was commended, being described as unusually comfortable. Contemporary road tests invariably praised the comfortable springing of the Bullnose. During the test there was a heavy downpour of rain, but the driver was able hastily to erect the hood whilst he was seated, a strong contrast to later four-seated Bullnoses. Once erected, the hood "served to keep off the major portion of the rain". Rather faint praise!

It was found that it was better to use both foot and handbrakes simultaneously with light pressure, as it was difficult to prevent skidding of the wheels if one brake was applied hard. It impressed the tester that both brakes operated in the rear hubs because this avoided all the unnecessary strain on the transmission caused by transmission brakes favoured at this time. The unit construction of the engine and gearbox was praised, which although now universal, was then a comparative rarity.

"The unit construction tends to simplification, and as a result there are only three points requiring the addition of lubricant. Oil poured into the engine serves for all lubrication as far back as the torque tube, and oil is introduced into the back axle." Everything so far is in favour of unit construction, but would not accessibility be bad? This problem had been overcome. "Special arrangements have been made by which it is possible to adjust the clutch springs without dismantling the gearbox, an easily detachable plate affording access. The later models have fewer plates and stronger springs in the clutch than the model we tried, and thus the slight trouble which we encountered due to the clutch sticking when cold has been entirely overcome."

The experience of a former owner of a Morris Oxford with this "slight" trouble is given at the end of this chapter.

So far W. R. Morris had appeared at the 1910, 1911 and 1912 Motor Shows in London in person, but without a motor car. He made amends at the 1913 Olympia Show, where he not only showed the models introduced in March 1913 but also exhibited an improved version known as the de Luxe. The earlier version was now referred to as the Standard Model. Basically the chassis of the two models differed in track, axle ratio, wheelbase length, radiator capacity, and steering layout. The de Luxe model had a 45 in. track as against 42 in. track for the Standard Model (originally 40 in.) and the steering layout of the two models was entirely different. The axle of the de Luxe was of the Elliott type instead of the reversed Elliott of the Standard Model, which is the commoner form of axle beam, and so that the de Luxe would not be heir to the inherent steering defects of the earlier car, its drag-link was above the axle. The desired results were obtained and the car no longer wandered when it hit a tram track or pot hole.

For the 1914 season the Standard chassis was fitted with one of two alternative torpedo two-seater bodies, one known as the "Standard Model" and the other as the "Commercial Model". The "Commercial Model" differed from the "Standard Model" in having a rather narrower body and a poorer quality finish. Four body types were available on the de Luxe chassis. These were a torpedo two-seater known as the "de Luxe model", the "delivery van" with a mahogany panelled body, the single-seater aluminium bodied "sporting model" and the "de Luxe model coupe", which had a folding leather hood. This model was later supplemented by the cabriolet coupe, which had rear quarter lights. For an extra five pounds "de Luxe" cars were available with nickel instead of brass fittings. A quick way of distinguishing a "Standard Model" or "Commercial Model" two-seater from a "de Luxe" model two-seater is by its doors; the doors on the Standard Models extend to the bottom of the body whereas the de Luxe models have shallower doors.

The de Luxe was a splendid car and probably well worth the extra cost although everyone did not agree. A Mr Reginald Daniels had something to say about Morris prices in a letter to the *Light Car and Cyclecar* in December, 1916. He discussed a light car which he did not name, but was obviously a Morris Oxford. The only fault he could find with the earlier models was that they had too narrow a track, and this had been overcome by the manufacturer adding to his range a de Luxe model with a wider track. Mr Daniels considered that the increase in price of the de Luxe model, £40, was scandalous, for £5, indeed 5s. should have covered the cost of track widening. Poor Mr Daniels then went on to complain about the cost of spares. He wanted to fit new clutch plates – 34 of them at 2s. 2d. each! And new piston rings – 12 at 2s. 6d. each, whereas if the car had been a Ford, piston rings would only have cost 9d. each! This letter complaining of Morris prices was, however, the exception. As mentioned, the only thing about which people generally complained was boiling or steaming and this occurred even though the little Bullnose radiator contained no less than 340 feet of 3/16 in. copper tube. On this subject the *Light Car* on 12th October, 1916 stated:—

"Mr Morris is confident – let his clients read, mark, learn and inwardly digest – that unsuitable sparking plugs are wholly responsible for the steaming from which some of his cars suffer in private hands."

W.R.M. Motors emphasised time and again that it was essential that only the recommended type and grade of sparking plug should be used.

After 4th August, 1914, Morris concentrated on assembling war equipment, mostly mine sinkers, but in a corner of the works he continued to assemble Standard and de Luxe Oxfords alongside his new car, the Cowley, although in very small numbers from left over parts. The Standard model was discontinued for 1916, and during the first half of 1916, the last half dozen or so de Luxe models were assembled. Two of these are still surviving in New Zealand.

During its production life, the modifications to the $60 \times 90 \times 4$ W & P engine/gearbox unit of the Morris Oxford were confined to the clutch and the universal joint. However, numerous experiments were carried out at the White & Poppe works from the introduction of the engine in 1913 until 1919 or 1920, well after production had ceased. The experiments were not altogether pointless because White & Poppe planned to produce a car of their own after the war, when armament work would cease. Poppe had a Standard model Oxford for personal transport, which was painted tetryl yellow and known in the works as the "Yellow Peril". His wife had a 1914 de Luxe model Morris Oxford. Probably the first of the experiments was the substitution of the "Yellow Peril's" standard multi-plate job for an adapted motorcycle cork clutch, but it was too small to be entirely successful; another of the works cars was fitted with a cork clutch in 1919. To increase the power output some engines were bored out to 65 m.m. and fitted with full forced lubrication, the pump being driven by the end of the exhaust camshaft. Boring out the engines was the only practical means of increasing the power output as the area of the passage from the inlet valve to the cylinder was smaller than the area of the inlet manifold. None the less after the First World War, valve timing experiments were carried out on the rather conservative original settings; the valve timing could be altered from the front of the engine although the camshafts could not be withdrawn from the front. To try to improve the cooling of the engine a flat radiator was fitted on one or two cars and some cars had an intermediate bearing fitted in the torque tube to support the prop shaft. The Standard Morris Oxford had no starter or electric lighting. A chain-driven Scott dynamotor was tried on a few cars but this was not a success as it gave rise to a vibration period. The last word in W & P $60 \times 90 \times 4$ units was one fitted with an o.h.v. conversion on the lines of the Rose designed Lea-Francis and Rileys, but this was a private venture on the part of some of the works personnel.

In his bicycle days Morris was better known for his racing prowess than for the machines he built. He was only a local assembler and not in the same category as the giants such as Humber or Singer. The Morris motorcycle clearly shows its constructor's capacity for practical and, where desirable, original thought on motor engineering. The White & Poppe engined Morris Oxford was primarily designed to combine reliability and a degree of refinement with economy and it soon gained an excellent reputation on these scores. The ready acceptance of the car was largely due to the fact that Morris advertised rather than disguised that it was built from first class proprietary parts. Furthermore Morris did not hesitate to adopt the ideas of others if they were good. His experience as a motor agent had taught him the merits of the Hupmobile enclosed torque tube final drive and the Belsize gearbox and a similar transmission was therefore adopted for the Oxford. From practical experience Morris avoided building the gearbox in unit with the back axle, a feature which bedevilled the otherwise excellent Singer and Fivet engined A.C. light cars. Morris would not sacrifice quality or reliability on price grounds and in fact the Oxford was more expensive than the A.C. and only a little cheaper than the small Singer. The W & P engined Oxford established Morris as a car maker, but he had a long way still to go to outsell the model-T Ford in Britain. Whilst there would always be a market for a small two-seater there was obviously a larger market for a family four-seater of comparable first costs, running costs and reliability. To meet this specification was a tall order, but Morris achieved it when in April, 1915 he announced his new model, the Cowley.

White and Poppe

Peter August Poppe was born on a farm in the wilds of Northern Norway in August (hence his second name) 1870. His workshop practice as a young man was gained on producing navigational instruments, and one of the users of his instruments was a personal friend, the polar explorer Fridtzof Nansen who stayed with him on a visit to Coventry after World War I.

P. A. Poppe first met Alfred James White in the late 1890s at the Austrian Steyr Werke. Poppe was visiting the Steyr Werke on behalf of the Norwegian Government to supervise a small arms contract and A. J. White, who was the son of one of the directors of Swift of Coventry, was visiting Austria to negotiate a licence for Steyr to manufacture Swift bicycles.

White and Poppe decided to go into partnership and accordingly White and Poppe Ltd. was registered on 30th September, 1899 to manufacture carburettors, engines and associated components. The nominal capital of the firm was £4,000 in £1 shares, and of the 589 shares taken up, one was bought by Poppe, one by a friend of the White family John Middleton and the remaining 587 by four members of the White family. White and Poppe, who were both skilled engineers, were joint managing directors, with White concentrating on the commercial side and Poppe on the technical side. A contract was drawn up between the firm and the two partners. A. J. White was to receive an annual salary of £260, plus expenses, to be paid weekly, plus a quarter of the total profits less £500. P. A. Poppe who was the works manager as well as a joint managing director was to receive an annual salary of £250 (£10 less than White), plus expenses to be paid weekly, plus a quarter of the surplus profits. Note the differences between their contracts.

The first factory of White and Poppe Ltd. was in Drake Street, Coventry, but in 1900 they moved to a new factory in Lockhurst Lane, Coventry, which also replaced 111 Little Park Street, Coventry (the address of the solicitors Hughes and Masser), as the firm's registered office. For so young a firm they did well to obtain a government contract during the Boer War (October,

1899 to 31st May, 1902) for the manufacture of fuse bodies. They also made fuse bodies during the Russo-Japanese War (early 1904 to 5th September, 1905) and as an offensive and defensive alliance between Great Britain and Japan was signed in London at the end of January, 1902 these presumably went to the Japanese. A full resumption to peace time activities saw the introduction early in 1905 of their very successful 80 m.m. bore by 90 m.m. stroke series of engines. These were available in single, twin, three and four cylinder form at first, and also in six cylinder form in 1906. The engines had a T-head, individually cast cylinders and a main bearing between each crankshaft throw (seven main bearings in the case of the six cylinder). Remembering the date, the absolutely outstanding feature of these engines was INTERCHANGEABILITY. None of the parts, such as pistons, was filed and fitted, they were made spot-on in the first place and as far as possible by machine. This fantastic accuracy and hence interchangeability, which was unique at the time in the car world, permitted White and Poppe Ltd. to produce a wide variety of engines from the minimum number of different parts. For example, all parts of the 80 × 90 series from the single to the six were common with literally only one or two exceptions. It was simply a case of using six times as many of most parts to make a six instead of a single. Naturally the pistons, conrods, valves and cylinders were common but so too were items like the crankcase parts, cams, crankpins and crankshaft webs. The high degree of interchangeability permitted built-up construction of crankshafts, which gave no trouble, but special jigs and hydraulic presses had to be used to assemble them and it was still well beyond the ability of any garage to dismantle one and then re-assemble it correctly.

At this time the lion's share of the proprietary engine market was held by the French, notably de Dion and Aster, against whom the Coventry firms such as Johnson, Hurley and Martin with their Alpha engines and Forman could make little impression. With the introduction of the W & P 80 × 90 series of engines there was at last a British firm which could really challenge the supremacy of the French. The 80 × 90 × 2 was used by Swift, Fairfax, Singer, Clyde and Horley. Clyde, Horbick, Horley, Singer and Swift used the 80 × 90 × 3 and also the 80 × 90 × 4. Other users of the 80 × 90 × 4 included Academy, Calthorpe, Climax, Globe, Rothwell and West and possibly Pullcar and Quadrant. In 1908, Herbert in a Singer with a W & P 80 × 90 × 4 covered a lap at Brooklands at 59·05 m.p.h., the first of many Brooklands appearances by W & P engined Singers which demonstrated the speed capabilities of W & P engines. The 80 × 90 × 6 sold in relatively small numbers, which makes one wonder whether the built-up crankcase was a little too long for rigidity, or if there were any other possible faults such as lack of balance. The 80 × 90 × 6 was used by Calthorpe, Climax, Heron, Horbick and West.

Alongside the 80 × 90 series of engines White and Poppe catered for the motorcycle market with an 80 × 85 single cylinder engine which had novel, though not very successful, detachable valve seats on pegs, but after only four were built the design was superseded by a really good 85 × 85 single cylinder T-head splash lubricated motorcycle engine which was supplied to Premier in 1909 and to Ariel until 1911, when the latter bought the manufacturing rights. In vintage days, Ariels were still making a modified version of this design. White and Poppe Ltd. also built a series of larger engines for commercial vehicles and for use in large cars.

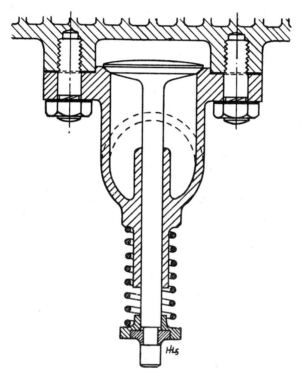

Novel, but unsuccessful, detachable valve and seat of the 1908 and 1909 80 m.m. x 85 m.m. single cylinder W & P motorcycle engine.

Good designs continued to come from the White and Poppe drawing boards. In 1908 the T-head 85 × 110 × 4 engine was introduced, being supplemented in 1909 by the larger bore 90 × 110 × 4. Then in 1910, the year in which the last 80 × 90 × 2, 80 × 90 × 3 and 80 × 90 × 4 engines were made, came the famous L-head 80 × 130 × 4 and 90 × 130 × 4. These engines were good enough to win White and Poppe the custom of famous firms such as Dennis and Siddeley-Deasy and lesser known concerns such as Withers. In 1911 a Siddeley-Deasy with a W & P 80 × 130 × 4 engine demonstrated reliability by covering 15,008 miles under R.A.C. observation at an average of 34·2 m.p.h., 23·14 m.p.g. of petrol and 1,184·49 m.p.g. of oil, which won them the Dewar Trophy. To demonstrate speed, in 1910 the Singer 'Bunny Junior' was raced with a 90 × 110 × 4 W & P engine and at the end of the season Herbert successfully took the 16 h.p. class flying start half mile at 81·26 m.p.h., which beat Coatalen's Sunbeam record of the previous month by nearly 10 m.p.h., and covered 10 laps from a standing start at 77·19 m.p.h. 'Bunny Junior' had a 40 m.m. W & P carburettor and 3·5 : 1 rear axle ratio, so the W & P engine was turning at over 3,000 r.p.m. In November, 1911 an 80 × 130 × 4 W & P engined Singer again raised the 16 h.p. class f.s. half mile, this time to 90·04 m.p.h. with Tysoe at the wheel.

Singers were after still more speed, because they had their sights set on the 1912 Coupe de *l'Auto* race. Poppe built three special engines for them, using the standard 80 × 130 × 4 as a basis. The stroke was increased to 149 m.m., the standard inlet and exhaust of the side valve L-head adapted to provide twin exhaust valves per cylinder and a special cylinder head designed, with over head inlet valves. This permitted the use of a single inlet valve per cylinder of no less than 2⅛ in. diameter. The crankshaft was of the bent-wire variety and the valve springs were said to have a surge period quite wonderful to behold. They were not successful in the Coupe de *l'Auto*, but after this race one was acquired by Percy Lambert who showed how effectively they could motor when he lapped at 89·25 m.p.h. at the 1913 Brooklands Mid-Summer Meeting.

In spite of Poppe's pre-occupation during 1911 and 1912 with the 60 × 90 × 4 engine/gearbox unit for W.R.M. Motors Ltd. and the 80 × 149 × 4 engine for the Coupe de *l'Auto* Singers, he still managed to work on an aero engine and his K formula. This formula, which he published in 1912, was devised to estimate the performance of different vehicles. It worked purely on engine bore and stroke, final drive ratio, road wheel size and loaded weight. The b.m.e.p. was assumed to be a constant and such things as streamlining and carburation were not considered at that time. In 1924 motoring publications still talked of this ingenious formula. The White and Poppe aero engine had been devised for the Government Aero Engine Competition held at Farnborough in 1912 which carried a £5,000 prize. The competition boiled down to two engines, the air-cooled W & P and the Green with a chain driven propellor. The chances of the W & P engine were ruined by a fractured engine bearer. Neither the W & P nor the Green, manufactured by Aster, saw Service life, but the W & P was used in the Alpha, Beta and Gamma airships, the Beta in its day reputedly being the fastest airship in the world.

By 1912 White and Poppe had expanded considerably from their humble beginnings and this reflected in their engine production. In 1908 they made 206 engines, followed in 1909 by 576 engines, then in 1910 production was up to 789, and in 1911 they produced 982 engines. Their carburettors were

3. P. A. Poppe with his wife's De Luxe Oxford coupe.

4. Competitive Cowley: Patrick Powell winning his class in his ex-Routledge 1924 Cowley in the 1970 Rhodesian rally.

5. 1913 export Oxford found in scrap condition in New Zealand and fully restored by Norman Findlay.

6. L. P. Jarman trying out a 1913 Standard model Oxford at a Bullnose Morris Club rally at the Cowley works.

The works of a 1913 White & Poppe engined Oxford impeccably restored by
the Herbert Art Gallery & Museum, Coventry.

The engine
proposed by Poppe for
the four seater long
chassis Oxford.

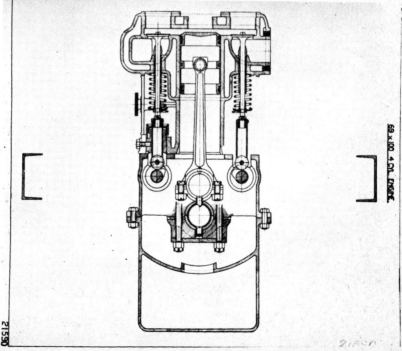

9. Two surviving 1913 Oxfords which have spent all their life in New Zealand.

also popular, despite the fact that they were devils to tune. Every entrant in the Baron de Forest cross channel air race of 1910 used one, as did successful competitors in the International Motor Boat Trophy. By August 1910 W & P had made 10,000 carburettors. Oddly enough, W & P carburettors reputedly were used on the Zeppelin which was shot down by Lieutenant William Leiefe Robinson over Cuffley on the 3rd September, 1916! The drawback of the W & P carburettor was that it could only cater for a comparatively narrow range of engine speeds. This was not a disadvantage prior to World War I but after it, it would have become more and more noticeable. Vauxhalls were a particularly good customer for carburettors.

Before World War I White and Poppe Ltd. had supplied Dennis Bros. with engines for their motor cars and commercial vehicles and one of these engines, the W & P 110 × 150 × 4 (later increased to 115 × 150 × 4) used in the Dennis 3-ton truck, was built to conform to the War Office 'subsidy' specification which stipulated features such as magneto ignition, big-end inspection covers on the crankcase and an engine speed governor. The W & P 'subsidy' engine and the B-type London General omnibus engine were two of the very few commercial vehicle engines with T as opposed to L-heads at this date. In 1914 White and Poppe Ltd. switched to war work. The demand from Dennis Bros. for the 'subsidy' engine rose rapidly to thirty per week and also, as anticipated, White and Poppe Ltd. received a sub-contract from Messrs. Armstrong, Whitworth & Co. Ltd. for 18-pounder shell sockets and Type No. 80 Mk. V aluminium fuse bodies. The demand for the latter rose steadily from 10,000 per week to 25,000 per week and then to 43,000 per week and so on. The company was appointed managers of the government shell filling factory literally around the corner from Lockhurst Lane in Holbrook Lane. White and Poppe & Co. Ltd. had expanded fantastically and included on their payroll some 12,000 people, many living on the premises in hostels. Many of these were Irish girls employed on shell filling who became known as the W & P Canaries because the shell filling stained their hands yellow. Many stories unsuitable for publication are told of the canaries' antics. In recognition of the part they were playing in the war effort the firm received a visit from Queen Mary and Princess Mary (now the Princess Royal) in 1917. Tactfully the Royal party arrived in a fleet of W & P engined Siddeley-Deasys, with the radiator behind the engine, Renault fashion.

White and Poppe & Co. Ltd. had bright post-war prospects. Vauxhall wanted carburettors, Morris was but one manufacturer wanting proprietary engines and the firm had plans for a car of their own with a really advanced 80 × 120 × 4 engine with inclined overhead valves operated by a single camshaft in the crankcase in a manner very reminiscent of the 328 B.M.W. All these plans came to nothing, however, because in December, 1919 White, who had the financial control of the firm, decided to sell to the rapidly expanding Dennis Bros., who not unnaturally wanted W & P to concentrate

on building engines for Dennis commercial vehicles. White and Poppe &
Co. Ltd. was finally wound up in 1934 and the manufacture of engines for
Dennis vehicles transferred to Guildford.

In 1924 P. A. Poppe resigned from the White and Poppe board and joined
Rovers as their chief engineer, acting also as consultant to Maudslay. Poppe
designed the complex but commercially unsuccessful 14/45 Rover with
inclined overhead valves. A single bevel driven camshaft under the cylinder
head and at the top of the block operated the inlet valves on the nearside via
roller ended rockers and the exhaust valves on the offside via pushrods. On
its introduction at the Olympia Show in 1924 the engine of the 14/45 Rover
was considered advanced although the fact that it had been designed by
Poppe six years previously (in 1918) was betrayed by the old fashioned
induction manifolding.

Poppe had a daughter, Ingrid, and three sons, Earling, Olaf and Gunnar.
The three sons were associated with the motor industry. Earling raced a
special 14/45 Rover at Brooklands lapping at 98·62 m.p.h. in 1927. Gunnar
has the distinction of having been an Austin 7 works racing driver (3rd and
class winner 1931 T.T.; class winner 1929 500 mile race, etc.) and Olaf became
the works manager and a director of Rovers.

Poppe had learnt about accurate manufacture and interchangeability from
armaments experience and applied these standards to engine production.
White and Poppe Ltd. should always be remembered as the pioneers and
absolute leaders of accurate machine manufactured parts and consequent
interchangeability in the petrol engine world. This was the key to quantity
production. They were the largest British proprietary engine manufacturer
prior to World War I, with the possible exception of Begbie Engineering
Co. of Willesden who built Aster engines.

Small cars of yesterday *by B. H. Davies*

(*An extract from an article which appeared in* The Autocar *of* 28*th December,* 1923.)

As much ridicule as interest was probably excited by the exhibition of the original 10 h.p. Singer in 1913. Destined to sire an enormous and distinguished family, its Lilliputian dimensions made everybody laugh. It was variously likened to a perambulator and a roller skate. I remember standing over it with a trio of eminent engineers, after a group of jeering laymen had disposed of it in a few sneers. One of my companions laid a finger on a rod connection – the rod swung in the vertical plane and had a horizontal yoke and pin joint. "Alter *that*, and this baby should make good!"

I did not buy one for another year, largely because one of them uttered a little dry cough outside my house and disgorged most of the contents of its bulgy back axle into the road; but I still remember the thrills of the little 1914 10 h.p. Morris Oxford, which I bought in its stead. It felt so fragile beneath one that we left the then modest little Cowley factory in momentary expectation of the chassis dissolving into spillikins under us. But when we got to the open road and gave the little White and Poppe engine its head, timidity gradually merged into glee. On the homeward run we chased, raced, and passed many leviathans of the road.

CATALOGUE OF TROUBLES. The tiny chassis, not yet burdened with the lavish equipment of today, probably scaled well under half a ton; and if small engines had not then attained their present efficiency, they had less load to pull. Fifty-five miles an hour was well within the compass of this small projectile, supposing one could keep its bounding hare-like leaps within the compass of the road. Changing down to second enabled hills to be shot up in a long crescendo scream. We provoked the laughter of beholders along the route, and not less so at the front door when we displayed the new purchase to the family. But, like the man who invented the first umbrella, we felt those laughed best who laughed last.

The first trip taught us the best of the 1914 small car. Ere long we were to learn the worst of it. The water spaces round the exhaust valves were somewhat throttled. Result, the sparking plugs were always rather too hot. The design of pistons and rings in 1914 was far below present levels, and oil could not be kept in its place. Plugs, blue with heat and intermittently drenched in oil, gave incessant trouble. Balance and r.p.m. being the fundamentals of the engine, as soon as one plug commenced to soot up inside its barrel, the road performance dropped to a kind of three-legged crawl. In an air test the guilty plug would probably fire at the official gap, only to misbehave on replacement.

After a few experiences I never took the road without a dozen plugs, preferably a brand new dozen. Seldom did a long run finish without plug changing, and it was always difficult to spot the culprit; shorting each plug in turn afforded little definite information, seeing that a large carburettor of a very sensitive and 'gulpy' type did not furnish too smooth a tick-over at the best of times. Sundry petty fakings of the piston rings, coupled with a superior plug, eliminated this trouble.

COOLING AND LUBRICATION. A second result of the same imperfection only became serious when the wind was astern. Relieved of wind pressure, the tiny Morris would race along like a scalded cat. Ere long the film of water round the exhaust valves flashed into steam, and seeking an exit would blow much fairly cool water out of the radiator safety vent. The entire radiator could empty itself in less than a mile under these circumstances. Experience soon made us revert to the customs of our motoring ancestors, and carry canvas buckets, wherewith to fetch water from adjacent ponds or streams. But until this counter was adopted, pathetic scenes were witnessed, such as two smart men scooping water out of potholes with their hats.

Winter introduced us to yet another failing. The lubrication was simplicity itself. An enclosed flywheel picked oil out of a sump, and flung it into bell-mouthed passages, whereby it flowed into engine, clutch and gears. The clutch was of the multiple disc type. Take the thick oil on which a tiny, high-speed engine throve best ten years ago; flood a multi-disc clutch with it; freeze the lot; and then try to get the clutch disengaged on a December morning.

One soon grew desperate. Finally, one revved up the engine, seized the gear lever in a firm grasp, and remorselessly forced in bottom gear with the clutch still solid. With a frenzied leap and a hideous clash the car shot out of garage, the driver clinging in terror to the wheel as he negotiated the circuitous paths of his back garden at speed, and dived out at the front gate into the traffic knowing that it would be impossible to declutch for at least five miles. After a few stunts of this kind, wisdom dawned, and at night the clutch pedal was chocked 'out' with a baulk of timber. Then the outraged clutch spring protested by taking a set. And so on.

STARTING FROM COLD. Starting up was a tricky business. Neither carburettor nor inlet pipe was designed for rational gas velocity at a low crankshaft speed, and the induction system contained one or two little traps in which pools of condensed petrol collected when at last juice began to quit the jet.

With a modern car, the first explosion on a December morning sounds as music in the ears; it marks the close approach of continuous firing, the end of yanking and sweating at the crank handle. Not so with the 1914 Morris. The first explosion probably implied that a large pool of petrol had just formed in one of the traps of the induction system. The final successful start was possibly more remote than ever. Still, one always triumphed in the end; and when once warmed up the little car was most joyful to drive, provided that the wind was not astern, and that sufficient plugs were aboard.

Her equipment was modest to a degree. No starter, no valances. Gas headlamps. Oil side and tail lamps. The minimum of tools. Single panel windscreen. No side curtains of any kind. But the lack of weight entailed by such additions endowed her with a performance which some of her descendants cannot reproduce. Like our first loves, she retains a tender niche in the memories of all those who are fortunate enough to have known her; and time has cast its healing gloss over her many faults.

Light car talk *by Runabout*
From The Autocar *of 9th May*, 1914

AN APPRECIATION OF THE MORRIS OXFORD. My 1914 Morris Oxford (*de Luxe* model) has now done 4,000 miles, a distance which is long enough to justify some confidence in the formation of a critical estimate. Let me say at once that the tiny vehicle has given supreme satisfaction. There is more of the Rolls-Royce *cachet* about it than most wee cars possess, and in general reliability, the silky ease of steering, the velvety efficiency of its clutch, and the operation of the brakes it is simply astoundingly good. It has the best balanced engine that a fastidious motorist could desire, vibration being non-existent up to 2,500 r.p.m., comparing very favourably indeed with most of its rivals. Compulsory road stoppages and mechanical breakdowns have been unknown, whilst the tyres are still perfectly sound, and very little worn.

The weak points are ultra-liveliness of the springing on really bad roads (reducible by binding the lower halves of the rear springs with trawl twine); quick wear of the brakes (my car has had an exacting life, and the footbrake is weak after 4,000 miles, though the side brakes are not quite ready for relining); distortion of the coachwork, leading to occasional jamming of the doors (probably inseparable from a light car body); under cooling, as indicated by frequent steaming in hilly country in hot weather with a following wind (I fancy these light cars really need pump cooling – a big radiator would mean over-cooling in town work); and a certain sensitiveness of the carburettor, which makes the car a little whimsical and moody. I have tried my own hand at adjusting the carburettor; the assemblers tried their hand; and the makers tried theirs; but I have never coaxed quite the consistency out of it which some users obtain from the same carburettor on bigger cars. One of the fitting agents tells me the best plan is to take it out on a pitch dark night, and play about with it till each cylinder ejects a straw-coloured flame from the compression tap, but as the Morris Oxford has no compression taps I shall have to wait until I can find a remote spot where I can run it minus the exhaust pipe at midnight. Still, all these minutiae are revelations of fastidiousness, and I dare to assert that if there is a better small car I shall be proud to invest in a sample.

2

The Morris Cowley – *"a car of superlative merit"*

"I wonder why the new car is called the Morris Cowley? Does the name conceal a horrid threat that Cowley will ultimately swamp Oxford, as Mr Morris already seems to tower over the Vice-Chancellor?"

The Autocar *of* 23rd October, 1915,

The Morris Oxford had sold well during its first year of production, 1913, and the addition to the range for the following season of a de luxe version with chassis and body improvements had increased its attraction still further. Even so, the Oxford had only a limited appeal, for a large section of the market were family men and the car could accommodate only two-seater coachwork. As early as 1913 W. R. Morris had been only too aware of this limitation and accordingly had planned a four-seater Morris Oxford for the 1915 season. This car was to differ from the two-seater in having a longer chassis, a bevel gear differential and a four cylinder, 60 m.m. bore W & P engine with the stroke increased from the standard 90 m.m. to 100 m.m. This proposed model had one drawback: its price. It would be appreciably more expensive than the two-seater and poor value in comparison with imported American cars. Morris was not at all happy about this and so that he could see for himself how the Americans built such attractively priced cars he visited the States towards the end of 1913 for three or four weeks with Hans Landstad, who had been with White & Poppe Ltd. for ten years and was now their chief draughtsman. Morris returned not only full of new ideas, but also with some extremely keen quotations for the supply of major components for his proposed four-seater.

The Continental Motor Manufacturing Company of Detroit had given Morris the drawings and a preliminary quotation for a four cylinder 69 m.m.

bore and 100 m.m. stroke engine. This initial quotation was about £18 per engine which was a staggering reduction on the price of about £50 for a W & P engine and gearbox unit. W. R. Morris visited P. A. Poppe and left him with the Continental drawings and quotation to indicate the type of unit he required. Poppe could see no obstacles to producing a technically comparable or even better engine, but how was he going to do it at the price? He could see no answer to this. Landstad suggested that the only solution was for him to take six months leave, go to America and take a job there in the motor industry to find out at first hand. Poppe agreed but decided to leave the final decision until that afternoon when he could get the opinion of Morris, who would be visiting them. Morris thought the idea a good one and considered that Landstad would have no difficulty getting a job in America. He invited Landstad to travel with him on the *Mauretania* which was leaving for New York the following week and Morris's parting shot was to ask Landstad to bring a drawing board, which amused Landstad greatly, because who in their senses would want to transport a drawing board from England to America?

The *Mauretania* sailed on Saturday the 18th August, 1914 with W. R. Morris travelling first class and Landstad travelling second class and paying his own expenses. Morris came down to Landstad's cabin on their first day out at sea, and although it was Sunday Landstad found it was not to be a day of rest, for Morris asked him to produce his drawing board. A draughtsman feeling sea-sick and a chain smoking motor car manufacturer started on the design of what was to be the British best seller of the twenties: the Morris Cowley. Their aim was to design a car which incorporated the various parts for which they had received preliminary quotations on their last visit to America.

On arrival in America W. R. Morris and Landstad called to see the Curtis aircraft factory at Buffalo before proceeding on to Detroit to finalize supply arrangements for sufficient components for 3,000 Cowleys. The contract for engines was placed with the Continental Motor Manufacturing Company of Detroit. The two important names in the early history of this company are Judson and Tobin, whose families were related by marriage. Ross W. Judson, as a student at the Armour Institute in 1898, began working on engines and in 1902 he worked on John W. Gates' Mercedes, which enabled him to study advanced design closely. Late in 1902 he began building four cylinder engines, financed by his sister, Ione J. Tobin, and her husband A. W. Tobin, with 2,000 dollars. In 1903 this partnership was incorporated as the Autocar Equipment Co. in Illinois and in May of the following year reincorporated as the Continental Motor Manufacturing Company, which was abbreviated to Continental Motors Company in February, 1916 with Benjamin F. Tobin as company president. Then on the 2nd January, 1917 the company was incorporated in Virginia as Continental Motors Corporation. The firm was highly successful and, for example, in 1915 produced 46,000 engines, many of them class B truck engines, declared a dividend of 100 per cent and increased their capital from 2,900,000 dollars to 5,900,000 dollars, which contrasts strongly with the original partnership's capital of 2,000 dollars. For 1916 they planned to increase production from 46,000 engines to 125,000 engines or more which called for extra factory space and so in May, 1916 they bought from a lumber and fuel firm a seven acre tract on the lake front at Muskegon, Michigan. By 1918 the firm had a capacity of 160,000 engines a year and employed 6,000. Ross W. Judson succeeded Benjamin F. Tobin as president and it must have been a proud moment for him in June, 1924 to approve the order for castings for engine number two million. Judson was by now a rich man and in 1927 invited President Coolridge to spend his holiday at his 128 acre estate at Grand Haven, Michigan. In 1932 Continental Motors Corporation formed a subsidiary, the Continental Automobile Co., to manufacture cars using, of course, Continental engines. The cheapest of the 1933 season range was the Continental Beacon two-seater at 355 dollars, with $3\frac{3}{8}$ in. $\times$ 4 in. four cylinder engine; a coupe and sedan were also available. Next in price were the De Luxe Beacons followed by the Flyers, with 3 in. $\times$ 4 in. six cylinder engines. The most expensive of the range were the Aces, with $3\frac{3}{8}$ in. $\times$ 4 in. six cylinder engines, which in four door sedan de Luxe form cost 865 dollars. For the 1934 season a new model, the Red Seal, with $3\frac{3}{8}$ in. $\times$ 4 in. four cylinder engine was planned but never materialised, because during 1933 operations were suspended and the company subsequently dissolved. The cars were a flop, but the engine side continued to prosper and in October, 1939, when activities were concentrated at Muskegon and the Detroit plant sold, the company had 1717 employees. Continental engines are reputed to have been used in over forty-five different makes of vehicle. It is quite a challenge to name them and the authors' list so far includes various models of Anderson, Beggs, Chandler, Columbia, Elcar, Huffman, Monitor, Noma, Paige, Sayers, Saxon and Stutz motor cars and Acme, Available, Bessemer, Corbitt, Day-Elder, Defiance, Huffman, Kleiber, Larrabee, Republic, Sandow, Standard, Traffic, Transport, Union and Wallace commercial vehicles. Even American motoring enthusiasts must find the histories of some of the makes shrouded in mystery.

Although the engine and gearbox were of unit construction the gearboxes were not made by the Continental Motor Manufacturing Company, but were obtained from the Detroit Gear & Machine Co. who also supplied them for cars such as the Scripps-Booth, Sterling and Monroe. The back axle, front axle and steering gear of the Cowley cost £16 5s. 6d., the gearbox cost £8 6s. 2d. and the engine £17 14s. 2d. Freight and insurance cost to Cowley on these items came to £6 10s. 0d., which did not inflate the purchase price too much. These prices were sufficiently low for John Pollitt Jnr. to make special reference to them in a letter to the *Light Car and Cyclecar* in 1916.

Landstad obtained a job with the Continental Motor Manufacturing Company, and after his day's work spent his evenings preparing the detailed drawing of the Cowley. Even weekends were busy as he visited the plants of other manufacturers including Ford, although whether the latter was an official visit or not is another matter. Landstad planned to stay in America for a while to gain experience in their manufacturing techniques, but after two or three weeks W. R. Morris decided to return to England. His passage was booked on the S.S. *Empress of Ireland*, but at the last moment he sailed from New York in a Cunarder. This was lucky, as the S.S. *Empress of Ireland* collided with a Norwegian vessel at the mouth of the St. Lawrence and sank.

War was declared on the 4th August, 1914. The general feeling was that it would not last long, but Tobin, the president of the Continental Motor Manufacturing Company, must have been a far sighted man, for he saw the implications immediately. He asked Landstad if Morris wanted them to proceed with his order for engines, because if there were shipping difficulties due to the war the production run of engines would be shorter than planned. Reduced production would be uneconomical for Morris because he would have to amortize the capital cost of the special jigs and tools, for which he was having to pay, over a smaller number of engines. Landstad sent Morris a cable advising him of the position, but Morris's cable in reply was short and to the point: he asked for the first engine to be delivered as soon as possible. Landstad stayed until October, 1914 to see the first engine through its tests and then, in view of the war, returned to his relatives in England. At the end of December, 1914 Landstad joined W.R.M. Motors Ltd. They acquired in Landstad a man thoroughly conversant both with the interchangeability of parts as a result of his experience with White & Poppe Ltd. and also with American production methods.

The first sample engines were delivered towards the end of 1914 and other parts were scheduled to arrive soon afterwards. By April, 1915 the first Cowley had been assembled and was shown to the Press, from whom it received an enthusiastic reception. The Continental Cowley received a lot of coverage in the motoring press throughout its production life, and part of the reason for this in the case of *The Autocar* may have been that a member of its staff, who wrote under the pseudonym "Runabout", owned one. The Cowley was announced at 158 guineas for the two-seater, which was cheaper than the smaller Oxford at £168. In the light car class the Cowley was obviously a strong competitor in terms of purchase price alone. Even in the respect of weight, the Cowley was within the light car class, but it departed from normal light car practice in the two important respects of chassis length and engine size. The chassis was unusual in being of sufficient length to carry a genuine four-seater body and the engine size was about half as large again as the engines of most light cars. Consequently it was not sheer optimism for W.R.M. Motors Ltd. to state in their 1916 catalogue that as the Morris Cowley "is on the border-line of its class, it will tap the field of both the modern light car and the car proper".

The Morris Cowley was obviously a car designed for the British market, but showed the American origin of its parts in one or two respects other than price. The engine was a four cylinder, 69 m.m. bore × 100 m.m. stroke type U Continental "Red Seal", which was summed up by "Runabout" in his own inimitable manner as being "an engine planned and specified to the tiniest detail by John Bull, but made in America under Uncle Sam's miraculous output methods". In spite of "Runabout's" assertion the engine was not only made in America, but also planned in its tiniest detail by Uncle Sam. All the evidence suggests that W. R. Morris and Landstad first set sail to America with nothing more than a bore and stroke in mind and this would have been fully in keeping with Morris's policy of letting the suppliers get on with the job because they were experienced and expert in their fields and after all he was paying them.

The type U Continental "Red Seal" engine was a side valve L-head unit with a three bearing crankshaft. The main bearings were pressure lubricated by a camshaft operated plunger pump, but the big-ends were splash lubricated. It had a detachable cylinder head, a feature which was by no means universal at the time, but the gasket was not the modern copper asbestos sandwich but a plain sheet of annealed copper, replacements costing 5s. each. The cylinder head had priming taps, a characteristic contemporary design feature, to ease starting from cold on the petrol then available, which was pretty inferior stuff of low volatility. The engine feature which the Press considered unconventional and particularly worthy of mention was the method of checking the oil level. *The Autocar* had the following to say on the subject:

"The standard oil gauge on light cars takes the form of an over-flow tap, which is necessarily so low down on the crankcase of an engine that it is difficult to see and awkward to clean out. A downward slanting tube is sunk in the side of the Morris Cowley crankcase, in which a knob-ended rod is a close fit, the lower tip of this rod is scribed with cross lines, and when the rod is pulled out the green stains shows exactly where the oil level is."

Yes, this was a dipstick! It seems incredible that the Cowley was one of the first British cars in serious production to employ so simple and yet so effective a device. The method of checking that the oil was circulating in the Continental engine was rather more messy. On most light cars of this time a button popped up when the oil was circulating. On the Cowley, a pipe led from the oil pump to a tap. With the engine running one knew the oil was circulating if a stream of it shot out when opening the tap. This messy system was hailed as an engineering refinement, for its simplicity rendered it infallible, whereas the button indicator, which was more expensive to manufacture, could suffer from internal troubles and was not unknown to rise on air pressure alone! The brass tap on the Cowley on the other hand would not have any of these troubles and had the advantage of releasing any air lock which might occur. Another additional advantage was that if the oil pump became gummed up it could be cleared by injecting paraffin into it through the tap (in those days adulterating the crankcase oil with paraffin seemed to be of little consequence). Engine cooling was thermosyphon, aided by a fan. The radiators of some of the cars were similar to those of the W & P engined Oxfords with a pronounced lip around the outside of the base of the header tank, but the later radiator shells were similar to the pattern which was to become so well known in vintage times and were of a solid nickel alloy. As W. R. Morris proudly claimed "You can go on polishing until you get right through to the water". Turning to the engine auxiliaries, the carburettor was a gravity fed horizontal Zenith and the magneto usually an American made Bosch, although sometimes the American Dixie was fitted.

The drive was transmitted by a double plate Ferodo lined dry clutch to the three-speed gearbox manufactured by the Detroit Gear and Machine Co. The ratios chosen, which were perpetuated by Cowley for over a decade and a half, are frequently criticised for their ineptness, but before such criticism is made one must remember the Saxon. In 1916 the Saxon light car used the same 1496 c.c. type U Red Seal Continental engine as the Morris Cowley, but had only a *two* speed gearbox! Although in 1921 the Saxon, which was an assembly job, was described by its producers as "a composite of the automobile achievement of the decade", before the end of the following year it was out of production. The central positioning of the ball change gear lever and hand brake lever betrayed the American origin of the Cowley gearbox. Centrally positioned control levers were common on American cars, but on most contemporary British cars including the Morris Oxford the control levers were on the right. Pressmen who drove the Cowley assured those who had only driven cars with right hand controls that they could soon get used to changing gear and braking with the left hand. On cars with right hand controls the driver usually finished up with a trouser leg full of control levers when entering through the offside door, but not so with the Cowley. The advantage of having a really usable driver's door on the Cowley was pointed out by Mr Clayton Wright of Joseph Lucas Ltd. in a letter to the *Light Car and Cyclecar*. He maintained that "when a lady passenger is comfortably seated and wrapped round with rugs, it is somewhat annoying to have to disturb her if the driver wishes to alight". Whether wrapped around with rugs or not, it was advisable for any lady to alight from a Cowley when it was being filled with petrol as the petrol filler of the scuttle mounted tank was inside the car on the centre of the dashboard.

The drive from the gearbox to the rear axle was totally enclosed and the universal joint, which was of bronze, was lubricated from the gearbox. This system had been an outstandingly good feature of the Morris Oxford. To illustrate how good, W.R.M. Motors had produced some 1461 Oxfords by December, 1915 and W. R. Morris claimed that they were still waiting to be asked to rebush a universal joint. One cannot do better than quote from *The Light Car* of the 10th July, 1917 really to drive home the advantage of the Morris universal joint:—

"The prejudice against metal universals is largely accidental. For example, you will not meet Morris Oxford owners afflicted by it, though no small car can boast a greater mileage or more owners, and every "M–O" has this type of joint. The average metal universal lurks somewhere under the front seat and, being lost to sight, is not to memory dear. Its owner oils it about once a year. After an oiling the pins squeeze out all the lubricant from the bushes, and when the car is at rest the disgruntled oil lies in a pool at the base of the casing – unless, indeed, the casing leaks, as it usually does, when it drips on the garage floor. As soon as the car is in motion the universal begins to spin wildly, and centrifugal force slops the oil ferociously against the casing. Its subsequent exit is irresistible. Some of it immediately makes amateur efforts at constructing a dustless road; the rest bespatters itself against the underworks of the car until the day when the owner commences an overhaul, when it daubs him vengefully. Meantime the bone dry universal – like the ideal and as yet uninvented golf-ball – squeaks until it's discovered, and then the foolish owner has the impertinence to denounce the poor joint. He should rather curse the designer, who has yet to learn that a metal universal astern of the gearbox is streets ahead of leather, and cannot be surpassed, provided it is adequately lubricated. If he wants to know how to lubricate it, tell him to study the Morris. If he retorts that this universal would be satisfactory if it were greased instead of being oiled, tell him to spend a hectic day greasing universals. The orifice is a pinhole, and though an extraordinarily diligent and painstaking man might fill the casing with rather thin grease in eight hours, none of the grease would ever enter the pin bushes, and if it did would soon be squeezed out. Meantime, the operator, the car, the adjoining house, and, in fact, the entire neighbourhood, would necessarily be greasy for weeks afterwards. Soaking the average metal universal in hot tallow is the only practical method of lubricating it, and at that it will be dry and squeaky within a few hours."

The Cowley back axle was American automobile engineering at its best. The casing was two pressed steel banjo sections welded together, a form of live axle construction which is now almost universal, and offered the advantages of cheapness combined with lightness and strength over the system of bolted up castings of most of the rear axles of British cars. The teeth of the crown wheel and pinion were helically cut. The first British car to have a helically

toothed crown wheel and pinion was the six cylinder, horizontal engined
Wilson and Pilcher of 1900 or 1901, but the Cowley was the first British
car which was produced in any quantity to have this refinement. The helically
cut crown wheel and pinion proved much quieter in operation than a straight
cut crown wheel and pinion and was as quiet in fact as a worm and wheel,
but unlike the worm drive fitted to light cars (including the Morris Oxford) it
did not have the tendency to "stick" on transmitting the drive during
acceleration.

The Cowley was the first Morris to have electric lighting as standard. A

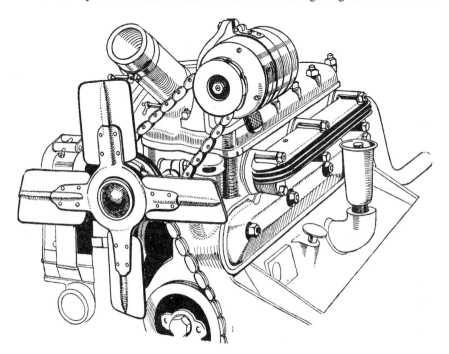

Continental Red Seal engine and Lucas dynamo.

Lucas five lamp set was used. The lighting equipment was expensive at
£10 10s. 0d. compared with £17 14s. 2d. for the engine. The six volt dynamo
had an output of six amps and was driven by a Whittle belt from a pulley
behind the fan. The dynamo was mounted on a bracket bolted to the
cylinder head studs which made the cylinder head nuts inaccessible. Slave
plugs were fitted to the chassis frame and windscreen pillars so that the car
could be used with its lights removed. There was no starter motor, which
was to be expected on a car of this price at this time, but in contrast with
many modern cars, a starting handle, at least, was provided.

Although Cowley chassis were assembled largely from American components, the bodies were British. It must be remembered that there was never such a thing as a Continental engined Oxford and it was only after World War I that the Cowley became simply an austere version of the Oxford. The Continental Cowley had none of this austerity and unlike the vintage Cowley it had diamond pattern buttoned upholstery in real leather, mahogany cappings and a driver's door. The spare wheel was mounted at the rear on the two-seater and on the offside running board of the four-seater, but this in no way impaired entry or exit through the driver's door, as the spare wheel was mounted well forward. The standard finish was chocolate brown with black mudguards and chassis and ebony black or nickel fittings.

One of the surprising things about the Cowley when it was announced in April, 1915 was the low price. The two-seater cost 158 guineas, which was cheaper than the smaller Oxford. Production, however, did not get under way until some months later and it was not until September, 1915 that the Cowley was generally available. Unfortunately this was also the month of the first War Budget of Mr Reginald McKenna, the Chancellor of the Exchequer, who imposed import duties on certain so-called luxuries. An import duty of 33⅓ per cent was imposed on private motor cars and their accessories with the exception of tyres. Consequently, in October, 1915 the prices of the Continental Cowley had to be increased and the price spiral began. The cost rose to 185 guineas for the two-seater, 212 guineas for the four-seater and 170 guineas for the chassis. Parts were arriving from America at a greater rate, but of the 3,000 engines despatched only 1,500 reached their destination, the remainder being lost at sea in enemy action. As Morris had ordered enough parts for 3,000 cars, this left him with 1,500 surplus of certain chassis parts! It was just as well that the delivery rate of American components had increased rapidly, for in March, 1916 the Government prohibited the further importation of American cars or parts unless for commercial vehicle manufacture. However, this did not prevent W.R.M. Motors adding a coupe and a delivery van to the Cowley range in November, 1916, and soon a fleet of the latter were in service in Glasgow delivering parcels and newspapers. The output of Cowleys could not satisfy the demand and this was ascribed by W.R.M. Motors to their difficulty in obtaining bodies, which may account for a number of Continental Cowley chassis being fitted with special bodies. The one thing which most of these special bodies had in common was that they were heavier than the standard bodies and consequently had the inevitable detrimental effect on performance. Some of these special bodies, such as Clayton Wright's coupe, were magnificently luxurious but the most handsome of all was the cruiser body fitted to the Cowley of W.R.M. Motors' works manager, H. W. Grey. The discovery and restoration of a Continental Cowley with a special saloon body is described at the end of this chapter.

Turning to the car's behaviour on the road, the first thing to be done of course was to start the engine, which had to be done by hand as no self starter was fitted. When the engine was new this was quite a task, as following normal American practice it met with little or no running-in. A red sticker on the windscreen warned purchasers that running-in of the engine was necessary, but if a safety league could have seen the wording they would have thrown a fit. It suggested that the legal limit should not be exceeded for the first 500 miles! It further recommended an oil change at 250 miles and another oil change at 500 miles! However, once run-in the engine invariably started first pull. In their 1916 catalogue W.R.M. Motors Ltd. remind us that the engine of the Morris Cowley "is very nearly half as big again as that of the Morris Oxford" and consequently claim that on the road the Cowley "differs from the Morris Oxford in one respect, viz., an ability to hang on to top gear up moderately stiff hills whereas the smaller car would require plenty of gear manipulation to maintain the engine 'revs'. Therefore it is equally economical, especially as the chassis and body are not unduly heavy." Advertising copy is not necessarily the most accurate source of information so it is wise to check whether the motoring Press substantiated these claims. They agreed that the engine was lively, but were more impressed by its fine pulling power. "Runabout" compared the hill climbing power of a 1916 four-seater Cowley with that of a 1914 Morris Oxford, 1914 Alder, 1914 G.P. Mathis, 1915 Singer, 1915 Sporting Calthorpe, 1915 Baby Peugeot, 1915 Raleigh and 1916 Calthorpe. Of these cars the 1916 Calthorpe and 1916 Morris Cowley were the only four-seaters. On the chosen test hill the Sporting Calthorpe was the fastest, but the second fastest was the Cowley, both cars making the climb on top gear. The only other car to climb on top gear was the 1916 four-seater Calthorpe. Other motoring correspondents claimed a maximum speed of about 46 m.p.h. which was considered satisfactory, and a petrol consumption of 31 m.p.g. in exceptionally hilly districts, which they considered would correspond to a consumption of 40 m.p.g. with ease in the Midland counties. This was with the engine fully run-in; before running-in the petrol consumption could fall to 20 m.p.g., which indicates just how tightly the engines were assembled. It was found that the oil consumption of the Cowley was modest, and the engine was notably oil-tight. Even after a lot of hard work the engine did not boil, which was a tribute to the efficiency of the themosyphon cooling system aided by a fan.

The Cowley had a lively performance, but the motoring Press considered that the really outstanding feature was its suspension and road holding, which proved a real advance on previous light car practice, as the rear end did not hop about. A trip in a Cowley so delighted "Runabout" that he wrote "Let nobody tell me in future that light cars cannot hold the road, for here, at least, is one which sticketh to it closer than a brother". The three-quarter elliptic rear springs were not considered responsible for this, because this method of suspension was not so very unusual, but rather the extra weight of the four-seater body over the rear axle, and the low tyre wear of the Cowley

D

was thought to be a consequence of the reduced bouncing. It was universally agreed that the four-seater was so capacious that it could really be regarded as a five-seater and although the room in the front of the four-seater, but not the two-seater, was limited, it was in no way cramping.

S. F. Edge had the politician's talent for convincingly presenting a half truth as the whole truth. In April, 1925 he told the Institution of Automobile Engineers:

"I object especially to accessibility for adjustment, and the less an owner can do in this direction the better, as some people appear to buy their cars for the pleasure of tinkering with them, while the real purpose of a car is to enable the owner to travel in it, and for these latter people I say that adjustability is undesirable."

Edge concluded his spirited dissertation by saying:

"My feeling on this question of accessibility is that a watch does not sell because it is accessible. I never yet went into a jeweller's shop and was sold a watch because it was accessible, but because it will go. In the same way I have never yet met a wireless man who says that a piece of apparatus is better because it can be taken to pieces. He sells it because it will work, and we have got to think of the motor car which will go with the minimum of attention. Therefore, let us think, as in clocks and wireless, not in terms of accessibility, but in terms of go-ability."

An article which really praised the Cowley appeared in the *Light Car* on the 29th March, 1916 under the title "A real owner-driver's car" and to live up to this description, despite Edge's views, the car had to be accessible for easy servicing. Thought, for example, had been given to routine greasing as the screw-down grease caps had hexagonal ends so that they could be given a turn with a box spanner instead of by hand. Allegedly this permitted routine greasing without so much as dirtying one's fingers – a likely story! "Runabout" of *The Autocar*, who was a notable Cowley enthusiast, as readers will have gathered, was so delighted with this excellent accessibility that he recommended that "some of the careless designers who clutter up the vital items of their cars by sheer want of thought, should study the Morris Cowley engine". Indeed in the respect of engine accessibility the only sinner he could find was the bottom water joint, but he mentioned that even this was get-atable as far as these things go. In all fairness one must add that if "Runabout" had turned his attention to the clutch he would have been hard pressed to think of one which was less accessible. Reverting to the accessibility of the engine, "Runabout" concluded that "not many big engines, housed under far roomier bonnets, can show such evidence of careful planning". So that owner drivers could take full advantage of the Cowley's excellent accessibility, in 1916 W.R.M. Motors once again led the way by producing a really comprehensive handbook, which informed the owner how to undertake such major tasks as adjusting the big-end bearings, the steering

. A 1926 Oxford with skylight open.

11. Before:
Norman Routledge's
1924 Cowley
towing home his
1916 Cowley.

12. After: The 1916 Cowley fully restored.

Humble Monarch: The Rajah of Perlis in his 1925 Cowley with appropriate extras.

Selling effort: 1926 Cowley with a Stewart & Ardern lady demonstrator.

15. Typical of the breed: A 1926 Cowley occasional four.

gear and the crown wheel and pinion without any professional help at all. *The Light Car* considered that this was especially valuable to owners of cars in remote corners of Britain, or those who found themselves dependent on native labour in semi-tropical colonies and in any case, as *The Light Car* pointed out, during the war there were few skilled civilians left for maintaining motor cars.

The degree of reliability of the Cowley could not be judged during a road test of a few hundred miles, nor indeed a few thousand miles. *The Light Car* admitted as much when one of their readers asked if the Cowley would stand up to its work and they prudently replied that only time would tell. Morris had competitors such as Calthorpe and Perry, but after a few years it was obvious that the Cowley was head and shoulders above any competitors in the respect of reliability. The clutch sometimes slipped because of a tendency for the rear main bearing to leak but otherwise the Cowley had no weak feature of note and would withstand the most shocking abuse without complaint. A motorist writing about his favourite car described it as possessing the silence of a Rolls-Royce and the reliability of a Morris Cowley! Probably the best indication of the worth of a Continental Cowley was that just after World War I it always commanded a higher second hand price than any other light car. Although only 1,450 Continental Cowleys were built it was sufficient to gain the model a magnificent reputation.

From this distance in time it is easy to see that the outstanding feature of the Cowley was its utter reliability and its ability to withstand the most shocking abuse. To summarise, one might almost say that the Cowley was a splendid tribute to the excellence of American automobile engineering and production techniques, as it should never be forgotten that the mechnical components of the Cowley were of American design and manufacture. On its introduction the Cowley had certain design features which reflected American practice but which were practically unknown on British cars. The Continental Cowley was, for example, about the first British car in serious production to have a central ball change gear lever, a pressed steel back axle casing, a helically cut crown wheel and pinion, and indeed the now universal dip stick. Quite rapidly these features appeared on more and more British cars. The use of American components had enabled Morris to introduce the Cowley at a thoroughly attractive price, but tariffs soon nullified the economic advantages of buying from the States. The true advantage of having all the Cowley's major components of American origin was that it ensured that they were of the right design for quantity production, which was of enormous value when the output of Morris cars was so dramatically increased during the 'twenties.

Few Continental Cowleys were built and the model's real significance is that it enabled Morris to enter the post-war market with a well tried design of excellent reputation and capable of mass production. The Cowley was one of the few British light cars capable of being manufactured in large quantities without much design modification or indeed complete redesign. It was absolutely right from the first. In the words of John Gilpin Jnr. of *The Light Car and Cyclecar* the Continental Cowley was "a car of superlative merit".

Light car talk *by Runabout*
From The Autocar, 23rd October, 1915

OXFORD, AND MORRIS OF OXFORD. Immediately before my last visit to Oxford I had read an impressionist volume on the city – you know the sort of thing, bound in pale green, with wide margins, and breathing a languid, literary atmosphere. I had hardly reached Carfax before I felt the impressionist had failed to catch the soul of Oxford, and I had not passed Magdalen before his defect was crystallised. He left out W. R. Morris.

W. R. Morris's ugly red 'buses disfigure all the grey ancient streets, doubtless ministering enormously to the convenience of their denizens, and thundering contempt of the prehistoric trams which they eliminated. W. R. Morris's red-boarded garages shriek defiance at the time-worn colleges. W. R. Morris's brass-prowed two-seaters flit about, blowing cobwebs from Oxford's brains; and, last, but not least, I imagine that W. R. Morris – via the aforesaid 'buses – is mainly responsible for a tardy but praiseworthy effort to substitute decent road surfaces for the shameful prairie tracks once masquerading as Oxford roads.

The leviathan who thus aggressively dominates the old grey town has his lair far out in the suburbs, where he is mainly busied at present in offering patriots a compromise, to wit, one of the very nicest small cars in the world, a British chassis, with an engine planned and specified to its tiniest detail by John Bull, but made in America under Uncle Sam's miraculous output methods. I wonder why the new car is called the Morris Cowley? Does the name conceal a horrid threat that Cowley will ultimately swamp Oxford, as Mr Morris already seems to tower over the Vice-Chancellor?

THE MORRIS COWLEY CAR.   Anyhow, the car strikes me as inaugurat-
ing a new era. I speak in all soberness, but it has never before happened that
I have sampled a new chassis without – secretly or explicity – picking some
holes in its road manners. Journalism stimulates the critical faculty, and
journalistic experience provides one with a basis for interminable com-
parisons. Above all things I am a critic; and here was a car I could not
criticise. Then I realised that I was handling the first offspring of a wedlock
between British ideals and American methods, begotten here – wholly; made
there – partly.

Let me particularise. The car is cheap. I know not what advances may
accrue from the Budget and war freights, but the original figure was 158
guineas for the two-seater. Nevertheless, its steering was blameless. Its
springs – devoid of shock absorbers – held the wheels glued to the road over
surfaces and at speeds hereinafter to be described. Its engine accomplished
the crescendo from zero to 4,000 r.p.m. without evincing a period, meanwhile
purring or bellowing out power beyond all expectation. Its brakes seized the
car, and held it pinned, without chattering, or pushing against the front axle,
as if the whole were delicately eager to obey.

The technical details bristle with originality, and combine every fad I had
ever mused over as wise and sound, the oil gauge gauges to a hair, be the oil
hot, cold, stationary, or bubbling; the oil indicator indicates to a drop; the
greasers hold a decent ration, and are operated by a tube spanner; the dynamo,
magneto, and carburettor are as accessible as sparking plugs. I could find
no fault at all.

A TRIAL RUN.   But let me outline the run. We started away as if we
were going to creep bourgeois-fashion along sordid, suburban lines. Suddenly
we took a dive to the right, and faced a hill, which presently degenerated into
a disused track, towering heavenward in single-figure steps. Its centre was a
made combat between living rock and multitudinous weeds; its sides, ruts in
which a novice could easily rip a wheel off the best hub made; its fringes,
undulating shoals of sun-baked earth and pebbles; and all the time the road
writhed madly up. The car – steered by a master, I acknowledge – roared up
the foothills on top; accepted second with a scream, and accelerated to
thirty; and seemed to sulk when first was snicked in to conquer a regular
pebbly bowl on a piece of about 1 in 5. Arrived at the summit of the old
London coach-road, the car sped over a grassy, roadless tableland, which
dips where a capsize seemed inevitable, with aged ruts where a wheel seemed
bound to jam, with pastures where tall thistles nodded drunkenly over the
side of the body.

"It's no use," said Morris tersely, "testing cars on the Holyhead road when
every mail brings Overseas orders." I suppose there are light cars which
could manage this obscene caricature of a road; I daresay some of my own
past 'buses – now sadly shrunk in my estimation – could do it; but the

miracle of the swoop lay not in the engine, though that was superb, but in the springing. For it is no shadow of an exaggeration to say that throughout this racing climb, and the subsequent voyage over the wild, billowy plateau beyond, the back wheels never once left the ground, nor did the body play cup and ball with its occupants.

When we got back I promptly went round to the stern, and examined the back tyres. I have hardly ever seen such treads. The cross-grooves were almost non-existent, for the tyres had seen hard wear, but the worn surface was innocent of the usual network of infinitesimal scars and criss-cross cuts; it was merely polished dead smooth, as if it had been ground down with an emery wheel. So the ocular test confirmed the witness of my skin. Let nobody tell me in future that light cars cannot hold the road, for here, at least, is one which sticketh to it closer than a brother.

Restoring a Continental engined Cowley *by N. D. Routledge*

The first five years of collecting old cars you have to seek them, after this they find you! People drop in to see you, mention th·y know where to find the rarest of old cars, and expect you to rush off at a moment's notice to buy them. Many of these turn out to be anything but as described, and much time and petrol can be wasted following up such "hot tips".

Thus, when the little man wandered in one day, and after the usual preliminaries, announced that he knew of a 1916 Morris Cowley, that was stored in an old brewery, I naturally assumed that he too had spent too much time in one.

However, I did not work Sundays then, and Boro'bridge is not all that far from here, so one Sunday a car full of sceptic Routledges set off in search of a 1916 Bullnose. Had it not been that during the war, Bill Boddy and I had previously hunted for a racing Hillman said to be in a brewery, I don't think I'd have thought any more about it, but the two stories whetted my curiosity and I had to have a go.

We arrived at Boro'bridge, and after much trouble found the man we had been told to contact. Yes, he had this car, and he remembered the Hillman. "About a twelve horse it was, had a pointed tail, and the numbers still on it, painted black they were, all aluminium body. They broke it up some years ago," he said sadly. We gently twisted his arm and asked, "Where's the Morris?" Still lamenting the Hillman, he led us to a yard behind an old mill.

When I first saw the old gentleman, never could regard this one as a "she", I got a shock. He was resting on tyres that were shreds of canvas and rubber, the top of the radiator had been cut off, and the body listed very badly to the nearside – brewery influence no doubt.

I looked, I boggled. What a job even to take it away I thought. New tyres would have to be got, and the wheels repaired before it would tow. The whole car would have to be rebuilt from scratch. "How much?" I said to the contact man. "Oh, these old cars are worth a mint of money" he replied. They usually are, I'm used to this one! So I told him that they were IF they were in good condition, and that this one wanted a mint of money spending on it, furthermore, I was the only fool in Yorkshire who'd consider buying it, and tackling the work – so what?

He thought that one over, it made sense to him. Offers were made, refused, discussed, and finally it was mine.

I scrounged some bricks, jacked up both axles, and took off all the wheels, which I brought home in the boot of my Alvis. These were sent to a tame wheel repairer, who sorted them out while I hunted for a set of beaded edge tyres to fit 'em. Had the stud centres been the same as my later Cowley the job would have been easier, but no such luck!

At long last a set of tyres materialised, not quite what I wanted, but tyres and they fitted. The wheels were given a coat of "Rustanode" after repair and sandblasting, the tyres and tubes fitted, piled into the rear of my Cowley four-seater, and one evening we went to collect the venerable old gentleman. On our arrival, we hastily fitted the wheels, applied a tow rope, and off we went, just beating the crowd that we knew would gather. I had a bit of trouble with the mechanic I took with me, although carefully prepared beforehand, the shock was nearly too much for him. I let him drive the four-seater, didn't want to shock him too much, and I tagged along at a very slow speed in the saloon. The springing was rather hard, the brakes didn't work too well, and as the screen had been shattered it was a little draughty in front. I amused myself by going through the pockets as we trundled down the Great North Road towards home. All the dust of decades swirled around me, I became thirsty, and some two miles from home we called at an inn for lubrication. The sight of a '24 tourer towing a '16 saloon was too much for the customers. The pub emptied, half of the customers to look and wonder, the other half to sign the pledge. It's fortunate that the landlord is a well known rally man, or I don't think we'd have been served, as by this time most of the dust had settled on me, and I looked much more odd than usual. Also I suffer from hay fever and the dust was making me sneeze!

When the dust was washed from my throat we proceeded to base where the Edwardian was put inside my garage, and I went home wondering if I'd done the right thing. Harry, the aforesaid mechanic did likewise, wondering if I WAS mad after all!

Later in the week, when we had time and had recovered from the shock, we took stock of our new acquisition. The body was rare, the front door being on the offside while the other door was on the nearside rear. The windows were raised and lowered, a la railway carriage, but with cord covered straps. The interior was in Bedford Cord, and trimmed with a fancy ivy leaf pattern which reminded me of the horse drawn cabs used for funerals when I was quite young. It was filthy and the front door pillar was badly fractured, which accounted for the drunken look it had when we first saw it. This pillar was removed and sent to a caravan maker friend of mine who had one made to pattern. His joiner who made it, said it was the perfect test of skill for the craftsman, as every type of tool had to be used to reproduce the original. Fortunately he was a craftsman, and the replacement fitted just like that! We pulled the body into shape and screwed the new pillar into place. The screen was repaired and fitted with "Triplex" glass. The whole body was cleaned up, internally with a vacuum and dry cleaning fluid, the woodwork was sandpapered down, and the outside was stripped and rubbed down, the mudguards being removed for attention to numerous dents and the odd broken stay.

While all this was going on, the engine had its share of attention. The head and sump were taken off, the valves removed, refaced and ground in. The big-ends were checked for wear. Very little was apparent, only the odd shim having to be removed and the pistons were "drawn" for inspection. All that was needed was a set of new rings, got from stock at the local Wellworthy agents! The engine was quite a straightforward job. I got the idea that whoever designed the Hotchkiss engine had seen at least one Continental engine. The differences are very slight. The webs in the Continental motor are open to the top whereas those on the later model are open to the bottom and look cleaner. The studding of the cylinder head is identical so that later type of cylinder head gasket fits, and the flywheel too would interchange. The cylinder head is flatter, the plugs protruding rather than being recessed as in the Hotchkiss, but they are so similar that I would call the Hotchkiss a "crib" of the Continental. The exhaust manifold is different, the take off being at the rear, from where a heave gauge pipe takes the gas to a robust silencer, and to a tail pipe far thicker than any I have ever seen. It appeared to be quite original. The magneto was in the accepted Bullnose location, the original had been swiped, so we had to fit a rather later one. Pity! But the sparks fitted the plugs so what?

The petrol tank was removed, checked and replaced. It was noted that the fuel gauge was of generous size, and its estimated capacity was about half a pint! Looked like the water gauge on a mill boiler! All the bright parts were sent for nickel plating and new side windows were ordered. These were of very thin glass and only by drastic alterations could thicker ones have been fitted, but, as they were in wooden frames, this was judged to be O.K. The wiring was replaced completely; metal bound wire was used, obtained by special order from Ripaults who thought us mad. No self-starter was fitted, but then it goes on the handle "just like that" so who cares? A six volt battery was fitted to the running board, fed from the engine mounted dynamo, to supply power for the lights. These too had been pinched, so we had to seek replacements of the same period. Very difficult it was too, but we triumphed in the end.

The road springs had excessive camber, but as they were sound and appeared to be original, they were greased and left intact. No shock absorbers were fitted, nor did we think them to be necessary.

The carburettor was stripped, cleaned and refitted. This was a very simple affair, made for economy rather than performance, as was most of this car. Several adverts for a radiator of the right age having proved fruitless, we reluctantly used a '23 Cowley one. The original differed slightly, having tubes in the block rather than film type block, and it had a band round the centre, running horizontally; this we omitted. It was hoped that one day we would find an original one – we never did!

The rear axle was of American origin as was the power unit, the braking system being similar to the later Cowleys – makes you think! The shoes were relined (at least the footbrake shoes were), shimmed up, and re-assembled. They were thought not much good, and this subsequently proved quite true!

The original clutch was the Ferodo lined "dry" type, but as this slipped like the very devil on the test run, some five hours before we were due to rally the car, the whole was replaced by an oil-immersed one from a Hotchkiss engine. "Needs must when the devil drives." I am not speaking about myself! We had the car mobile again just in time for the event, which I couldn't miss, as the local Morris folk had laid on a new Cowley saloon to show the contrast. The car was sold with this clutch still fitted; it never gave any trouble so we left it well alone.

Beyond draining, washing out and refilling the gearbox it wasn't touched. It was the usual three-speed and reverse ball change thing, fairly wide ratios, but then it WASN'T a sports car. It drove via an enclosed propeller shaft inside a torque tube. Somebody once said "There's nothing new under the sun" and this car proves that!

All the spring shackles were in good shape, I don't think the car had done a great mileage, the steering was tight and had little play, but the wheel was too small for my liking, and made the car feel a bit like a "Dodgem", although it was adequate for the rest of the outfit. The front axle was very "rear wheel braked Bullnose", with the same drop in the centre, but the wheels and hubs were, as stated earlier, of a smaller size. A speedo was driven from the front nearside hub, via a little gearbox and flexible drive. The instrument read up to 60 m.p.h. – but never during its life on this car!

Finally, when we had sorted the old man out, it was decided to repaint him as near the original colour as could be, so we hied ourselves to a coachpaint manufacturer in Leeds who matched the samples we showed him. It was two shades of brown with black mudguards. The valance had been black leather, but we used leathercloth. It was more easily obtainable and cheaper. The running boards and the aluminium beading round them had to be renewed and new rubber fitted. The interior woodwork was in black enamel, and very nice it looked too.

I was particularly pleased with the results we had on the Bedford Cord interior, it came up really well. As some vandal had nobbled the front seat squab, this had to be replaced and never really matched the rest. Just one of life's little disappointments!

I ran the car for a few months, attending the local check point when the Anglo-American Rally passed through Yorkshire. It was amusing to drive, very comfortable, but so top heavy! I never felt really happy in it. I like a bit more speed than it had. It was fascinating with its lumbering, dignified gait, but I could never have grown to love him as I do my four-seater. Moreover one can have too many cars, so, reluctantly, for he had a little charm in a "bath chair" kind of way, I sold him to an enthusiast in London to whom I delivered him one day in March.

We left Leeds at crack of dawn, about six in the morning (I only hear it crack when it cracks late!) and made our stately way down the Great North Road. Doncaster was reached in about an hour – 30 miles, and so we rolled on through Newark and Grantham without incident to Stamford where it was deemed advisable to fill up with petrol. After some delay answering all the questions we moved on to Alconbury Hill where we left the North Road for the A14 on to Royston, where A10 was joined. Progress was steady, and at 2 p.m. we had arrived at Chingford absolutely without incident of any kind, something to be said for the old stager after all.

I got no end of pleasure from rebuilding this car, especially as it was saved from a fate worse than death. I enjoyed my brief spell of ownership, but it could not complete with my little "maid of all work," the four-seater. I found her in a barn where she had lain for fifteen years. I may fool myself, but I honestly believe that she goes so well because she is so pleased to be out of that barn, after all those years. During the ten years that I have had her she has done everything I have asked her, and some of my demands have been very unreasonable – but that is another story!

3

Post-war developments

"A Morris owner is as unconscious of his clutch as a healthy man is of his liver." *The Motor in Australia – January* 1917.

W.R.M. Motors sold 1,133 Continental engined Cowleys and 316 W & P engined Morris Oxfords during World War I, but car assembly had been a sideline because the factory primarily had been occupied manufacturing mine sinkers and other military equipment on a cost plus basis. With the return of peace, the military contracts ended abruptly and Morris was able to concentrate on car assembly again. The switch from munitions to motor cars required only minor re-organisations, and Morris got off the mark quickly, but he was hampered by the difficulty of obtaining parts, and for the time being had to rely on his limited stocks of American components left over from the 1915 Cowley programme. As these components were used up he could not replace them with further supplies from America because duties and government restrictions made it either uneconomical or impossible to do so. Even if this had proved only a temporary setback it would have been of little help because The Continental Motors Corporation of Detroit had decided to discontinue the manufacture of their type-U Red Seal since they considered that the American market for a 1495 c.c. engine was too limited. Thus Morris, having gained an initial advantage over his competitors, whose change over to peace time production was more fundamental because they manufactured most of their components as opposed to merely assembling, found himself in the anomalous position of having to reduce production during the post-war boom due to a lack of parts.

Morris had to rely on British suppliers. At first body supplies were not a major headache because W.R.M. Motors had always used British ones.

Raworths of Oxford, who had made the bodies for the W & P engined Oxford, and Hollick & Pratt of Coventry, who had supplied the bodies for the Continental engined Cowley, were natural choices. Morris knew Raworth well, because the latter had been in charge of painting at Cowley during the war, but one presumes that he set an altogether higher standard of finish for cars than for the mine sinkers! It soon became apparent that the two firms could not meet the demand and therefore in 1919 Morris set up his own body shop at Cowley, with Pratt in charge, and from then on the standard touring bodies were made at Cowley and Raworths and Hollick & Pratt supplied the more specialised ones such as coupes and saloons.

Morris had always used British radiators and his suppliers had been the Doherty Radiator Co. Ltd., Coventry Motor Fitments and Randles of Coventry. After the War Dohertys could supply part of Morris's needs, but not all. To overcome this Morris bought the old roller skating rink in Osberton Road and Dohertys set up a branch there. Shortly afterwards Morris helped two employees of Dohertys, Messrs. H. A. Ryder and A. L. Davies, to buy the Oxford branch, which was renamed the Osberton Radiator Company. At first the Company bought in radiator shells from Fisher and Ludlow, but then started to make their own and entered other branches of the pressings field.

The rear axle assembly of the Continental engined Cowley was of American manufacture and consequently a British substitute of similar design had to be found. Wrigleys had supplied Morris with complete rear axles and steering boxes for his W & P engined Oxfords, but could not produce these components for the post-war Cowley because they had already heavily committed themselves to Angus Sanderson, as related in Chapter 7. Morris was not perturbed over his inability to purchase complete rear axles or steering boxes in the quantities he required because war-time experience on assembling mine sinkers had shown that it was now possible to purchase from different suppliers individual items such as gear wheels, axle casings (from Fisher and Ludlow), shafts and bearings which could then be assembled at Cowley into larger units such as complete rear axles. For success this method depended upon the maintenance of rigid purchasing specifications, but its adoption enabled Morris to overcome the problem of rear axle and steering box supplies and also to contract with the smaller specialists.

Morris's most pressing need was to find a supplier of engines and gearboxes, and in his search he had two facts to consider. On the debit side he had little money and so could not afford a large deposit. To his credit however he had the design rights and some jigs and tools of the Continental type U engine, so that all he needed was to find an engineering firm capable of producing, but not necessarily designing, engines (at his price!). The obvious firm to approach was White & Poppe of Coventry who had supplied the engine/gearbox units for the earlier Morris Oxfords. Just after the outbreak of World War I Poppe had submitted to W. R. Morris a design of engine for the Cowley as an alternative to the Continental Red Seal. The engine had been designed by Poppe and his chief draughtsman Hanche during a business-cum-holiday trip to their homeland, Norway, in 1914, but which was unfortunately cut short by the outbreak of war. The proposed W & P unit for the Cowley was a fairly conventional four cylinder L-head design of 60 m.m. bore and 100 m.m. stroke, but interesting features were a dynamo driven in tandem with the fan and a water outlet over the centre of the cylinder head. Since initially drawing up the engine Poppe had decided on a few design modifications. He had concluded that off-set big-ends resulted in tapered crank pins and bell mouthed big-ends and therefore substituted in-line big-ends. In spite of Poppe's deductions it is interesting to note that some present day models still have off-set big-ends. Poppe eliminated the water spaces under the valve seats on the portions remote from the cylinder barrels because he concluded that with them the valve seats were more liable to crack under heavy load conditions without provision for fitting reliable inserts. Although this engine never left the drawing board, W. R. Morris had such confidence in White & Poppe Ltd. that he was anxious to conclude arrangements with them for its supply. Poppe was also eager to have Morris's business, but the deal fell through because Poppe's co-managing director, Alfred White, was against it. There are two possible reasons for this. One is that White & Poppe already had plans of their own for the production of a car, and the other is that Dennis Brothers may have already made a tempting take-over bid.

In view of the unwillingness of White & Poppe & Co. Ltd. to supply engines, Morris started negotiations with Oldhams of Coventry, who during the war had manufactured large guns, but the talks came to nothing because the works representatives could not agree with the management that the price Morris offered was economic. Next Morris approached Dormans of Stafford, the proprietary engine manufacturers, who sent along a sample engine. Landstad stripped down the engine and advised Morris against using it because the finish of the parts was too rough, but what really scotched the possibility of a Dorman engined Morris was that the Stafford firm required a £40,000 deposit. Morris was also approached by Mr J. H. Pick of the New Pick Motor Co. of Stamford, but the latter had insufficient production capacity. Then he had a stroke of luck. Hotchkiss et Cie heard that he was looking for engines.

Many armament firms have turned to making motor cars as a side line. In Great Britain cases in point have been B.S.A., who made Daimlers and Lanchesters as well as cars bearing their own name prior to the acquisition of their car interests by Jaguar, Vickers Ltd., who made Wolseleys before Morris acquired them in 1927, and Armstrong Whitworth. Belgium had the F.N. and Nagant and Switzerland the Martini. In France there was the

Schneider and those non-commercial propositions, Cugenot's steam vehicles and the C.T.A. – Arsenal Grand Prix contenders. Marc Birkigt reversed matters by designing his celebrated 20 m.m. Hispano aircraft cannon after many years of car manufacture. And there was Hotchkiss.

Hotchkiss et Cie started manufacturing their famous machine guns and quick-firers during the Franco-Prussian war in their newly built factories at Saint Denis and Levallois-Perret in the Seine district of France. During World War I, when it looked as though their Saint Denis factory would be overrun by the Germans, they hurriedly transferred production to a new factory in Gosford Street, Coventry. By the end of the war the Coventry branch of Hotckhiss et Cie had produced over 50,000 machine guns, but afterwards contracts dried up. They were left with a first class works manager in Ainsworth, a pool of experienced engineering staff skilled in quantity production techniques, and excellent equipment, but, alas, little work. Consequently, as soon as the rumour got round that Morris was seeking an engine supplier Benet, the Hotchkiss Managing Director from France, two other Frenchmen and Ainsworth, were on his doorstep. Morris had never set eyes on them before, but they walked into his office and got straight to the point. Did Morris want engines? Morris countered by asking Ainsworth about the type of engine he had in mind and Ainsworth offered to make one to Morris's designs if preferred. This suited Morris admirably. The Continental Red Seal engine, of which Morris had acquired the rights, had proved splendid and here was a firm prepared to copy it. Next, the question of price was raised, and Morris warned Ainsworth that he would want engines at less than £50 a piece. Ainsworth replied that at first the engines might cost as much as £100 each, but once production got under way these prices would most certainly come down. Now for the sixty-four thousand dollar question! Did Hotchkiss et Cie require a deposit? Benet, their managing director, was on the point of suggesting a suitable sum when Ainsworth interposed and said that no deposit was required, as they had sufficient financial resources. The business was clinched. Although the Coventry branch of Hotchkiss et Cie had never built a motor car or motor car parts, nevertheless Morris could have full confidence in them. He received sample engines in July, 1919 and in September, 1919 Hotchkiss started to supply the production versions.

In his post-war range, Morris planned to make the Cowley a basic, minimum of frills model, which would be an austerity version of the Continental engined Cowley, having for example upholstery in leather cloth instead of leather. He also intended to offer a de luxe version of the same car for which he revived the name Oxford and which would have leather upholstery, a superior finish in a wider choice of colours and larger section tyres. By introducing these two versions Morris hoped to widen the appeal of his products, the Cowley catering for the light car market whilst the Oxford suited those requiring touring cars. The post-war models had been advertised as early as September, 1918 but full details did not appear in the Press until August, 1919 because sample Hotchkiss engines were only available the month before.

The differences between the new cars and the Continental engined Cowley were few. Indeed, in comparing the Hotchkiss and Continental engine the striking thing is their extreme similarity. The differences included a slightly increased stroke, except possibly for a few of the sample engines, a cylinder head without priming taps and a new layout for the oiling system. There was in addition provision for a starter. An interesting but almost imperceptible variation between the American built and the British built engines was that the latter had French Standard metric (not International Standard metric) threads, as the Hotchkiss Coventry factory was equipped throughout with French metric tool heads. However, so that Whitworth spanners could be

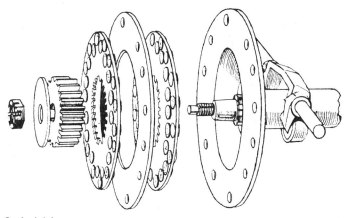

Cork clutch.

used, the metric nuts and bolts had Whitworth heads. To drive home the similarity between the two engines a 1926 Cowley cylinder head gasket is interchangeable with that of a 1915 model.

The only real difference between the chassis of the Continental engined cars and the early Hotchkiss engined cars lay in the clutch and the electrics. In the majority of engines the top halves of the main bearings are supported in the crankcase and until a few years ago the crankcase was split at the centre line of the crankshaft. In the case of the Continental Red Seal engine the crankcase was split well above the crankshaft centre line and the main bearings were mounted on plummer blocks beneath the cylinder block. This permitted an economy as the housing for the starting handle could be cast with the sump (in 1927, for ease of maintenance, the housing was separate), but the saving at the front end must have been lost at the back as the rear main bearing oil sealing arrangements were complicated. This complex oil seal had only one fault: it did not work. In the case of the Continental **Red Seal** engine this was serious because it caused the Ferodo lined dry clutch to slip. Morris, himself, thought of the solution, which was to fit a clutch which ran in oil intentionally instead of accidentally. This was one of the few occasions when Morris concerned himself with detailed design and it clearly shows his practical ingenuity. The new Morris clutch had twin plates running in oil and the lining medium was a multitude of little cork discs. The Hotchkiss engine was such a close copy of the Continental that the complicated rear oil seal was retained, but a hole drilled underneath it for clutch lubrication! Later, a flap valve was fitted to limit the flow of oil into the clutch pit on steep hills in order to avoid starving the engine of lubricant.

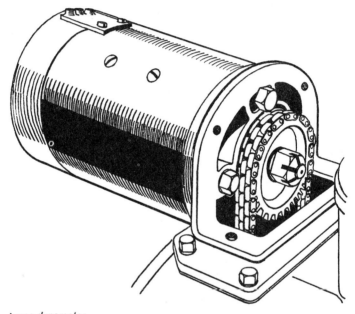

Lucas dynamotor.

Wet clutches were rare on cars, but common enough on motorcycles. To allay any suspicions caused by the novelty of the clutch, after only a year's experience, Morris Motors were bold enough to claim that it was good for 50,000 miles at least without attention, providing the clutch case was kept full of oil, and no undue slipping of the clutch was indulged in. This was just as well, as to give the clutch attention it was necessary to remove the back axle and gearbox or, alternatively, start from the other end and remove the radiator and engine. The reversion to a wet clutch harked back to the W & P days and like the W & P metal to metal wet clutch this new design of wet clutch could drag abominably if the clutch plates were bent or misaligned and was also prone to drag when the oil was cold and thick. To be fair, the new design of clutch has since proved to be an outstandingly good Morris feature, combining durability with lightness and smoothness of operation and freedom from any tendency to slip.

The electrics of the Continental engined Cowley have already been described in Chapter 2. Turning to the Hotchkiss engined cars, the Cowley had a 6 volt B.T.H. mag-dyno which supplied current for the 3-lamp lighting set, but starting was by handle. The more luxurious Oxford had to have a self-starter, because it was demanded by the more affluent purchaser for whom the car was intended. The type chosen was the Lucas dynamotor, which combined the starter with the generator. The dynamotor was sited above the gearbox and driven by an inverted tooth silent chain (either Bamber or more usually Reynold) from a sprocket immediately in front of the flywheel. This unique positioning of the dynamotor was possible because the chain drive was properly lubricated from the wet clutch.

The Hotchkiss engined Morris has one rare refinement; because the engine oil circulates through the clutch compartment, the dipstick not only shows the oil level but any odd particles of cork on it gives early warning of impending clutch slip.

4

The cuckoo in the nest

"Morris, obviously lost to all decent feeling, scooped the cream of the motor trade into his cup by sticking to the unfashionable belief that the best way to expand business, in times of depression, is by lowering rather than raising prices." *A. Bird & F. Hutton-Stott in* The Veteran Motor Car Pocketbook, 1963.

It was a poor reflection on British manufacturers that the best selling car in their country just before and again after World War I was imported; it was the model T-Ford. Although Morris had made a good start as a motor manufacturer, he aimed to increase his sales to a level comparable with those of Ford in Britain. He knew that he must not simply rely on price and quality to sell his cars in quantity; he needed a first class selling organisation.

When W.R.M. Motors Ltd. had been formed in October, 1912, its appointed agents were Stewart & Ardern Ltd. for the London area, H. W. Cranham for the North of England and W. H. M. Burgess for the South of England and all exports. The last two were natural choices at the time, being already White & Poppe distributors. However, Morris wanted more than two distributors outside London to cater for the scale of production he envisaged and he also needed a direct control over exports. To rid himself of his agency agreements with Cranham and Burgess, in July 1919, he dissolved W.R.M. Motors Ltd. and formed a new company, Morris Motors Ltd., with a nominal capital of £150,000 to acquire its assets. In the new company, £25,000 worth of 7 per cent £10 cumulative non-voting shares were issued to Morris's original backer, the Earl of Macclesfield and Mr H. W. Young and Gillett, the Oxford banker, took up £2,000 worth each. Of the ordinary

A 1924 Cowley.

A 1926 Oxford.

18. Luxurious survivor: Margaret Thomas's beautifully preserved 1925 Oxford coupe.

19. One of the last: A 1923 11.9 h.p. Oxford which scorned the larger alternative 13.9 h.p. engine.

A 1924 Oxford with a special Morris Garages body.

22. W. R. Morris by a 1924 Oxford. Note the Morris Service sign.

shares W. R. Morris and his auditor, Thornton, bought one each while Morris, who was permanent Governing Director, was issued with £75,000 worth as a consideration of the net assets of W.R.M. Motors Ltd. The formation of the new company served its purpose but regrettably, according to *The Motor* of 24th December, 1929, led to Burgess suing Morris for a breach of agreement and Morris having to pay compensation in settlement. Happily, the rift between the two was not permanent and Morris chose Burgess as his metropolitan S.U. distributor shortly after he acquired the firm.

In 1919, after the formation of Morris Motors Ltd., W. R. Morris appointed new distributors, who included such now famous names as Kennings of Clay Cross, Derbyshire, Joseph Cockshoot & Co. Ltd. of Manchester and W. Watson & Co. of Liverpool (Watson had won the 1908 4 inch T.T. on a Hutton). Stewart & Ardern of course remained the sole London and home counties distributor, and, not unnaturally, the Morris Garages were appointed for Oxford. In addition there were numerous agents. In February, 1924 the business journal, *System*, published a series of articles by W. R. Morris called "Policies that have built the Morris Motor Business". In these articles Morris had some interesting comments on his distributors and agents. He considered that the main difficulty of his sales department at Cowley was not so much actually selling cars but in educating retailers to accept the Morris principle of expansion. A retailer who sold a hundred cars one year had to be convinced that if he rested on his laurels, he was missing opportunities and his aim should be to sell two hundred cars the following year. Such expansion needed money and for this reason Morris was a firm adherent to retail price maintenance. He made strenuous efforts to ensure that his retailers maintained the official Morris published prices and thereby made sufficient profit for expansion.

The natural rapid growth in the demand for motor cars between 1914 and 1919 had not been satisfied, because production was practically at a standstill during the war years. The demand was accentuated because a large number of people had become mechanically minded during the war and these people, with war gratuities to spend, could afford cars. The result was a boom; anything on wheels would sell. The number of groups which jumped on the band waggon and joined the established manufacturers was enormous.

Some of the designs on the market were shockers and a study of them is full of entertainment, providing that it is purely academic. The owners of the products of these optimistic designers no doubt felt that the matter was far from humorous and that the mechanical jokes were in the height of bad taste. Under such circumstances there was a ready market for cars of proved design such as the Morris Cowley and Morris Oxford, even at the revised prices. When the Cowley had been introduced in 1915, the selling price was announced at 158 guineas for the two-seater and 185 guineas for the four-seater, but by 1919 the price for the more austere two-seater version had risen to £295 and the four-seater to £310. The more expensive 1919 Oxfords were listed at £360 for the two-seater and £390 for the four-seater. These were steep price increases, but even W & P engined Morris Oxfords which had cost new between £175 and 190 guineas were advertised in 1919 for as much as £350, second hand.

Despite his excellent start in 1918 when he sold 198 cars, at the height of the boom in 1919 Morris actually had to reduce production due to the shortage of parts. Two or three sample Hotchkiss engines were delivered in July 1919 but production versions only started to come forward in October 1919. Consequently, of the 360 cars Morris sold in 1919, only 79 had the new Hotchkiss engines. 1920 promised well for Morris, as components were fairly readily available and any optimism he may have felt was justified in the first nine or ten months of the year. In October, 1920 due to rises in costs and labour he put up his prices, the Cowley two-seater for example rising from £390 to £465, the Oxford two-seater from £450 to £535, and the four-seater from £495 to £590. The price increases, 19 per cent in the case of the Cowley two-seater, were not confined to Morris but common to the majority of the British motor car manufacturers, with the notable exception of Bean, at about this time. However, in America the picture was very different. The boom conditions they had been enjoying had collapsed and prices were tumbling. Ford, in particular, had reduced prices and this of course meant that the model T prices in Britain had been correspondingly reduced. If American events foreshadow British trends, the writing was on the wall. In 1920 Morris assembled 1,932 cars, but towards the end of this year conditions changed dramatically. Morrises were at last in free supply, but the boom conditions collapsed.

By January, 1921 Morris was becoming thoroughly alarmed. His factory was full of unsold motor cars and the prospects of selling them seemed small. He then took the most momentous decision ever made in the British motor industry. He decided to cut the price of his cars and not by just a small amount but by making a radical reduction. He felt it would be better to get rid of the cars in the factory rather than stop production, because no motor car manufacturer can make a profit without selling his cars. The price of the Cowley four-seater was cut the most drastically. It was reduced by £100, from £525 to £425. The two-seater was reduced by £90 to £375. The prices of the Oxford two-seater and four-seater were reduced by £25 to £510 and £565 respectively and to bring the price of the Oxford coupe more into line with that of the other Oxford models it was reduced by £80 to £595. Even to Morris the results of these price cuts were quite startling. The sales of his cars went up overnight and his revised system of distributors coped ably with the demand. In January, 1921 Morris sold 68 cars. In February the figure leapt to 244 and in March to 377 cars. Morris's decision to cut prices was his alone and must have taken enormous courage. His colleagues were not in favour of the action and he had no encouraging precedents to rely upon because, in fact, only a few months earlier Beans had reduced their prices without any notable increase in sales.

No other British manufacturers of note followed Morris's lead, they just waited for things to improve. This was surprising, but enabled Morris firmly to establish himself. By the October 1921 Motor Show Morris's competitors had got the message and prices of British cars were on average 17 per cent lower than the previous year. However, they had no sooner made the reductions than Morris made yet another on the eve of the Show, although his models were improved. The biggest cuts were made to the prices of the Oxfords, the two-seater being reduced from £510 to £415 and the four-seater from £565 to £446. The two-seater Cowley came down from £375 to £299 and the four-seater from £425 to £341. To appreciate the size of these price cuts, the February and October reductions must be considered together. In nine months the price of the four-seater Cowley had been reduced by 35 per cent and that of the four-seater Oxford by 21 per cent. The results were that in 1921 Morris sold 3,077 cars against 1,932 cars in 1920, and in comparing these two figures it must be borne in mind that 1921 was not only a slump year for the motor car industry, but probably the worst year it has ever experienced. The results of the policy of Morris to cut prices was seen not only in increased sales but also in increased profits. Afterwards, he admitted that the immediate consequences had been greater than he had ever thought possible.

At this time and indeed before the outbreak of war the best selling car in Britain was the model-T Ford. Since Morris was attacking the Ford share of the market, the Bullnose and model-T were competitors, although they were very different cars and competing for the market in a different way. Reams have been written on the now legendary model-T. Compared with the Morris it had hopeless brakes, bad steering and grossly inferior electrics. It could be a devil to start, backfiring viciously if the ignition was not correctly set, and on a cold day the oil drag in the gearbox was so great that one rear wheel had to be jacked up when starting the car as otherwise it would edge forward. On the other hand, the model-T offered exceptional reliability coupled with a good spares service. It was however of 1908 design and the chief reason it remained saleable was that it was cheap, exceptionally cheap. There was a joke that no one who could afford a car bought a model-T, but this only emphasises the cheapness of a Ford. In 1921, for example, the Morris Cowley four-seater, after the October price cut, cost £341, but the model-T, a full five-seater, cost a mere £195, some 43 per cent less.

After the war it was expected that the makes which would provide some really strong opposition to Ford would be the 14 h.p. Tylor-engined Angus Sanderson (see *Motor Sport* of January, 1961), the 16/20 h.p. Cubitt (see *Motor Sport* of July, 1958) or the Bean. Beans came nearest to this and it is hoped that the notes on this make given in the section at the end of this Chapter will show the fine dividing line between success and failure. Angus Sanderson and Cubitt never lived up to their promises of vast outputs and indeed Cubitts ended up by building a copy of the Anzani engine for A.C.s around 1925. This arrangement bankrupted British Anzani, but well before-hand the astute S. F. Edge had taken the precaution of selling the holding of A.C. in the firm, which must have been a relief to Vauxhalls, who held a large number of A.C. shares. In comparison, Morris Motors finances were simplicity itself.

After February, 1921 sales figures alone made it obvious that Ford's biggest competitor would be Morris. The Cowley was about 80 per cent more expensive than the model-T, but it was an up to date design, equally reliable and cheaper to run. Then Morris had a gift from the Chancellor of the Exchequer. In 1910 Lloyd George had introduced a Road Fund for highway improvement, which was raised by taxing petrol. In 1921 the duty of 6d. per gallon was removed from petrol and to raise revenue for the Road Fund in its place the £1 per R.A.C. h.p. per year system was instituted. (Cynics said that the tax was bound to be reimposed on petrol sooner or later and of course it was, in 1927). Overnight, by a piece of government legisla-tion, the Morris Cowley which was of only 12 R.A.C. h.p. gained an enormous advantage over the model-T, which was 22 R.A.C. h.p. It was more than a matter of straight economics; the Cowley had the incalculable psychological advantage of being subject to £10 per year less tax. Now to capture more of the Ford market, Morris had only to narrow the price gap.

The pattern of the 1921 Motor Show was repeated again in 1922. Prices were down and on average the prices of American cars were 20 per cent cheaper than in the previous year, Continental cars 12 per cent and British cars 15 per cent. The only British cars to remain unchanged in price were two of the Daimler range, the five-seater open Austin 20 at £695 and the 40/50 h.p. "Silver Ghost" Rolls-Royce, which in chassis form cost a cool £1,850, but which was supplemented by a cheaper 20 h.p. model. It may have been sound policy on the part of Rolls-Royce to leave the price of their "Silver Ghost" unchanged, but in the case of the Austin 20 one gathers that Sir Herbert had no option in the matter because it had initially been costed incorrectly at too low a price.

Many exhibitors offered definite technical improvements in combination with lower prices. Sunbeams for example included front wheel brakes on their 24 h.p. six-cylinder model as an optional extra at £125 and were one of the first British constructors to do so. Morris offered a 13·9 h.p. engine as an optional extra for the Oxford. The Humber stand was full of technical interest, inlet over exhaust valve engines having replaced the side valve units on their 15·9 h.p. and 11·4 h.p. models, and even more interesting, the display of a new model, the pretty little 985 c.c. three speed 8/18. When the price of the new Humber 8/18, £275 for the "Chummy", was announced before the Show it was £3 5s. 0d. less than the Cowley two-seater and many people considered this good value for a car of greater economy and excellent quality. Morris had similarly announced his reduced prices for the 1923 season beforehand but on the eve of the Show he once again took the wind out of his competitor's sails at a time when they must have thought he had reached rock bottom prices. His second price reduction within six weeks was announced. The new prices were sensational, the two cuts combined amounting to a reduction of about 24 per cent. Compared with the previous year, the price of the four-seater Cowley at £255 was reduced by £86 or 25 per cent, and the two-seater Cowley price by £74 to £225. The reductions in the Oxford range were even greater, the two-seater being cut by £84 to £330, the four-seater by £111 to £355 and the coupe by £110 to £390. 1922 ended on a high note with the sale of 6,937 cars; a record. Morris was now the largest British manufacturer. After the war he had ranked with such light car makers as Calthorpe (see *Motor Sport* of April, 1959) and Calcott (see *The Vintage and Thoroughbred Car* of July, 1954) but these firms were going under against Morris competition. The very small firms such as Gilchrist (see *Old Motor* of January, 1963) and Warren Lambert (see *Motor Sport* of January, 1960) were in a hopeless position; they did not have the manufacturing capacity to rival Morris production and thereby meet Morris prices. Bunny Tubbs, in his book *Vintage Cars in Colour* summed the matter up best: "Morris was the cuckoo in the nest."

The effectiveness of the 1922 Motor Show price cuts is shown by the sales for the year. 6,937 cars were sold in 1922 compared with 3,077 in 1921 and of the 1922 sale more cars were sold in the last quarter than in any one of the preceding three-quarters, which is proof positive of the soundness of Morris's policy. As well as being a successful year, 1922 was also an eventful one, the most important happening being the breaking up of the partnership between Morris and the Earl of Macclesfield, the former returning the Earl's investment to the full. The authors do not know the full reasons for this parting of the ways, but it is said that Morris felt that the Earl's interest in the detailed day to day business of the company often amounted to interference. Whatever the reasons, the result of the financial support of the Earl of Macclesfield during the most difficult period of the Morris motor car venture, its first ten years, must never be underestimated. Without the Earl's help, the Morris car might never have survived. W. R. Morris was a man of outstanding ability and courage and the Earl of Macclesfield had that all too rare quality of recognising such attributes in others. He gave Morris the chance he deserved.

The other important events of 1922 for Morris concerned his suppliers, an increasing number of whom were finding themselves in the undesirable position of having him as their only customer. Osberton Radiators was just such a firm. Morris was virtually their sole customer and in turn they were his sole supplier of radiators. This placed both parties in a dangerous position. Morris therefore acquired the business for £15,000, keeping in charge Ryder, who previously managed it as part owner. Another firm which was wholly dependent on Morris orders for survival was Hollick & Pratt Ltd., the coachbuilders. On 1st August, 1922 their factory was burnt down and although Pratt and Morris were close friends Pratt pointed out quite reasonably that it was ridiculous to rebuild his factory with the insurance money when Morris was his only customer. A bargain was struck and Morris paid Pratt £100,000 for Hollick and Pratt Ltd., £40,028 for the ordinary shares and £55,822 in instalments for the preference shares. Pratt remained in charge of the body side and later became second in command of Morris Motors Ltd. with the title of deputy governing director. In the latter post Pratt proved ideal and was respected by all, but regrettably he held it for all too short a time, for he died at Stratford-on-Avon at the early age of forty-four on the 19th April, 1924.

Hotchkiss et Cie were in a different position from Morris's other suppliers because being a French firm they were more interested in expansion in France than Britain. Also, although by 1922 they were largely dependent on Morris orders to keep their Coventry branch going, they were determined not to become wholly dependent on him. In addition to doing a considerable amount of armament and engineering contract work, they supplied two other car firms; B.S.A. were provided with a flat twin air-cooled engine and Gilchrist, a Scottish firm whose product was competitive with the Morris in most respects other than price, with an exciting overhead valve development of their four cylinder 69·5 m.m. bore and 102 m.m. stroke engine. Although these concerns were only taking a small proportion of the Hotchkiss output, it irritated Morris that Hotchkiss were supplying them at all. Morris was in a difficult position. Supplies of engines during 1922 were just sufficient to meet requirements, but increased engine supplies to permit further expansion of car production were unlikely and furthermore, for the reasons already outlined, Hotchkiss were not prepared to do much about it. The matter was resolved by Morris making an offer to Hotchkiss for their plant and works complete. The offer was a high one and Hotchkiss accepted. This was no knock-down bargain which Morris acquired, but he was prepared to pay, as he felt the Hotchkiss works at Coventry had unsuspected potential which he could realise by re-organisation. The terms of sale gave Morris the option to purchase the ordinary shares of the Coventry branch of Hotchkiss et Cie for £150,000 and Morris exercised this option in May, 1923, the total purchase price of the firm amounting to £349,423. Until Morris purchased the ordinary shares, Hotchkiss had the right of representation on the board of Morris Engines Ltd. which did not suit Morris at all. *The Garage and Motor Agent* of 13th January, 1923 in fact reported that the new company was to be named Morris-Hotchkiss Engines (Ltd.), but W. R. Morris set matters right at the eighth annual dinner of Hotchkiss et Cie in February, 1923 when he announced that the new company was to be named Morris Engines Ltd.

Morris could face the 1923 season with confidence. He had supplies of major items such as radiators and engines under his control and at his new low prices he could expect to capture more sales from the Ford model-T although the latter was still some 40 per cent cheaper. However, during 1922 two things occurred to complicate the picture. One of little immediate consequence was that Sir Herbert Austin announced his famous "Seven". Although unquestionably one of the most important designs in motoring history, its full impact was not to be felt until the later twenties. The public were not yet ready for the ultra small car. For example, Humber up to the time of their take over by Rootes never sold as many of the little 8/18s, 9/20s and 9/28s as their larger models and Morris himself always expanded into the higher horse power range until the introduction of the Minor in 1929. The other noteworthy event of 1922 was the decision of the Wolverhampton concern of Clyno Engineering, who already had a very long and successful history of cycle and motor cycle manufacture behind them, to start car manufacture. This was of real and immediate importance to Morris because from the start Clyno ambitiously set out to compete directly with his cars on price. Until their demise in 1929 Clyno gave Morris strong competition. They offered a car of excellent design. Most of the engines used were the Coventry Climax which had a two bearing crankshaft in comparison with the Morris three bearing job, but, to offset this, it could be claimed that the Clyno had the edge over the Morris in performance and braking. Also, it had possibly a better gear change and most certainly steering, which was in a class by itself. Against the Clyno was the impression that its low price was only achieved by skimping on details, an impression which the Bullnose never gave. The story of the Clyno is recounted in Lord Montagu's book *Lost Causes of Motoring*.

Ainsworth stayed with the parent Hotchkiss company when Morris acquired the Coventry branch in 1923 and Frank G. Wollard, from the ailing firm of E. G. Wrigley & Co. Ltd., was appointed works manager in his stead. A Hotchkiss employee retained by Morris was Leonard Lord and a new apprentice was George Harriman, whose father was chief foreman. Their day was yet to come. After completing Hotchkiss contracts, including those for guns, Wollard started in earnest to re-organise engine manufacture and within six months had increased production by 66 per cent. Increased engine production allowed increased car production. Compare the 1923 sales with the sale of 6,937 cars in 1922. In 1923 Morris sold no less than 20,024 cars. It was a golden year. He had established himself as quite easily the largest motor manufacturer in England.

1923 marked the turning point for Morris but towards the end of this year the whole British motor industry had a fresh challenge to face. An

election was pending and the Labour party under Ramsey MacDonald had
pledged that they would remove protective tariffs if elected to Parliament.
The tariffs of particular interest to the British motor industry were the
McKenna duties. These duties, although temporary, were renewable every
year, and always had been since their introduction in September, 1915.
Morris did not disguise his sympathies under a cloak of impartiality, but
pledged that if Baldwin's Conservative government was returned to power,
he would employ a further 500 men at Morris Engines, Coventry, and another
500 at Cowley. Alternatively he would present a sum of £5,000 to the
Radcliffe Infirmary, Oxford, but he was not called upon to do either, because
in January, 1924 Labour were elected. In April, 1924 the worst happened.
Philip Snowden, the Labour Chancellor of the Exchequer, announced in his
budget that the duties would not be renewed. He made one concession
however; the duties would not cease forthwith but would remain operative
until 1st August to give the industry time to re-organise itself to meet the
threat of duty free imports from their foreign rivals. For the 1924 season the
two-seater Morris Cowley was priced at £198 and the Model-T Ford, with
the newly introduced two-seater "Runabout" body, at £105 duty paid. The
British price leader was $88\frac{1}{2}$ per cent more expensive than its American rival
which was subject to duty. In the uncertain period between the election of the
Labour Government in January, 1924 and the presentation of their budget in
the following April Ford did not wait to see if the McKenna duties would be
removed, but to maintain sales assured pre-budget purchasers that "Ford
passenger cars will be reduced in price when these duties are discontinued.
Refund of the whole difference will be made through the authorised dealer
supplying". From 1st August, 1924 the McKenna duties were removed from
imported cars. This may have suited Henry Ford, but caused real consterna-
tion among British manufacturers.

Herbert Austin invited Morris and Dudley Docker of Vickers, which
controlled Wolseleys, to a meeting in May, 1924 and proposed that their
motor companies should merge to combat the threat of foreign competition.
Wolseleys had not learnt from Argyll's mistake and were suffering from the
same trouble of being over capitalised, having sumptuous showrooms and a
magnificent and well-equipped factory, but insufficient output to carry the
high overheads. Austins were picking up with some good designs, but were
still feeling the effects of their financial debacle just after the Armistice. It
was proposed that the new company should have its headquarters at Long-
bridge and that the holding in the new Company should be on the basis of
the assets handed over and not on earnings. Under this arrangement
Wolseleys, who were actually running at a loss, would have been laughing,
but not so Morris, who was making three times the profit of Austin. Morris
was offered managerial control of the new company, but he simply could not
see what was in it for him and so the proposed merger came to nothing.

Instead, to combat the threat from imported cars Morris pursued his policy of offering more and more for less and less and in 1924, sales leapt from the 20,024 cars of 1923 to 32,939. These figures would suggest that Morris was worrying unnecessarily about the removal of the duties and that *The Autocar* had had a point when it opined "it seems unreasonable to despair, if only because the average prospective purchaser regards first cost as but one of the important factors to be faced. Annual taxation and running costs are often even more important, and if the British factories continue to produce reasonably priced, highly efficient, and really economical cars for which they are now world-famed, a reduction or even the total disappearance, of the McKenna duty – serious and most regrettable as it would certainly be – will not, we are confident, prove so disastrous as some of the more pessimistic are inclined to fear." The removal of the duties it so happened was only short term, because in November, 1924 Baldwin's Conservative Government regained power and the then Chancellor of the Exchequer, Winston Churchill, re-introduced them in the next budget. Morris strongly opposed the lifting of the McKenna duties because he felt it was wrong to risk British car workers' livelihoods during a depression. Whilst the duties were lifted imports of foreign vehicles rose from 23,746 in 1924 to 47,667 in 1925, and at the Hollick and Pratt annual dinner in January, 1926 Morris said that his company had set out in 1924 with a production target of 35,000 cars, but because of the removal of the duties they only achieved sales of 27,000 cars. The re-imposition of the duties emboldened him to plan for the production of 70,000 cars in 1926.

True to form, prices for the 1925 season were reduced, the Cowley four-seater for example at £195 showing a reduction of £30 over the previous season. The lower prices now included 12 months' comprehensive insurance, which made the cars truly ready for the road. Morris was not the originator of such a scheme and for the 1921 season for instance the British market price of £525 of the American 18/22 h.p. Maxwell included tax and insurance. The Morris insurance scheme was underwritten by the General Accident, Fire and Life Assurance Corporation Ltd., Perth. This proved rather an expensive undertaking for them and the claims record was such that after a year or two this free motor policy had to be discontinued. 1925 was a bumper year for Morris. As far as production was concerned, the output of specialist bodies (e.g. coupes and saloons) at Hollick and Pratt during the twelve months was 28,618 and the output of Morris Engines Ltd. was over 60,000 units. As far as sales of cars were concerned, they reached 54,151, a record, which was 41 per cent of British private motor car production. To put this figure in perspective, seven years previously the annual output at Cowley had been 387 cars, or 99 per cent less. Morris had indeed made advances.

Following the usual pattern, prices for the 1926 season were cut. The difference between the 1925 season and 1918 season sales may be striking, but prices were no less contrasting. In October 1920 the two-seater Cowley had cost £465 or 174 per cent more than the 1926 two-seater Cowley at a mere £170, although the latter was a better equipped car and included in its price were four wheel brakes and a year's free comprehensive insurance. A most unusual optional extra was offered for the 1926 season: a motor house. The Cowley model, which was 14 feet by 8 feet, cost £15 15s. 0d. and the Oxford model, which was 16 feet by 8 feet, cost £17 0s. 0d. Fire risk for one year was covered by the comprehensive insurance issued with new cars.

Morris success had been achieved by a private company, Morris Motors Ltd. There were rumours that Morris was now thinking of going public,

The Morris Motor House.

but on this subject *The Garage and Motor Agent* of 20th February, 1926 had the following to say:—

"The references made in the Press lately to the effect that Morris Motors Ltd. are being converted from a private to a public company are officially stated to be entirely without foundation and wholly inaccurate."

However, a public company, Morris Motors (1926) Ltd., was registered on 29th June, 1926 to acquire the assets and goodwill of the private companies, Morris Motors Ltd., Morris Engines Ltd., Osberton Radiators Ltd., Hollick and Pratt Ltd. and Morris Oxford Press Ltd. The new company had an authorised 3,000,000 £1 7½ per cent cumulative preference shares and 2,000,000 £1 ordinary shares, all of the latter being issued to W. R. Morris, who thereby retained effective control of his companies. Morris was Governing Director of the new company at a salary of £5,000 per year. This public issue gave Morris Motors (1926) Ltd. more liquid assets and Morris was prepared to make such an issue because he felt that his companies were sufficiently secure to guarantee the safety of investors' money.

Sales during the first half of 1926 were a disappointment. They were actually less than in the corresponding period of the previous year, only 26,550 cars compared with 28,331 cars. The general strike and coal strike could certainly be blamed in part for this, but another reason was the "Bullnose" itself, which was showing its age. To remedy this, design changes, including a flat radiator, were made for 1927.

Attached to the first annual trading report of Morris Motors (1926) Ltd. was a slip which stated that the following concerns were entirely separate from Morris Motors (1926) Ltd.: Morris Commercial Cars Ltd., Wolseley Motors (1927) Ltd., Société Française des Automobiles Morris-Leon Bollée; the Morris Garages, and Morris Collieries Ltd. All of these businesses, it was modestly explained, were owned by Mr Morris personally.

Some notes on Beans

The first Morris was sold in March 1913 and yet within a decade Morris Motors were established as the largest British motor car manufacturer. The drawback of any history of W. R. Morris is that it makes his success seem inevitable, whereas it was only achieved in the face of fierce competition. For example, John Harper Bean could see like Morris that the market for a cheap car of high quality was enormous and the object of these brief notes on Beans is to show the fine dividing line between great success and failure.

The parent Bean Company was established in 1826 and the original products of the first works at Dudley (Worcs.) were mainly hand-forged fire irons and other hardware. In 1900 drop stamp shops were laid down in Smethwick (Staffs.) and a year later the company was registered as A. Harper & Sons Ltd., but in 1907 the name was changed to A. Harper, Sons & Bean Ltd. They built up a considerable trade in supplying the motor industry with stampings, forgings and castings, but switched to war work in 1914. Their four factories were the Wadhams Pool Works and the National Projectile factory at Dudley, a fuze plant at Tipton (Staffs.) and the drop forging works at Smethwick.

After the war A. Harper, Sons & Bean Ltd., decided to manufacture motor cars. They sold the shell factory at Dudley and built spacious modern shops and a large foundry at Tipton for their new venture. From the outset Beans intended to mass produce and by this they meant an output of 50,000 vehicles per year, even in 1920. To enter the industry quickly they considered it best, like Darracq earlier in the century, to buy a design and in May, 1919 announced that they had "purchased the jigs, tools, drawings and spare parts pertaining to various models of cars produced by the Perry Motor Company Ltd".

Perry & Co. Ltd. were established in 1823 by Sir Josiah Mason and James Perry and in 1876 were incorporated as a limited company. They built up a large business in pens, pencil cases and stationers' sundries and subsequently added the manufacture of cycle parts to their activities. Their chains, hubs and free-wheels became world famous and one of the few bicycles that the authors have ridden which stopped properly was fitted with a Perry "back-pedal" hub brake. Porter's Motor Trade Directory of 1902 quotes Perry & Co. Ltd. as motor car manufacturers, which is intriguing, but it is not certain how many (if any) cars they built. However, it is quite clear that it was not until 1912 that they decided upon car manufacture in earnest.

The Perry Motor Co. Ltd. was registered on 25th September, 1912 and of the £60,000 capital £50,000 was invested by Perry & Co. Ltd. The new Perry cyclecar was the work of C. T. Bayliss and *The Cyclecar* of 4th December, 1912 reported him as saying:—

"It was the old Humberette which first wakened me to the enormous possibilities of the light and simple four wheeler, I at once set to work to design a machine. This was three or four years ago, just before the Bedelia was introduced into England. I gave the French cyclecar a trial, and this combined with my motor cycling experience (for you must know that I am an enthusiastic motor cyclist, and have carried out numerous experiments on my T.T. Triumph) gave me a good deal of material upon which to work." Bayliss was only twenty-one or twenty-two when he gave *The Cyclecar* this interview and so the preliminary designs of the first Perrys were made by a teenager. In January 1913 it was reported that the Perry Motor Co. had almost completed their new works at Tyseley, Birmingham, and that it would only be a matter of a few weeks before a start was made on the first batch of cyclecars, although by this time they had decided upon a new style of body.

The Perry cyclecar was a small 6·4 h.p. machine with a water cooled 72 m.m. bore and 108 m.m. stroke parallel-twin engine, which was unusual in that the designer placed more value on even firing which necessitated the pistons moving up and down together as on the de Dion twin, than the alternative arrangement of having the crank throws at 180° to one another for better balance. The makers of the Perry claimed that they had largely overcome the balance problem by the use of very light reciprocating parts. Another noteworthy feature of the engine was the flywheel, which weighed no less than ¼ cwt. In unit with this 875 c.c. engine, which developed about 10 b.h.p. and propelled the car at close on 40 m.p.h., was a cone clutch and three-speed gearbox. An open propeller shaft took the drive to the live rear axle, which had worm gearing in 1913 but bevel gearing from 1914 onwards. Also for 1914 worm and segment steering replaced the former direct steering

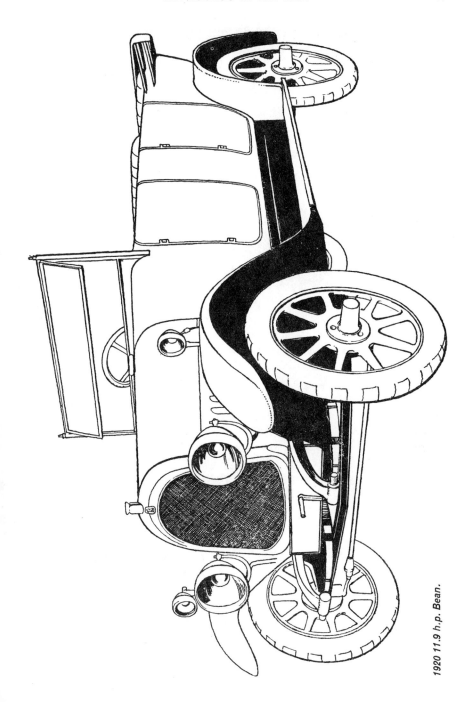

1920 11.9 h.p. Bean.

layout. There was also a special sporting model with raked steering and the seating so arranged that, in the words of *The Motor* of 21st October, 1913, "the popular semi-recumbent position can be obtained". At £137 in 1913 and £10 more in 1914 and its final year 1915 it was cheaper than the W & P engined Morris Oxford.

In 1915 Perry's announced an 11·9 h.p. four cylinder model of 69 m.m. bore and 120 m.m. stroke with a three-speed gearbox and shaft and bevel final drive, but at £221 in 1915 and £260 in 1916 it was considerably more expensive than the comparable Cowley which was introduced at £158 in 1915. Chassis numbers, which can be thoroughly misleading, indicate that no more than 500 four cylinder Perrys could have been made in 1915, only 200 at the most in 1916, and few if any at all after 1916, but nevertheless the cars made an impression on A. Harper, Sons & Bean Ltd., who absorbed the company in 1919. The new owners, in addition to organising a service and repair department for the cars already made, advertised that they were also "arranging to produce a car similar in design to the 11·9 h.p. Perry, but incorporating several necessary modifications". This car, which embodied features "to appeal strongly to the owner drivers and to ladies", was put on the market in the latter part of 1919 as the 11·9 h.p. Bean. Further improvements were made for 1920, the chief one being a complete redesign of the three-speed gearbox with larger bearings and stiffer shafts.

A. Harper, Bean & Sons Ltd. were producing a car which was comparable with the Morris, but in contrast to the Cowley firm they made nearly all their own components. Financially they were the opposite to Morris, in that they were in a strong position, but, for apparent greater stability, they decided to climb under a large umbrella with their few outside suppliers, other motor car companies and a motor car selling organisation. To this end a holding company, Harper Bean Ltd., was registered on 7th November, 1919, and on the first of the following month they issued their prospectus. The new holding company had the enormous capital of six million pounds divided equally into £1 cumulative participating preference shares and £1 ordinary shares. The preference shareholders were entitled to a fixed 8 per cent per annum cumulative preferential dividend and £25 per cent of the surplus profits of each year (after providing for the payment of a dividend of 10 per cent on the ordinary shares) and in a winding up to the repayment of their capital and all arrears (if any) of dividend in priority to the ordinary shareholders, and to 25 per cent of the surplus assets remaining after repayment to the ordinary shareholders of the amount of ordinary share capital, but to no further participation in profits or assets. The ordinary shareholders were entitled to a fixed non-cumulative dividend of 10 per cent per annum and to 75 per cent of the surplus profits for each year. The new holding company, Harper Bean Ltd., acquired all the shares capital of A. Harper, Sons & Bean Ltd., approximately 75 per cent of the shares of Vulcan Motor & Engineering

Co. Ltd., of Southport, who had been making cars since about 1902, 51 per cent of the ordinary shares of Swift of Coventry Ltd., originally a sewing machine firm which had turned to bicycles and then to cars in 1899, half the issued capital of the British Motor Trading Corporation Ltd., which became the sales organisation for Bean cars, 166,666 shares of Hadfields Ltd., the famous steel firm, 100,000 ordinary shares of the Birmingham Aluminium Castings Co. Ltd. and large interests in Harvey Frost Ltd., Rushmores (1919) Ltd., Jigs Ltd., Regent Carriage Co. Ltd., Gallay Radiator Co. Ltd., Aeromotor Components Co., Alex Mosses Radiator Co. Ltd., Ransomes and Marles Bearing Co. Ltd., Marles Steering Co. Ltd., Cooper's Mechanical Joints Ltd. and last, but not least, A.B.C. Motors (1920) Ltd. The directorate of Harper Bean Ltd. were Hubert John Whitcomb (chairman), chairman of the British Motor Trading Corporation Ltd.; John Harper Bean (managing director) managing director of A. Harper, Sons & Bean Ltd.; Robert Burns, director and general manager of Swift of Coventry Ltd.; Major Augustus Basil Holt Clerke, managing director of Hadfields Ltd.; James Armstrong Wilding, a consulting engineer, Charles Benson Wardman and Jonathan Edward Hodgkin. Wardman was managing director of Vulcan and came to the rescue of Lea Francis in 1922. It is unlikely that Beans, Swifts or Vulcans carried any insurance loading for being inherently dangerous because Jonathan Edward Hodgkin was a director of the Motor Union Insurance Co. Ltd.

Although a few 11·9 h.p. Beans were made towards the end of 1919, and indeed exhibited at Olympia of that year, production did not really get under way until January, 1920, when 100 cars were produced. In February, 1920 a further 125 cars were made, and in the following month *The Autocar* showed a batch of twenty Beans which had been produced in one day; a healthy output, as it was equivalent to 6,000 cars per annum compared with the 1920 Morris sale of 1,932 cars. During the first three-quarters of 1920 the 11·9 h.p. Bean four-seater at £650 was more than double the price of the comparable Cowley at £310 and even the Oxford at £390 was £260 cheaper, but this was of little immediate consequence as demand still exceeded supply. In October, 1920 the tables were turned. The four-seater Bean was reduced in price by an incredible £105 to £545 whereas the cost of the four-seater Cowley went up by no less than £215 to £525, and now there was only a price difference of £20. As important, the Bean was £45 cheaper than the Oxford. The Bean price cut was attributed to "the economical point of manufacture now having been reached", although the price reductions were timely in view of the rapidly slumping market. For some reason which is hard to explain the Bean price cuts did not have the same impact as those made by Morris in February, 1921 although they were greater. Beans were in a strong position and in November 1920 could advertise that their car was the lowest priced 11·9 h.p. model on the market. They were to remain in this proud position until

February, 1921, when Morris made his sensational price reductions. Beans did not follow suit at once, but waited for the Motor Show, by which time Morris made further price reductions. The turning point had been reached and Beans never made up the ground they had lost, although for some years they remained priced in between the Oxford and Cowley.

Bean sales had fallen below expectation and the slump had also hit Swift and Vulcan. The holding Company, Harper Bean Ltd., were in trouble and relinquished the majority of their shares in A. Harper, Sons & Bean Ltd. These were acquired by Mr John Harper Bean and Hadfields, who had discovered manganese steel, and in April 1922 the receiver was withdrawn. The revived Bean company opened a service station at 4a, Cambridge Street, off the Edgware Road, and new showrooms at 11a, Regent Street. Beans seem to have given up hope of competing directly with Morris on price and to remain competitive made their cars more attractive by introducing a four-speed version in April 1923.

Beans abandoned their principle that successful mass production centred around a one model policy and at the 1923 Motor Show introduced the "Fourteen". On the original 11·9 h.p. model the dynamo and fan had been belt driven, but on the new fourteen there were two silent chains, one of which drove the camshaft and water pump and the other the dynamo, magneto and three blade fan. Dual ignition was available as an extra at £7 10s. 0d. and most notable for a conservative British make in 1923, front wheel brakes were available for an extra £25. A basic price of £395 for the 1924 five-seater tourer put the Bean Fourteen in the same class as the Austin 12/4 at £375 rather than that of the Morris, when the comparable Cowley cost £225 and the Oxford £320.

The robustness of the Bean Fourteen was illustrated by the successful double crossing of Australia, a total distance of 6,200 miles, by a five-seater. The journey was made to investigate projected railway routes and the load carried by the car, which had already covered 14,000 miles, was equivalent to sixteen twelve-stone passengers. With a record like this, it is scarcely surprising that overseas sales almost equalled home sales. The Bean Fourteen was never noted for its liveliness and *The Motor* test team recorded a maximum speed in a tourer on the level of slightly less than 50 m.p.h. Writing about the 14 h.p. tourer Edgar N. Duffield in *The Automotor Journal* stated, "she is not intended to be a flier" and the authors remember suffering the indignity of having to change down in a "Long Fourteen" saloon to climb the almost imperceptible gradient of a Thames bridge, but to be fair the engine was well worn and the ignition incorrectly set. Another thing they remember about this car was its greed; in addition to petrol it used oil at the rate of less than 50 miles per pint, which was mysterious as the exhaust was clean, and not only the radiator, but also the tyres and even the battery needed topping up weekly. They found two features noteworthy; the horrible steering and

23. Leg room: John Holyoak's immaculate 1924 Oxford.

24. Prizewinner: Miss M. G. Chiesman, M.B.E., with the 1925 Oxford with which she won the novice's cup in the Civil Service Motor Club Championship Trial in 1926.

25. Modern competition: Mr. and Mrs. Best taking part in a Bullnose Morris Club rally at the Cowley works in their 1924 Oxford.

26. A 1926 Oxford.

27. Good clean fun:
A 1924 Oxford.

28. The Morris Garages: It cost the owner of this 1925 two-seater 2d. per tyre or 6d. per set to have them inflated.

29. Just run in: A 1928 Oxford being checked over.

the superb brakes. Bean brakes were in a class by themselves, which is understandable because Beans were the sole makers of the Perrot-Bendix system in England. In contrast to other makes, Beans were designed to stop and not to go.

In October, 1924 A. Harper, Sons & Bean Ltd. were advertising that they were entirely separate from their old holding company Harper Bean Ltd. of 132 Long Acre, London, and that the affairs of the latter could not affect the Bean car organisation in any way. Harper Bean Ltd. after some stormy shareholders' meetings went into voluntary liquidation early in 1925. A. Harper, Sons & Bean Ltd. were also running into trouble and early in 1926 Hadfields acquired the controlling interest in the firm from John Harper Bean, who resigned his post and joined the board of Guy Motors Ltd. The ponderous Fourteen had proved the wrong model; a car with a little more speed would have been required to save the day.

The name of A. Harper, Sons & Bean Ltd. was changed to Bean Cars Ltd. and H. Kerr Thomas, the President of the Institution of Automobile Engineers, was appointed general manager. Kerr Thomas had trained with J. & E. Hall Ltd. of Dartford and ultimately had full responsibility for the design and manufacture of their Hallford Commercial Vehicles. In 1909 he went to America on the behalf of D. Napier and Sons Ltd., but when their scheme to manufacture cars in the United States fell through, he joined the Pierce-Arrow company and remained with them until 1919, when he returned to England.

Production was moved to Tipton and Bean Cars Ltd. introduced the six cylinder 18/50 model for the 1927 season, which differed from normal Bean practice in that the engine was not of their own manufacture but made by Meadows. Kerr Thomas replaced the old-school Beans with the new 14/40 in 1928, which in 1929 became the 14/45 and the 14/70 Sports. The cars were now called Hadfield Beans and had a 75 m.m. × 130 m.m. four cylinder engine which Ricardo had a hand in designing. The new Beans certainly performed better than any of the previous models, but no one would believe it and production of cars stopped in 1929. The 30 cwt. Bean Commercial continued to be made until about 1931, after which Bean Cars Ltd. was liquidated. A far cry from 1920, when the firm had been competitive with Morris.

5

Bullnose variations

"I think we shall probably avoid an entirely new design." *F. G. Woollard*
February 1925.

When Morris acquired the Gosford Street, Coventry, works of Hotchkiss
et Cie in 1923, the factory was producing 300 engines per week (in addition
to other sidelines), but by December 1924, when there were 2,200 employees
and 786 machines, production had risen to 1,200 engines per week. Frank G.
Woollard, the works manager of Morris Engines, told the Institution of
Automobile Engineers in February 1925 how their high output had been
achieved in an excellent paper, "Some Notes on British Methods of Continuous Production". Woollard quoted the following as being the savings in
making 1,200 engines per week compared with 100 engines per week:—

		100 *engines/week*	1,200 *engines/week*
Men	per engine	4	1·83
Space	per engine	53 sq. yds.	15·6
Machines	per engine	2·1	0·64
H.P. used	per engine	3·5	1·27

To obtain these high outputs a twenty-four hour day of three shifts was
worked, but the savings in overheads were largely consumed in overtime pay
and extra heating and lighting bills. One point on which W. R. Morris was
emphatic was, in his own words, that "no factory can turn out cheap cars on
low wages". He was proud that he probably paid as high wages as anyone in
England and he felt this was to his advantage. Morris stated:
"The monotony of working from morning to night, going home at night
with no money to spend, and therefore having to stay at home, getting up the

next morning and going to work again, day after day, must have a bad effect upon production. If a man can leave work, say, at 5 o'clock and go home and change and have money to go into town and amuse himself, he will come to the works next morning full of keenness. I have tried to put my men in that position, and the result has been extremely satisfactory."

Woollard was equally enlightened, as can be seen from his statement:—

"Low wages do not necessarily make for low production costs, though even now the low wage school has still many adherents; it cannot be too strongly emphasised that it is not the amount paid for, but the amount given in return that matters. . . ."

There were no petty restrictions in the Morris Engines factory and smoking was permitted at any time in non-dangerous areas. Sir Herbert Austin was in entire disagreement with this policy, but it is relevant to note that Sir Herbert was a non-smoker whereas Mr Morris chain smoked. On the vexed question of smoking Woollard said:—

"I have no regrets whatever in allowing smoking all day in the works, except in danger spots, but that does not in effect mean that there is too much smoking. On the other hand, it does mean definitely that there is practically no lounging in out of the way places where visibility is not high."

Woollard achieved high outputs at low cost by the efficient use of machines. The Morris Engines factory was highly automated and contained, for example, a giant cylinder-block machine which was 181 feet long, 11 feet 4 inches high, 11 feet at its greatest width, weighed upwards of 300 tons and employed 81 electric motors with a combined rating of 267 horsepower. From rough castings obtained from the Cowley foundry this machine produced finished cylinder blocks including bearing blocks, crankshaft bearings and all studs at the rate of one every four minutes. The actual time it took a block to pass through the machine was 224 minutes, during which time it had 40 lb of metal removed and went through fifty-three different operational stages completely automatically. The rate of production of other engine parts was geared to the rate of cylinder block production of one every four minutes.

Ford claimed that the car driven away on Thursday night had been iron ore on the previous Monday morning, which was quite easily a record in turnover from raw material to the finished product, but in Britain Morris held the record. It took rather less than fourteen days from the receipt of the raw materials to produce a finished engine and at no time were there more than 2,500 cylinder blocks on the ground. The financial advantages of having so comparatively little capital locked up needs no elaboration.

Hotchkiss organised the Gosford Street factory so that machines of the same type were grouped together, which had the advantage that they all could be supervised best by a foreman with a knowledge of the particular type of machine, but what Woollard was after was continuous production, so machines were sited where they were needed on the line; the machine had been taken to the workpiece. Ideally all the machine tools worked in balance, but Woollard admitted that this could not be achieved in practice. The machine tools were frequently replaced. In Woollard's opinion "many manufacturing concerns have endangered their future by holding on to machinery which should have been scrapped in a previous generation". He continued: "for an automobile shop demanding the highest accuracy it is plain suicide. No operator can produce accurate work on worn tools at full speed; either accuracy or production must suffer. Economy, in other words, is not saving: it is wise expenditure." To support these comments Woollard could have cited the case of Calcott; large dividends at the expense of re-investment found them out in the end.

Continuous production from this elaborate equipment demanded regularity; regularity of supply of raw materials, regularity in demand for the finished product and regularity in specification. To guard their raw material supplies Morris Engines, where possible, obtained a given line from two or three different local suppliers and Woollard reported that as production expanded supplies became less of a problem. There was a steady demand for engines, so Woollard was lucky, and also fortunate because the engine was of excellent design and called for few modifications. It was an expensive luxury to stop production and reset machines to make a small change, even though it might make a certain part cheaper and so otherwise anachronistic features were retained. There could be no risk of hold-ups and therefore it was frequently more economical in the long run to use the best materials and work to very fine limits to minimise rejections due to cumulative errors. It was this policy which determined the use of a steel flywheel instead of a cast iron one and should stamp out the fallacy that large scale production necessarily meant poor materials or indifferent workmanship. Seven per cent of the staff were employed on inspection and before despatch each engine was tested and run-in for four hours. It was first loosened up by an electric motor, then run on town gas and then fitted with its own carburettor and run on petrol.

The Morris chassis was made by continuous production methods which demanded continuity in specification whereas bodies gave little scope for the application of such techniques. Consequently, the Morris policy was to make changes to the chassis only when they became necessary and to avoid changes, if they simply offered marginal technical or sales advantages. For bodies the policy was different and additional styles were offered as the years went by to give the cars wider appeal. The Oxford showed more changes than the Cowley. On its re-introduction in 1919 the Oxford had been a luxury version of the Cowley, but during 1923 and 1924 it grew up, and although bigger it was of very similar design to the Cowley and the two models had many common parts; in fact the Oxford had become nothing more than a long-wheelbase Cowley with a bored-out engine. Until the end of the 1926 season the only notable changes made to the Cowley and Oxford chassis were the adoption of four-wheel brakes and balloon tyres. Many manufacturers made more changes than these to their designs in one season.

During the 1923 season for an extra £10 the Oxford was available with an 1802 c.c. 13·9 h.p. engine as an alternative to the 1548 c.c. 11·9 h.p. engine. This new motor was only an 11·9 h.p. engine bored out from 69·5 m.m. to 75 m.m. and so presented no manufacturing difficulties, but to distinguish between them 13·9 h.p. engines were painted blue and 11·9 h.p. engines red.

The majority of Oxford purchasers opted for the larger engine and therefore it was standardised for the Oxford for 1924 and the 11·9 h.p. reserved for the Cowley. Two other specific Oxford changes for the 1924 season were an increase in radiator size to overcome the tendency of the 13·9 h.p. engine to overheat and an increase in wheelbase from 8 ft 6 in. to 9 ft to accommodate the larger and heavier bodies which the more powerful engine could propel satisfactorily.

In February 1925 S. F. Edge said of well base tyres:—

"I believe the Dunlop wheel will sweep everything before it, because it has all the advantages of a detachable rim plus the advantages of a detachable wheel, with the weight only of the detachable wheel. It is the old Welch bicycle rim brought into motor car use, and it has been lying dormant all this time, after the patents have run out."

Edge was on safe ground because for the 1925 season Britain's largest car maker, Morris, had already standardised on the new Dunlop low pressure well base balloon tyres, sometimes referred to as "comfort tyres". The development in multi-cord casings, which superseded the old canvas casings, had made the low pressure balloon tyre a practical proposition. Balloon tyres made a definite contribution to comfort, although they robbed many of the earlier steering layouts of their delicacy of control and magnified any tendency to wheel wobble, a problem of sufficient importance to merit a paper on it by Dr F. W. Lanchester which he read before the Institution of Automobile Engineers.

Morris led many of his competitors in the adoption of balloon tyres and by British standards, if not Continental ones, he was not left far behind in the use of front wheel brakes. They were fitted as standard to the Morris Oxfords for the 1925 season, although customers who considered them dangerous could specify the old two wheel brake layout for £10 less. For the 1926 season Oxford customers got front wheel brakes whether they liked them or not and front wheel brakes also were standardised on the Cowley, although Cowley customers could opt for rear wheel brakes only and thereby save £7 10s. 0d. The only difference between the rod-operated braking system of the Oxford and the Cowley, made by Alford and Adler under Rubery patents, was that the Oxford had 12 in. drums whereas the Cowley had 9 in. drums. Morris front wheel brakes have a most commendable characteristic: they work! A feature of Morris brakes was that they squeaked, which was a gift to the manufacturers of anti-squeak bands, but Morris liked the brakes that way. On leaving the despatch bay the cars had to run down a ramp and brake at the bottom near Morris's office. Every time Morris heard a squeak he knew another car was on its way. The adoption of front wheel brakes brought one or two other changes in its train. The chassis frames of the cars were made of deeper section, a tie bar was fitted between the front dumb irons and the front springs were made wider to resist the additional braking stresses. At the same time the front axle was redesigned. The new axle was of the Elliott type, with ball and socket steering joints, and one suspects that the use of balloon tyres dictated the change as much as anything, although the cars with rear wheel brakes only but balloon tyres continued to be fitted with a reversed-Elliott axle, with pin and bush steering joints.

The very few changes made to the Bullnose engine between 1919 and the end of 1926 fall into two categories: firstly, those made on technical grounds and secondly, those made to reduce production costs. The first change to improve performance was to switch from a three port to a four port exhaust system, which necessitated modification to the cylinder block, at engine number 18061 on 22nd February, 1922. The biggest improvement in performance was obtained in January, 1923 by boring out the 11·9 h.p. engine to 13·9 h.p. for use in the Oxford. In the opinion of *The Automobile Engineer* a design weakness of the 11·9 h.p. engine was that the connecting rods at 190 m.m. were too short for the stroke, and with the desaxe crankshaft offset 10 m.m., tended to increase the secondary unbalanced forces. Nevertheless, Hotchkiss increased the length of the stroke from 100 m.m. to 102 m.m. when they took over the Continental design. Furthermore the big-end bearings, although satisfactory, left but little margin for safety. The larger bore Oxford engine certainly gave more power but with its heavier reciprocating parts was a thoroughly rough job. Primarily to improve the smoothness rather than the performance of the 13·9 h.p. engine, very soon the 20½ oz. cast-iron pistons were replaced by 11 oz. aluminium ones (split skirt Aerolite at first, but later of Morris taper design) and carefully designed 10¼ oz. duralumin connecting rods replaced the former 18½ oz. steel stampings. The duralumin connecting rods had big-end studs to avoid flats having to be machined on them to accommodate the heads of big-end bolts. In the new duralumin connecting rods strength had been sacrificed for lightness and it was imperative that they were used in conjunction with aluminium pistons. Steel connecting rods and cast-iron pistons continued in use on the commercial vehicle, industrial and marine versions of the engine, where strength was of more importance than smoothness. The lighter reciprocating parts certainly improved bearing life, smoothness and performance of the 13·9 h.p.

engine and happily the latter was allied to four wheel braking. For the 1925 season $9\frac{1}{2}$ oz. aluminium pistons replaced $18\frac{1}{2}$ oz. cast-iron pistons on the Cowley, but the steel connecting rods were retained, which was a happier combination for the Cowley because after thirty years of active service the duralumin rods have been known to disintegrate, with shattering results.

The Cowley and Oxford were first class products and if constant modification had been necessary to make it saleable it would have been impossible to cut production costs. Production costs were reduced by improving manufacturing methods and not by introducing economics into the basic design. The only parts modified to make them cheaper were some of the castings and although these changes in no way affected reliability it must be admitted that they adversely affected ease of servicing.

For example, the oil filler on top of the flywheel housing was eliminated, rendering it necessary to remove the clutch inspection plate to refill the clutch after an oil change. Routine decarbonising also became a little harder and involved fiddling with hose clips because the water outlet flange gave way to a water outlet cast in one piece with the cylinder head. The biggest engine production economy came with the elimination of the big-end inspection plates. Big-end inspection plates, for example, were specified for the World War I "subsidy" lorry engines and in many instances these inspection plates were in the crankcase sides which reduced crankcase and crankshaft rigidity. In the case of the Cowley and Oxford the big-end inspection plates were in the sump, so their elimination was in the interests of cost and not bottom-end rigidity. The "Bullnose" sump was a lovely aluminium casting, the hall mark of a true vintage car in the opinion of the Editor of *Motor Sport*, and Woollard said of it:—

"Take the case of pressed-steel parts ... for instance, a pressed-steel underpan versus a cast aluminium sump! Accuracy may be present in both cases, yet the solid job has an appeal to the engineer, which is wanting in the case of the lighter pressing."

However the Bullnose sump had the severe practical disadvantage that it necessitated an oil tight seal being made on two surfaces at right angles to one another – a difficult operation.

With respect to "Bullnose" electrics, the main change after 1919 was more one of attitude than technological advance and by 1926 a dynamotor, the replacement cost of which was about 10 per cent of a new Cowley, was justifiable on a car catering for the mass market. The big advantage of the dynamotor was that it gave completely silent starting due to its being permanently connected to the engine. Dynamotors, which had been chosen for Oxfords in 1919, have been criticised as being a poor compromise because if ideally geared as a starter motor they revolve too fast as a dynamo and vice-versa. This criticism was not too important in respect of the "Bullnose", because the engine was never noted for high revolutions, and the objection that the dynamotor was too highly geared for a starter motor and could not turn the engine really effectively when the oil was thick was not serious because most owners still expected to give the engine two or three turns on the handle to loosen it up in really cold weather. Whatever the objections to dynamotors on theoretical grounds, even the most vociferous critic had to admit that the Lucas A 400 unit used on the 1919 Oxford had robust windings, because under normal running it functioned perfectly although becoming impossibly hot to the hand; the insulation would soon have been found out if it could not have withstood the British Standards' specified 95°C. The dynamotor on early Oxfords projected into the driving compartment after the fashion of the starter motors on early Austin Sevens, and may have been a welcome source of warmth in winter but felt like an uncontrollable furnace in summer. To overcome this, for the 1921 season Hotchkiss et Cie repositioned the dynamotor from the top to the nearside of the gearbox and the inverted tooth silent chain dynamotor drive was then taken from a sprocket on a tubular extension of the clutch pressure plate. This entailed increasing the length of the gearbox casing. Admittedly the clutch bell housing casing was only lengthened by an inch or two but so was the unsupported length of the gearbox mainshaft which, together with the added side thrust from the dynamotor drive, put more strain on the front bearing. This bearing wears much more rapidly than the other gearbox bearings, but it is of little immediate consequence because the gearbox carries on working although more noisily. When new, even by the standards of 1920, the gearbox was noisy on the indirects and was criticised by *The Autocar* on this score. However, one can say that the noises were not of the unpleasant variety! George Oliver, writing on Bullnose Morrises in the *Manchester Guardian* of 10th March, 1958 summed up the matter beautifully. To quote:—

"The car-spotters of my generation had at least two advantages not available to the young fry today. The cars of the twenties had more individuality of shape than most of those we now know, and they produced sounds sufficiently distinctive for the boy-expert to identify many makes before he even saw them.

"Best known and best loved – I think the superlative is justified – were the sounds made by the "Bullnose" Morris, especially when running in one or other of its indirect gears. First produced a pooh-like hum, rich and deep in tone. Second was altogether higher in pitch; not a whine and not a scream, yet having some affinity with the human voice; this sound had great carrying power and could be heard long before – or after – the car itself was sighted."

The growing up of the Oxford and the adoption of front wheel brakes and balloon tyres on both the Oxford and Cowley were the major changes on the "Bullnose". The proprietary equipment fitted was also altered from time to time and the item which varied the most was the carburettor. Like the earlier Continental engined Cowleys, from 1919 to 1921 both Oxfords and

Cowleys used Zeniths. For the 1922 season the mixture was metered by that splendid device, the bronze S.U. "Sloper" with leather bellows. S.U. is a contraction of "Skinners Union", which the brothers G. H. Skinner and Carl T. Skinner jocularly called themselves. They founded their firm in 1910 in Kentish Town, London, and, at first, doubts were expressed about their use of leather for the carburettor bellows, but such fears were needless because the brothers were connected with the famous shoe firm of Lilley and Skinner, acknowledged leather experts. The S.U. carburettor was used on the Bull-nose for the 1922 season only because some of them were faulty (the bellows were blameless), but Morris could see the merits of these carburettors and in December 1926 he bought the concern. For the 1923 season Morris swapped to Smith carburettors; the straightforward bronze single-jet instrument

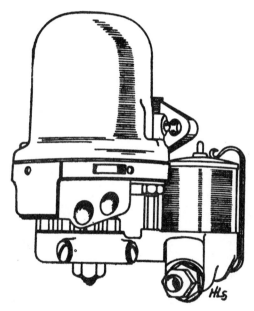

Smith "straight-through" 5-jet carburettor.

working on Zenith principles was chosen for the Cowley and the five-jet five-choke instrument which worked on the constant vacuum principle like the S.U. was selected for the Oxford. The depression in the manifold operated a piston which admitted more mixture by successively uncovering the five choke tubes and fixed jets, whereas in the S.U. the piston increased the choke tube area and operated a jet needle. The 1923 edition of the Smith five jet was not very clever, as the five jets and choke tubes were at different angles to the carburettor's main passage and consequently the mixture was tied in a reef knot on its way to the induction manifold. For the 1924 season both the Oxford and Cowley had Smith five-jet carburettors, but of improved design; the choke tubes now pointed the same way and the mixture had only to bend through a right angle on its way to the inlet manifold. The Smith five-jet continued to be used in the 1925 and 1926 seasons but the choke tubes now pointed towards the induction manifold, which gave the mixture a bend free run. The five-jet was a good carburettor, good enough for the touring Bentleys and superbly engineered Lanchesters, and continued to be used on Morrises until the end of the 1928 season. The carburettors fitted to the Oxfords were very smart cast-aluminium jobs whereas a cast-iron version was used on the humbler Cowley. Ironically

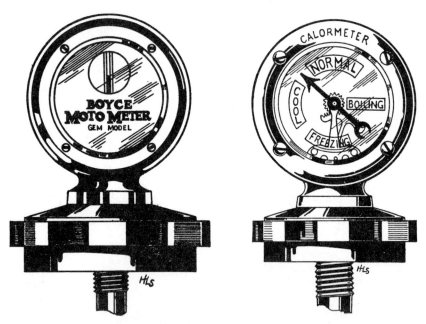

enough the piston dashpot never wears on the Cowley but does so on the Oxford. This calls to mind the plain pressed steel valve chest cover on the Cowleys which did its job, and the fancy cast aluminium ones of the 13·9 h.p. Oxfords, which due to having unmachined faces were not nearly so satisfactory, despite appearances.

The "Bullnose" engine ran at near boiling point, which partly accounts for its very long bore life and surprisingly good economy, but with a water capacity of four gallons (an Austin A 60 holds $11\frac{1}{2}$ pints) it took a long time to warm up. To overcome this a Smith "Thermet" thermostatic water flow controller advertised for 32s. 6d. including two hose clips, was fitted as standard in the top hose of the 1926 Oxfords. One would have thought that the Oxford owner would have found this an invaluable fitment for shopping trips, but strangely enough the authors know of no surviving Oxford with this accessory.

So that the owner could tell just how near the boil his car was running, the 1925 Oxford and Cowley had as standard a "Gem"-model Boyce Moto-Meter, which was manufactured under licence in Britain by The Benjamin Electric Ltd. of Tottenham, London. They were also available at 21s. 0d. for earlier Morrises. In 1926 both the Cowley and the Oxford were equipped with water temperature measuring instruments, but for this season Morris had placed his business with the Wilmot Manufacturing Company (later Wilmot-Breeden) for their Calormeters. To put it mildly, Boyce must have been a little upset over loosing their largest account to Wilmots and the matter finally culminated in Boyce suing Morris for patent infringement, the case being heard by Mr Justice Astbury in the Chancery Court at the begin-ing of December, 1926. One of the grounds on which the defendants (Morris) alleged that the Boyce patent was not valid was by reason of prior user, wherein thermometers placed in the radiators of cars had been used for testing the performance of cars and settling their designs. Further, it was alleged that the invention was not useful because certain advantages which were alleged by the patentee (Boyce) were not in fact obtained. The court held that the device had a real and practical advantage in communicating to the driver at the right moment the existence of danger and that there was a real exercise of the inventive faculty. The alleged prior user was held by the court to be at the most a mere casual accidental or incidental user in the course of a completely different investigation, and unfortunately for Morris Motors it was held that they had infringed the Boyce patent. Despite the court's ruling, Morris continued to fit Calormeters and he got away with it in a surprisingly simple but ingenious manner. Boyce described their device as "comprising a thermometer, the heat responsive element of which is exposed to the temperature conditions prevailing within the so-called air space immediately above the normal surface level of the liquid". They claimed that the advantage of this was that variations in pressure which affected the boiling point were taken into account because the thermometer only shot up when the water was actually boiling and thereby raising steam. Morris got round this patent quite simply by fitting Calormeters with longer stems so that the temperature of the liquid itself and not the temperature of the air space above it was measured.

The Morris policy was to offer comprehensively equipped cars at modest prices. For example the tool kit of the 1926 models consisted of a cold chisel, a half-round file with handle, a 9 in. adjustable spanner, a 6 in. steel punch, a pair of pliers, a hammer, a tyre lever and an oil can, which indicates that too much mechanical finesse was not required for satisfactory maintenance. A particularly pleasing feature was that the petrol can contained two gallons, the value of which was 3s. 0d. The 1925 and 1926 season's cars wore a black can with a magnificent golden scallop embossed on the side, whereas earlier cars had to be content with a rather plain red-painted can with SHELL MOTOR SPIRIT embossed in black letters on the side. The oil filler of the Morris engined Bullnose carries the Shell trade mark and it is alleged that Shell provided a full two-gallon can of petrol per car in consideration of this. The 1926 season Oxfords were cheaper than their predecessors, but better equipped and boasted of Barker dippers as an original fitment. This was a true luxury touch not found on most cars many times the price of the Oxford. For the benefit of owners of earlier Oxfords who wanted to bring their cars up to date Barker & Co. Ltd. offered these dippers for £3, or £3 10s. 0d. if fitted at their works. In the Barker system the headlamps complete were literally dipped and the idea has been revived since by Citroen for the 2CV admittedly in a slightly different form. The big advantage of Barkers is that the headlamps can also be raised, which is handy for reading tall signposts in dark country lanes or checking the height of low bridges.

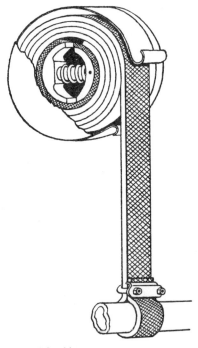

Gabriel Snubber.

In 1926 the only items of American manufacture on the Oxfords and Cowleys, which were themselves basically of American design, were the Gabriel Snubbers. These were manufactured in Cleveland, Ohio, and marketed in Great Britain by Brown Brothers Ltd. Despite a suggestion of celestial glory, a Gabriel Snubber was in fact a single-acting spring damper, the principle of which was that the road spring, on rebounding to its normal position after deflection, had to compress an auxiliary coil spring. Gabriel Snubbers were certainly available as early as February, 1912, but it was not until the 1923 season that Morris considered them a worthwhile extra rather than a frivolity and offered them as standard on the Oxford and as an extra at £6 4s. 0d. per set on the Cowley. For another 4s. 0d. one could buy a Gabriel Snubber adjusting lever, a handy tool for taking up the slack in the belting. Gabriels were standardised on both the Oxford and Cowley range for the 1925 season with the exception of the F-type Six, and at last full advantage was taken of the inherently excellent Morris suspension.

If an established Morris supplier produced an improved product at little or no extra cost, quite naturally Morris adopted it. Probably the best example of this is balloon tyres, but the remarks also apply to the smaller items such as greasers. The Continental Cowley and early Hotchkiss engined cars were fitted with screw-down greasers, but these were changed for screw-on type nipples when they were introduced by Enots and in turn they were superseded in 1925 by the present-day push-on grease nipples. This was only a small change, but it must be emphasised that the alterations made to the Morris chassis from year to year were few. Read what *The Motor* of 1st September had to say about the hand throttle of the 1926 season cars:—

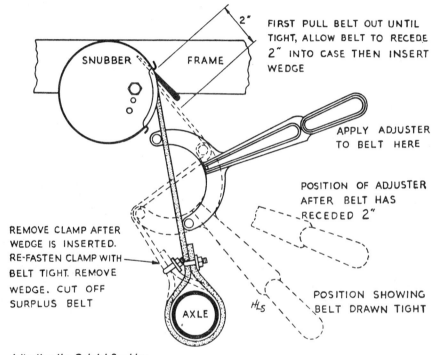

FIRST PULL BELT OUT UNTIL TIGHT, ALLOW BELT TO RECEDE 2″ INTO CASE THEN INSERT WEDGE

2″

SNUBBER   FRAME

APPLY ADJUSTER TO BELT HERE

POSITION OF ADJUSTER AFTER BELT HAS RECEDED 2″

REMOVE CLAMP AFTER WEDGE IS INSERTED. RE-FASTEN CLAMP WITH BELT TIGHT. REMOVE WEDGE. CUT OFF SURPLUS BELT

AXLE

POSITION SHOWING BELT DRAWN TIGHT

Adjusting the Gabriel Snubber.

"The old slow-running throttle control has been replaced by a neater type. With the old one, it will be remembered, there was no indication as to which way to turn the knob for slow or fast running. This has been overcome by fitting an ebonite disc of approximately the size of a five shilling piece. On this disc, which is attached to the fascia board, are arrows and lettering 'slow' and 'fast' showing the proper direction in which to turn the control (now fitted with an ebonite instead of metal knob) so as to achieve the correct engine speed."

That *The Motor* should devote so much space to such a trivial change emphasises that most changes made to the Morris chassis were only small, but nevertheless of interest because it was the British best seller. In the calendar year 1925 it represented *forty-one per cent* of the total U.K. motor car production.

Morris certainly reduced the costs of body building by having many of the components jig-manufactured and jig-assembled, but most of the construction relied on hand operations rather than machine tool operations and consequently, even though continuous production methods were applied as far as possible, stability of design was not critical, as in the case of engines, to keep costs down. Body components such as mudguards, running boards and bonnets were standardised, but this still left room for Morris to introduce more and more body styles to increase the appeal of his cars. Two additional body styles that were added only to the Cowley range were the occasional four and the doctor's coupe whereas the additional body types that only appeared on the Oxford chassis were the cabriolet, coupe, landaulet and saloon landaulet. It is strange that saloons were the only body styles common to both chassis to be added to the "Bullnose" range after the Armistice. Raworths of Oxford and Hollick and Pratt of Coventry built the special bodies and the Morris body shop at Cowley built the standard two- and four-seater open touring cars. In body items, changes were made to economise on materials and the door handles, for example, got smaller and smaller although never so small that it became impossible to operate the lock, and then in the late 'twenties there came the master stroke: hollow door handles. The changes in upholstery are the best illustration of the constant eye kept on costs. The Continental engined Cowley had buttoned leather upholstery. Buttoned upholstery was also used on the Hotchkiss engined cars but from then on leather upholstery was to be an Oxford feature and the cheaper Cowley had to make do with leathercloth. The upholstery continued for about an inch over the body top and the first economy move was to dispense with this extra inch. Next, the upholstery was no longer buttoned on the doors and body sides. Then the seat bottoms and backs had only one row of buttons each instead of two, until, for the 1925 season, the buttons gave way to pleated detachable upholstery, the Oxford of course still in leather and the Cowley in Rexine leathercloth. The advantage of detachable upholstery was, in the opinion of Morris Motors, that when the cars were used to carry loads after the manner of a commercial vehicle the upholstery could be removed first and damage to it avoided. In the "Flat" Cowley, Morris Motors found final fulfilment in upholstery economy: no longer buttoned, no longer pleated, but flat, non-detachable sheets of rexine.

The best selling body styles were the two-seater and four-seater tourers which were available on the "Bullnose" Cowleys and post-war Oxfords throughout their life span. It was not on their introduction, but at the 1925 Motor Show, that the "Bullnose" saloons were a sensation. Morris Motors

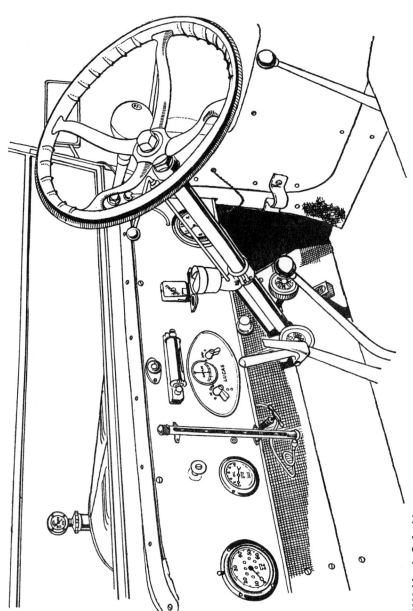

1926 Morris Oxford tourer

Ltd. announced that in future they would concentrate on cheap saloons rather than open cars; Morris Motors once again led the way, with the others following a good way behind. The first Morris saloons were offered as standard in early 1924 on more expensive Oxford chassis, which is what one would expect, because, besides being more expensive, they were available at option with a larger engine which could drag the extra weight about better. The Bullnose was available in chassis form and prior to this saloons were among the coachwork built on Morris chassis by specialist coachbuilders.

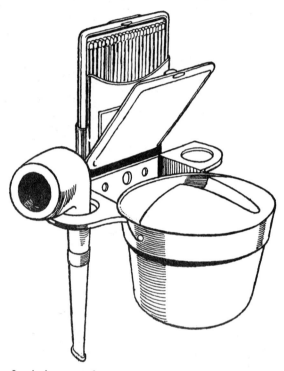

Smoker's companion.

The standard 1926 Oxford saloons were wonderfully luxurious, and although one of the cheapest available, they were upholstered throughout in Bedford cord with deep pile carpets to match and had as standard equipment accessories such as a luggage net in the roof and a Wilmot "Smoker's Companion," which was very much more than a mere ash tray. Although beautifully built they had a rather ungainly and heavy appearance, but appearances can be deceptive, because they weighed only 2 cwt. more than the relatively spartan five-seater Oxford tourer. The Cowley saloon had been introduced during the 1925 season and although lacking the luxury of the Oxford, it was prettily proportioned, and avoided the latter's heavy, clumsy appearance. In

1926 and 1929 Morris publicity matter.

31. & 32. 11.9 h.p. Light Van with its distinctive radiator.

33. 11.9 h.p. Light Van. Note the non standard scuttle.

34. A 1929 Morris 5 cwt. van.   The unusual radiator suggests this was the prototype.

35. The 30 cwt. Morris commercial charabanc.

complete contrast to the 1925 Cowley saloons the 1926 Cowley somehow seemed austere and were downright ugly. Bullnose Cowley saloons had only two doors and the year of manufacture can be determined by their positioning. 1925 models had one door on the front nearside and the other on the rear offside. The 1926 saloons had both doors on the nearside.

The Cowley occasional four was added to the Morris Motors range for the 1924 season. Actually the first Morris to have an occasional four or "chummy" style body was a 1914 W & P engined de Luxe Oxford. The body was specially built by Raworths to the order of the Morris Garages and was not *a standard W.R.M. Motors body style*. The 1914 W & P engined Oxford "chummy" was a flash in the pan and it was not until after World War I that "chummy" bodies became popular, largely thanks to the Rhode. Morris Motors claimed that the "chummy" had many advantages over the two-seater. To quote from their catalogue:—

"The space behind the rear seats is eminently suitable for carrying luggage, commercial travellers' samples, golf clubs and other items that are normally out of place in the boot of a two-seater."

There is no explanation why golf clubs, etc., are out of place in the dickey of a two-seater, but to continue:—

"The space at the rear whether occupied by passengers or packages is under the hood in rainy weather, thus ensuring proper protection. This makes a big appeal to the man with a big family. Children, moreover are safer in a chummy model than they are in the dickey of a two-seater."

Admittedly, children were safer in a "chummy" than the dickey of a two-seater, but the advantages of the Cowley "chummy" seemed to have been more imaginary than real, as shown by the model's short life, for it was discontinued when the new style of Morris Cowley with a flat radiator was introduced for the 1927 season. One can't help feeling that probably the reason for this is that for an extra £10 the purchaser could obtain a full four-seater Cowley, and a full four-seater offered real leg room for the rear seat passengers. The Morris Oxford offered even more leg room, the rear seat passengers having no less than 25 inches, which compares with the $7\frac{1}{2}$ in. to $17\frac{1}{2}$ in. of a 1964 Rolls-Royce Silver Cloud. The Cowley doctor's coupe was introduced for the 1925 season and differed from the 1926 season model in that the latter had rear quarter lights. The 1926 season Morris catalogue describes the doctor's coupe as having

"been produced to meet the demand for a really comfortable and thoroughly weather-proof, low-priced two-seater. Fully equipped and tastefully upholstered, it represents a new ideal in two-seater luxury. . . . The coachwork is non-drumming and rattle-proof, and weather protection is assured by the double windscreen with its storm gutter and wiper."

The first post-war addition to the Oxford range was the two-door saloon and two-door cabriolet for the 1924 season. The saloon had mechanically operated front windows with the two back windows sliding, grey cord cloth upholstery and adjustable front seats, all for £395. The cabriolet at £10 less had mechanically operated frameless windows, upholstery in antique grey leather and adjustable front seats. It was not until the 1925 season that these models were fitted to the chassis of 9-foot wheelbase.

A coupe was added to the Oxford range of two-seater, four-seater, four door saloon and cabriolet for the 1924 season. The Oxford coupe represented real luxury for two; nothing was spared. The leathercloth hood was lined with West of England cloth and upholstery was in Bedford cord. Smoker's companion, pile carpets, flower vase and deep pockets were fitted, and of course wind-up windows; none of that fiddling with side curtains in pouring rain. However, the dickey seat was still jolly cold and draughty.

For formal occasions a landaulet was available in 1925 and 1926 on the Oxford chassis. The landaulet was available in any colour to choice providing it was blue, and yet the two-seater Cowley at half the price had alternative colour schemes. The designer of the Oxford landaulet was fully aware of the dangers of pampering the servants. The poor chauffeur had no windows or side curtains at all, whereas the passenger compartment had every luxury, including wind-up windows. For the 1926 season, the landaulet was supplemented by the rather more expensive saloon landaulet. This model appealed to the more enlightened employer and certainly to the chauffeur as the front compartment had wind-up windows. Many passengers who occupied the rear compartment of the saloon landaulet must have marvelled at the way that the Morris designers seemed to have thought of everything. To quote but one example of this thoughtfulness from the 1926 catalogue:—

"by an ingenious arrangement all the three rear windows are provided with blinds so that privacy for town nightwork is assured."

On the road with the 14/28 Morris Oxford by Edgar N. Duffield
(*Reprinted from* The Automotor Journal *of* 18th *December*, 1924.)

There are two Morris-Oxford chassis for 1925, of 8 ft 6 in. and 9 ft wheelbase, the shorter being employed for the open two-seater and two-seater coupe, while the other is reserved for the open four-seater, four-seater cabriolet and four-seater saloon. Naturally, detail modifications have come into practice, but these are so very trivial as to be quite imperceptible to anybody but a Morris expert, apart from the standardisation (as an optional feature) of four-wheel braking, and wheels which will carry 28 in. by 4·95 in. Dunlop low pressure tyres. Except for the engines used, the lengths of the frames and the fitting optionally, of four-wheel brakes, the differences between Morris-Oxford and Morris-Cowley are merely of bodywork and equipment, and therefore in trying the new 14/28 Morris-Oxford I may be said to have been trying the complete range. Obviously the Cowley's four cylinders of 69·5 by 102 m.m. will develop less energy than will four of 75 by 102 m.m. on the Oxford, but the less costly model has a motor which justifies the use of the same gear ratios on either model, so that the difference of engine output is offset, I suppose, by the greater weight of the more expensive, due to its more elaborate coachbuilding and equipment.

I have always, on previous visits to Cowley, driven down, but on this occasion I trained. My friend in the works sent a car to Oxford to meet me, and I reached his office to find him too busy to show me what I had gone down to see, too busy for an hour.

How could I kill time? "Oh, take a car, and have a run around," he said; "Do you good after a two-hour frowst!" "What shall I take?" I asked. "Any one; they are all the same. Take that service car which brought you up from the station, or I'll give you a chit and you can go over to the running-shed and take ANY car which has been used. Which do you prefer? We have no 'specials'; they are all alike."

We went out to the car in which I had ridden up from Oxford. "Yes, that's one of the latest," said my friend. "Let's see if she has plenty of petrol." He investigated, by a glance at the tubular gauge on the instrument board. "Two hundred miles," he said. "You won't do MUCH more, within the hour will you?"

He waved his hand, I got aboard, and was off.

Now all this sounds very casual, and the car handed over, though obviously not very much used, had clearly been in service. With no knowledge of the local geography, I buzzed her on second until I had cleared the last of the traffic around the works, and hit the trail. I had an hour to kill. Inside that hour I added a little over thirty-five miles to the tally on the speedometer. Where I went, only the car knew, but I found some good, clean, hard roads, some squidgy ones, some decided hills, and some winding lanes. I was rather glad to be alone, because I particularly wished to examine the Morris gearbox. I knew that it was very good on third and second (4·4 to 1 and 7·6 to 1, I think), but I wanted to see what happened when one put one's foot hard down on first, which is 17 to 1.

Like everything else of the Morris but the tyres, wheels and accessories, this gearbox was designed in the Morris works. I believe Morris Motors Ltd., still buy their metals, 'raw', but everything that it is commercial to make they do make, and although I shall never be an enthusiast concerning central control, for reasons frequently stated, I certainly want to know about a better gearbox than this.

The engine will enjoy 26 m.p.h. on first, 41 m.p.h. on second, and – this particular car being a touring four-seater – 56 m.p.h. on third, one up. Doubtless if I had felt more dashing I'd have done better on each gear, but at the speeds named I had no apprehension as to anything dropping off.

The car had its standard 'balloons' on, but they were properly inflated, so that it steered excellently. It was also equipped with the rebound dampers which are standard equipment, so that its springs did only what they were required to do, and I registered a decision that there was still much to be said for three-quarter elliptics in the rear, rightly applied, although we so seldom see them on the new chassis nowadays.

Reverting to the gearbox, it is the best of the centrally-controlled type that I know. I should say that only those of the Star and Talbot compare with it (of those which I have tried, I mean, of course) for niceness of operation. The lever does not jump out of any gear, it does not dither like a joy-stick gone mad, and it does not in any way inconvenience anybody sitting along-side the driver. Admittedly, a third person sharing the front seat would be a little in the way of the driver's left hand, or elbow, but even in the first and third positions it and its head are so far forward as to offer the least possible encroachment upon seating space, or knee room.

The new brakes can be anything one likes, from velvety-soft to toothily-drastic. They are manufactured under the Rubery patents. The forward pair are adjustable in the simplest, most accessible fashion, without tools, and the grease gun lubrication of the few articulations is also an easy, speedy matter. I regard their provision as more of a concession to clamour than anything else, because the rear wheel braking of last year's Morris-Oxford and this year's Morris-Cowley is all that I personally should ever require, but in the case of a manufacturer in the unique position of Mr W. R. Morris, I think it is highly creditable to provide what so many people at least THINK they want, without making his customers pay for it whether or not they want it. What I have in mind is the fact that you can buy this car, with four-wheel braking, for £295. If, however, you do not like, or do not want four-wheel braking, you say so, have your car without it, and pay £10 less for it. Like everybody manufacturing on a really ambitious scale, Morris Motors Ltd. tell you plainly that in all other respects you must take the car as it is. They will not fit you up with what the irreverent call a "Leonard" instrument board, bedight with a dozen useless dill-dolls; but they will give you your choice of two-wheel or four-wheel braking, and will charge you less for the former than the latter. That seems to me real policy, infinitely preferable to that of another (and at present even more famous) manufacturer, who decides for himself what people should want, gives it to them, and sees that they pay for it, whether or not they really wish to have it. That is the difference between Mr Morris and The Other Guy. Any three cheers for the little difference!

I will confess, now, that I am a little mad on Morrisism. I honestly believe that this manufacturer deserves every ounce of his success. I believe that he owes less to 'luck' than does anybody else in the history of mechanical transport. He never gave us an ugly, crude, unmechanical, "because I say so, and I know" machine. Even in 1913, when I first saw one of his cars, it was of its date and price a very personable, presentable little thing. And as I sat in solitary state, on this 1925 Oxford at £285, all on, even to the ruddy Oxfordshire mud on its tyres, I came to see that if there were not so many Morrises morrising about the world and its highways and byways, we should all look at any one of them that we chanced to meet, and say "That's rather a neat looking, inconspicuous, workmanlike sort of rig. Nobody could quarrel with very much of its appearance!" This is so, and I believe that its creator has scored not merely because he had the courage to jump right into the deep end, and risk a big splash, as he did, and has done. I believe that he has come through because he started right – started with the knowledge that, no matter what HE thought people wanted, they would say, and show him. He therefore did what one man can to approximate the ideas, the appeals, of all buyers of contemporary motor cars within twice to two-and-a-half times the price of his, and strove to put into his all possible merits and 'points'.

My hour was nearly up, and I was hungry. I stopped on the top of a handy eminence, and took my bearings – a stranger in a strange land. I caught a glimpse of a main road (that running toward Henley, Maidenhead and London), along which were running a train, a stream, of Morrises, one about every fifty yards. That road showed me where I was, roughly, and I beat it for Cowley.

I had tried this little car on the level, uphill and downhill. Encouraged by a perfectly dry stretch of clean, hard surface, I had stood upon its four-wheel brakes in such a fashion as to put a Marcell wave in the LONGERONS of any but a perfectly rigid and robust frame. I had then wickedly abused the four-plate oil-bathed clutch by making it take up the load on top gear, which it did without a squeak or a shudder anywhere in the transmission. I had certified the real freedom of all bearings by a delirious clutch-out coast down a very sudden slope. I had tried to knock the gear-selector mechanism out of engagement (by giving the lever nasty little knocks of the kind that might be given by a clumsy footed passenger, new to cars and fidgety). In this I had failed singly. There is a very nice spring-check on the selectgear – not enough to offer any resistance to a deliberate effort to change positions, but sufficient to be proof against accidental knocks.

I had listened for body noises, to hear none. I had unlocked the nearside front door, and let it flap, only to find that it slammed itself into security with a click like that of a rifle bolt. I had done lots of other silly, superfluous things. I then looked at the mileage recorded on the Smith speedometer. 1267·3. Yes: just a nice running-in.

By now I was back at the works. I walked round and round the car. Washed and polished, it would have been a new car. Radiator top just pleasantly warm. Brake drums, fore and aft, icily cold. Engine running; I could FEEL that it was running; but anybody who could HEAR that it was running was a keener-sensed person than I was. Then I wondered if this might be a Morris Silent Six? I opened the bonnet, to find only four plugs, and that is generally quite a good indication.

As my friend was still engaged in conference, I ticked over the equipment, trying to find something 'cheap'. Smith carburettor, Lucas magneto and lighting set and starter, Lucas mirror, Lucas bulb and electric horns, five Lucas driving lamps, one ditto 'festoon' ditto on the instrument board, Wefco spring gaiters, Dunlop low pressure tyres of 28 in. by 4·95 in., a Boyce radiator thermometer, a Smith speedometer and clock, an oil gauge, petrol gauge, graduated in gallons, a spare can of fuel in carrier, a licence holder, an automatic windscreen wiper, four shock absorbers or rebound dampers (to make the best of both worlds), a smoker's 'companion' with ash-receptacle, a can of engine oil, a kit of really useful tools – all this and an insurance policy covering all risks, for £285!

I left it, and went into my friend's office, as the clock struck one.

"What do you think of the car?" he asked. "I don't" I replied. "I do not WANT to think about it. There is nothing to THINK about. But I feel that I begin to know why people buy them!" And I did, and do.

Anybody who has not, so far, tried a 1925 Morris has a lot to learn about motoring. That might have been said early last summer, but there is nothing else to say now, of this year's output. Everybody should try one, no matter what he owns, or drives, or thinks of buying. He will then see why Mr W. R. Morris does not REALLY like people who buy other than British cars, and at the same time he will see – But let him try one.

6

Morris publicity and "Imshi"

"An 'interest' film covering the whole process of manufacture of a standard Morris car from metallurgical tests to coachwork is now being shown at high grade cinema halls."

From a Morris advertisement in The Motor *of the 17th May,* 1922.

Morris's object was to make cars people could afford. He was insistent that prices did not come down romantically with large scale production unless every sort of economy, great and small, was practised. To this end he claimed that he never spent a penny unnecessarily on selling or publicity.

Prior to the outbreak of World War I Morris did no advertising in the trade press, although he occasionally advertised in the national daily papers. For example, an advertisement for a W & P engined Morris Oxford appeared in the *Daily Mail* of Saturday, 8th August, 1914 showing both styles of coupe, the cabriolet coupe with a folding leather hood and hard-top limousine coupe. Six years later the two names, Morris and *Daily Mail*, were again linked, this time by "Imshi". Nearly all the advertisements for Morris cars, including those in the trade press, were by Stewart and Ardern and they often mentioned Morris successes in minor events as evidence of the soundness of the new *marque*.

After World War I W.R.M. Motors started advertising their new models of Oxford and Cowley, although they were not as yet in production and from now on Morris advertising coverage steadily increased.

At the end of February, 1920 Morris advertisements stated:—

"Important Notice: Morris Motors Ltd., Cowley, Oxon, are the sole makers of the Morris Oxford and Morris Cowley light cars. This company carries on its manufacture at Cowley, nr. Oxford; NOT IN LONDON, and has no connection with any other firm of a similar name. Every car bears one distinctive badge as shown above."

This left little doubt that the car in question was the Morriss-London, which was a four cylinder machine of 85 m.m. bore and 127 m.m. stroke and cost about £350. It was manufactured by Century Motors Co. of Elkhart, Indiana, and imported into England by H. E. & F. Morriss of 4, Athelstane Mews, Stroud Green Road, in North London. According to Doyle and Georgano in their *The World's Automobiles* Frank Morriss was the official car repairer to King Edward VII, and specialised in modifying early Daimlers. By 1921 Morris advertisements really carried news with announcements of the first of a series of fantastic price cuts.

The best publicity Morris ever received was gratis. John Prioleau, the motoring correspondent of the *Daily Mail*, planned a motoring adventure which would take him through France, Italy, Morocco and Spain. His object was not to break records, but to tell the *Daily Mail's* readers of the

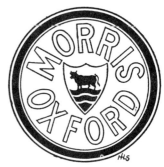

places he saw and how post-war motoring conditions overseas compared with those of the pre-war days. Prioleau's scheme received the blessing of Lord Northcliffe, the proprietor of the *Daily Mail*. For his journey Prioleau chose a light car, which he christened and always referred to as "Imshi", which is arabic for 'get a move on'. Imshi received no special preparation for her dash into the wilds, although she had already covered nearly 14,000 miles since Prioleau had purchased her new in January, 1920. Prioleau left London on 19th December, 1920 and next day crossed from Dover to Calais. Trouble struck soon for he had got no further than Gisors when the petrol pipe severed, but repairs were effected within a quarter of an hour. French road conditions at the time contrasted strongly with their present excellence and over a six mile stretch to Chalon-sur-Saone Imshi broke both front springs and sprang numerous leaks in her radiator. In Prioleau's words:—

"Like a lame duck, poor Imshi waddled and groaned, weeping hot tears, up a hill to the never-sufficiently-to-be-advertised garage of Monsieur B. Rogier."

M. Rogier explained that springs were rather at a premium as most travellers coming from Chagny (12 miles away) at more than five miles an hour usually needed a full set! Four hours later, and a cost of roughly £3, Imshi had new front springs and a repaired radiator. Superb service!

Some six months later Prioleau was growing distinctly suspicious of Imshi, as "why should this now venerable vehicle suddenly pretend she is brand new and delight the very road-weary heart of her owner? I have done nothing to cheer her up – most of the time I have been too busy resting. She has really been distinctly neglected." At the end of his travels Prioleau had nothing but praise for Imshi, who had covered nearly 21,000 miles, 7,000 of them in the six months of his overseas tour through France, Italy, Morocco, Algeria, Tunisia and Spain. In some places the roads had been atrocious and in other places there had been no roads at all, but Imshi had come through with flying colours. The only repairs and replacements necessary were as follows:—

at 13,850 miles: petrol joint repaired

at 14,150 miles: two new front springs fitted

at 17,000 miles: one new leaf in front spring

at 19,000 miles: two new brake springs, two new steering pins

at 19,500 miles: nut and washer holding off differential ball race replaced.
   Four new brake linings. One new spring leaf

at 19,985 miles: magneto overhauled and repaired

at 20,110 miles: off-side front spring clip replaced.

In addition, the engine had been scoured of carbon five times and the valves ground in once.

Soon after the start of his journey scores of people wrote to ask the make of Imshi and since then there had been a steady demand for this vital knowledge, but Prioleau said he would wait until the very end of his travels before disclosing it. This built up tremendous interest. In June, 1921 Prioleau gave up his secret. Imshi was a 1920 11·9 h.p. Morris Oxford two-seater. The publicity value for Morris was enormous and came at just the right time. Four months earlier Morris had made his startling £100 price cut and allied to low prices here was proof of the excellence of the Cowley products. The demonstration had been all the more impressive because Imshi was not only practically standard, but also well used. Prioleau said:—

"I particularly wish to lay stress on Imshi's unpreparedness for this rush into the blue, if only in bare justice to Mr Morris, who was casually informed, by telephone I think, forty-eight hours before I started, that Imshi was off into the wilds. I remember asking him to send me some valve springs. His reply was to send two of his best engineers to London with a perfect dump of spares of every possible kind. The only ones I have used have been gaskets, one petrol pipe (a 'spare' beyond price in Africa, let me tell you) and a magneto. The remainder of the beautiful stock is untouched."

Prioleau's newspaper articles were published in April, 1922 by Jarrolds in book form under the title, *The Adventures of Imshi*, and with the delightful sub-title "A two-seater in search of the sun", which gives the adventures a holiday air. This book still remains one of the best on motor travel and instead of grumbling about mishaps its author had the gift of making them all seem an essential part of a great adventure. Prioleau was a veteran motorist and added spice is given to the account of his and Imshi's travels by comparing motoring in 1921 and at the turn of the century.

After her adventures, Imshi returned to Morris Motors where she was fitted with a later radiator and different windscreen, repainted maroon and equipped with a copper dashboard, which when polished brought many a blush to damsels of the short-skirt era. Imshi spent some time on display at various Morris dealers and then was sold for £7 10s. 0d. to a motor dealer, who used it as a general hack and motorcycle transporter. In 1933 a 14/40 Vauxhall took Imshi's place and poor Imshi, due to lack of space, had to be scrapped. Its last journey was to a breaker's yard near Bletchley.

There was a sequel to Imshi. Imshi II was a new 11·9 h.p. dark blue standard four-seater 1922 Oxford in which Prioleau intended to tour Holland, the Rhineland, South Prussia, Bavaria, Czechoslovakia, Prague, Hungary and Budapest, but a collision in France with a locomotive, which won the argument, delayed him. Imshi II was duly straightened out and completed its journey, which is described in *Imshi in New Europe* published in October 1924. There was even an Imshi III. The latter Imshis behaved well, but the novelty and therefore much of the interest was gone. *Imshi in New Europe* makes poor reading compared with *The Adventures of Imshi*.

Increased sales demanded and could support a large publicity programme. When Morris was describing the features of a new model to the Press, he was irritated to see that one of the journalists, Mr W. M. W. Thomas, D.F.C., who was the editor of *The Light Car and Cyclecar* was not bothering to take notes, but when the articles appeared he considered Thomas's to be the best. Morris was impressed and the upshot of the matter was that he placed him in charge of Morris publicity including a new venture, a magazine called *The Morris Owner*. The first issue of *The Morris Owner* came out in March, 1924, and although now renamed *Motoring*, it has appeared at regular monthly intervals ever since. *The Morris Owner* claimed to be the only all-British motoring magazine and it never mentioned foreign cars. A Morris slogan was "Buy British and be proud of it", which reflected his opinion that it was immoral to buy a foreign car when so many members of the British motor industry were unemployed or on short time. Quite naturally, Morris preferred people to buy his cars but if they did not buy a Morris they should buy another British make. Surprisingly, advertisements for other makes of British cars, including the highly competitive Clyno, appeared in *The Morris Owner*. Advertisements for cars such as the A.C. and Armstrong Siddeley were aimed at the Morris owner who could now afford something a little better. In August, 1925 a subsidiary called the Morris Oxford Press Ltd. (renamed the Nuffield Press Ltd. in September, 1942) was formed to print the increasing volume of Morris publicity matter including *The Morris Owner*, handbooks and *The Morris Owner's Road Book*, which was a touring guide. W. R. Morris's faith in W. M. W. Thomas, D.F.C., now Sir Miles Thomas, D.F.C., was justified and he was appointed to the board of Morris Motors in May, 1927.

Morris literature was characterised by good photographs. In 1919 R. W. Barnes, an engineer, left his birthplace London to work as a jig and tool designer with Hotchkiss et Cie in Gosford Street, Coventry, later to become Morris Engines. He was known as a good amateur photographer and on occasion took pictures for Morris Motors. These were so successful that towards the end of 1923 he was invited to accept an appointment to be created for him at Cowley as official photographer for Morris Motors. As an engineer he was the ideal man for the job. He then turned to industrial films, a field in which he was a pioneer and he not only shot them but wrote his own scripts, and edited. In 1924 he produced one of his earliest films, which showed how Bullnoses were built. Barnes kept meticulous records, for which the authors are grateful, because it so simplified the illustration of this book.

7

Morris commercials

Morris increased his sales from 6,937 cars in 1922 to 20,024 in 1923, an achievement all the more remarkable when it is remembered that this was accomplished during a trade depression. The increased sales gave Morris profits for further investment but since he was already well able to meet any anticipated rise in demand for Oxfords and Cowleys, he began to consider branching out with a different type of vehicle.

Commercial vehicles based on the Morris private car chassis were available, but were only suitable for light work. W.R.M. Motors offered a 5 cwt. light van based on the W & P Oxford chassis in 1913 and 1914, a very handsome affair, too, with its mahogany panelling. Continental engined Cowleys were only available in small numbers, but one or two with lorry bodies were used during the war as factory hacks for transporting Morris assembled mine sinkers and a few with van bodies were used by a Glasgow firm for delivering newspapers. A Morris light van of 8 cwt. capacity was officially listed for the 1923 season. The chassis, of course, closely followed that of the Cowley car, but an immediately noticeable difference was the radiator, which looked like a Bullnose radiator with the front inch or so sawn off. When the cars went square for the 1927 season the vans partially resisted the change and continued with the same radiator shape. In addition the Morris Cowley commercial traveller's car, which became available in 1925, must be mentioned. It was very similar to the two-seater Cowley but had a big box at the back instead of a dickey seat and the Morris publicity literature describes it as a car "particularly well adapted for the carrying of samples, while the seating accommodation has all the comfort of the standard two-seater, the upholstery being deep and the cushions well raked.... It is sold rubbed down ready for painting and lettering. A net weight of eight cwt. can be carried." It was not an aesthetic success.

Ford's Model-T may have had its defects, but in one respect, other than price, it had a big advantage over the Bullnose; its chassis was equally suitable for a 7 cwt. commercial, a touring car and, with a few cheap modifications such as lowering the final drive ratio, a 1 ton commercial. In respect of touring cars, Morris could hold his own but the Model-T remained unbeaten in the expanding 1 ton commercial vehicle market and it was in this range that Morris finally decided to challenge Ford. (Having burnt his fingers with the Oxford "Silent" Six, he resisted the temptation, if indeed there was any, to develop higher horse-power cars.) To produce his own 1 ton commercial, Morris knew he would have to design a vehicle specially for the purpose, but the use of the $13 \cdot 9$ h.p. Oxford power unit, clutch and gearbox would help him to keep the price down, so essential when trying to sell against Ford. The use of the standard $13 \cdot 9$ h.p. Oxford engine was possible because at last they were freely available. In 1922 there were difficulties over engines supplies from the Hotchkiss et Cie for an annual output of 6,937 cars, but since Morris acquired their Coventry branch in 1923 the factory had been re-organised to such effect that the output was trebled with production capacity to spare.

Morris considered that the Cowley works should concentrate on cars and that the commercials should be built in a separate factory. Obviously entry into the commercial field could be effected more rapidly if an existing plant was bought instead of a new factory built and specially equipped. In this Morris was lucky for in 1923, E. G. Wrigley and Co. Ltd. of Soho, Birmingham, were up for sale.

Founded in 1898, E. G. Wrigley and Co. Ltd. were an engineering firm, who began specialising in transmissions and they displayed rear axles and two- and three-speed gearboxes at the Olympia Show as early as 1906. In 1913, they made plans to join the cyclecar boom with a 7 h.p. machine which had a twin cylinder engine, air or water cooled at option, two speed and reverse gearbox combined with a worm drive rear axle and Sankey wheels. *The Cyclecar* of the 5th March, 1913 stated that: "at present the machine is only coming out of the experimental stage, but in a few weeks will be ready for delivery." One doubts whether the machine ever left the experimental stage and it seems more likely that very sensibly Wrigleys continued to concentrate on supplying the motor industry with axles, gearboxes, steering boxes and similar components. In 1913 one of Wrigleys' new customers for their worm and wheel rear axles was W. R. Morris, who used them on his W & P engined Morris Oxford. (In contrast to Mr Morris, Dr Fred Lanchester had only one use for a Wrigley worm and that was fishing!) After World War I, Wrigleys lost Morris's business, but at that time they must have felt more than compensated by obtaining the Angus Sanderson contracts for gearboxes, steering boxes and complete front and rear axles. Angus Sanderson rather than

Morris was favoured as the British firm which would really strike a blow at Ford, and with this in mind Wrigleys geared up for large-scale production. Wrigleys anticipated that Angus Sanderson requirements would so tax their production facilities that in 1919 they were advertising that they could accept no more orders. To their cost, Wrigleys had backed the wrong horse too heavily and Angus Sanderson never lived up to their promise of vast output despite the torrents of words devoted to them by the motoring press. Things looked black for Wrigleys with orders falling off from other motor car manufacturers, who were having to cut production in face of Morris competition. In February, 1922 their authorised capital was written down by order of the High Court and in 1923 Wrigleys were up for sale. The quality of their products had never been in question, but the market had evaporated.

W. R. Morris bought E. G. Wrigley & Co. Ltd. for £213,044 and moved into their works on New Year's day, 1924. On the 4th February, 1924 Morris Commercial Cars Ltd. was incorporated and it is interesting to note that it remained Mr W. R. Morris's personal property until October, 1936 when it was acquired by Morris Motors Ltd. The Morris Commercial one tonner was announced in May, 1924. Suspension was by half elliptic springs all round, and included in the specification were five stud wheels and a radiator with a cast aluminium shell. The engine, clutch and gearbox were almost identical to those of the 1,802 c.c. Morris Oxford and final drive was by torque tube to an overhead worm axle. To enable the engine to cope with loads of up to one ton, the final drive ratio had been lowered from $4 \cdot 75 : 1$ or $4 \cdot 42 : 1$ of the Oxford to $7 \cdot 25 : 1$. Prices were modest, the chassis costing £185, the lorry £225, the standard van £235 and the van-de-luxe £250, the latter being described by the manufacturers as "a commercial vehicle of the highest class, suitable for transportation of the best quality goods." The vehicles were supplied to the customer in grey primer and standard equipment included number plates, a practice which could well be copied by present day manufacturers. Prices had been kept down as the usual commercial vehicle practice of fitting no starter or front wheel brakes was followed, but even so the Model-T one tonner was still roughly 25 per cent cheaper.

During their first four months, February to May, 1924 Morris Commercial Cars Ltd. made a loss of £22,000 but this was scarcely surprising since there was no production. During the summer months sales were slow and further money had to be put into the business, but by May, 1925 a profit of £39,000 had been made and Morris Commercial Cars Ltd. were firmly established. Trojans may have distributed Brooke Bond Tea, but by 1925 Kardomah tea was delivered in Morris Commercial one ton vans and Maypole tea in Morris eight cwt. vans. The Co-operative Societies also favoured Morris Commercial one tonners, the Ten Acres and Stirchley Co-op having one fitted out as a mobile butcher's shop and the Portsea Island Mutual Co-operative Society Ltd. used half a dozen standard Morris vans for local deliveries in the Portsmouth area. Neither were Morris Commercials over-looked by public authorities such as the local councils and the police. Two one-tonners were bought by the Stratford-on-Avon town council in 1925, one of which they had equipped as a dust cart and the other as a tanker for sewage drainage. The bodies of both vehicles were built by Messrs. Tuke and Bell of Litchfield, still existing today as a leading firm of sanitary engineers, and who were, incidentally, responsible for the belt-driven single cylinder Aster-engined Globe cyclecar of circa 1912–16, which was built at their Tottenham works. The Paisley police had a chocolate and brown Morris Commercial patrol waggon and the Perak police bought a one-tonner with a body specially designed and constructed by Malayan Motors for riot duty! It had not escaped the attention of the Morris Commercial distributors, the Colmore Depot, that the G.P.O. were using foreign vehicles and the latter were persuaded to try Morris Commercials as a replacement. The trials were carried out in the Birmingham area and were eminently successful. By 1925 the users of Morris Commercials were legion and included "Kensitas", M.A.C. Fisheries, the Birmingham Brewers, Davenport C.B. Ltd., Carrs the biscuit firm, and the Western County Creameries. Thomson Bros. (Bilston) Ltd. built a baby tanker on a one ton Morris Commercial chassis for Shell Mex and B.P., for oil and petrol deliveries.

By March, 1925 a twelve/fourteen-seater charabanc and bus were available from Morris Commercial Cars Ltd. on their one ton chassis. They could be equipped with an engine-driven Maxfield tyre inflator as an extra at six guineas. A sixteen-seater charabanc was also offered and space for the extra two seats was obtained by having an inside gangway entrance to the last two rows of seats and omitting the outside entrance over the wheel arches. In 1925, Hants and Dorset Motor Services Ltd. were using four Morris Commercial buses on the narrow roads of their district, which were banned to heavier buses. The drivers of buses were frequently in trouble for exceeding the 12 m.p.h. speed limit and sometimes even passengers came up against the law: in September, 1925 one motoring journal reported that passengers had been charged, convicted and fined under new byelaws which prohibited, among other things, the throwing of coins to children in the road and the trailing of streamers.

The success of the one-tonner was such that Stewart and Ardern, the London distributors, opened a special "Commercials Only" depot at 371 Euston Road, London, in June, 1925 and by the following month they had to cater for an addition to the Morris Commercial range, the 12 cwt. The 12 cwt. was a scaled down version of the "Tonner" and used the 11·9 h.p. Cowley engine. The specification included five stud wheels with 32 × 4 straight side tyres, a 7½ gallon fuel tank, 14 in. rear wheel brakes and a choice of either 7·33 : 1 or 6·25 : 1 final drive ratio. There was, of course, neither starter nor front wheel brakes, but even so the chassis at £165 and the van at £215 were good value, although still more expensive than the Model-T Ford. As to performance, one of the advertising slogans for the 12 cwt. was "faster than the Tonner". In November a 12 cwt. and a Tonner ran from Land's End to John O'Groats under R.A.C. observation without once stopping their engines. The 12 cwt. carried a load of 1,833 lb. and averaged 21·19 m.p.g. or 41·23 ton miles per gallon. The Tonner carried a heavier load, 2,604 lb. and recorded a poorer m.p.g. figure of 19·48 but a better ton miles per gallon figure of 49·43.

A 12 cwt. chassis was used as the basis for a special known as "Coppernose Connie". The normal radiator of the 12 cwt. chassis was replaced by an outsize one in copper which was hand-beaten by Mr Davis who was then works manager of the Morris subsidiary, the Osberton Radiator Co. The Morris Garages built a large fabric limousine body on to this chassis and in this guise Connie plied for hire in the streets of Oxford from about 1925 until 1930. Only a year or two ago the dear old lady was reported to be still going strong. One can only hope that no mischief has befallen her since.

Morris Commercial Cars Ltd. continued to expand rapidly and by the 1931 Motor Show had a wider range than any other British commercial vehicle manufacturer, offering everything from an ambulance and taxi-cab to 6–7 tonners and double decker buses.

37. Two of fifty made: The F-type six cylinder Morris Oxford.

38 & 39. The F-type six cylinder Morris Oxford.

0. *Reflections in Bripal cellulose: 1928 Oxford luxury.*

1. *A genuine Empire Oxford on test prior to export.*

42. *A 1922 Sports Cowley.*

*43. Mrs. Fernihough standing
by L. P. Jarman's 14/28 M.G.
which her husband owned
when he held the world speed
record for motor cycles.*

8

Not so successful

"Students of design are to be enormously intrigued by the news that the makers of the Morris Oxford and Morris Cowley cars are projecting a small six cylinder model."

The Autocar, 30*th October*, 1920

Technically the six cylinder Bullnose Oxfords were bad, the Morris Leon Bollees good and the 'Empire' Oxfords mediocre. The thing all three had in common was that they did not sell; they were failures. They are consequently of enormous interest to the vintage enthusiast because they are in complete contrast to other contemporary Morris models, but it is essential to preserve a sense of proportion when studying these cars and acknowledge that these failures were trivial and nothing as compared with W. R. Morris's success. The envious like to read of mistakes of men who have made their mark, but they will receive little satisfaction here, because this chapter only emphasizes that Morris was a man of extraordinary qualities. He had the rare attribute of recognising an error very quickly and at once taking remedial action. He did not suffer from a false pride which drove him to greater efforts to try and prove himself right; he knew such efforts would only make the mistake more costly.

Six Cylinder Bullnoses

Morris was experimenting with a six cylinder engine as early as 1915 and the sole example built is reputed to have been a side valve unit designated the D-type. After the war, experiments were carried a stage further with the construction of two overhead valve 2,355 c.c. six cylinder engines of 70 m.m. bore and 102 m.m. stroke. These engines were equipped with a Zenith carburettor, Thomson Bennett magneto and water impeller; Morris normally relied on thermosyphon cooling. One of these engines was fitted into a specially designed chassis of 9 ft 3 in. wheelbase, which was 9 in. longer than that of the 11·9 h.p. cars. The E-type chassis is really interesting because, besides being the first Morris to have an overhead valve engine, it was also the first Morris to have centre lock wire wheels with 765 × 105 tyres instead of artillery wheels, and half elliptic rear springs instead of three-quarter elliptic rear springs, which were a feature of all four cylinder Morrises from March, 1913 until the introduction of the flat fronted Morris for 1927. This E-type chassis was fitted with a small saxe blue saloon body and black mudguards and exhibited with its spare engine on Stand 97 at the 1920 Olympia Motor Show. The Morris record book shows a car with the chassis number E 100, which is presumably this E-type saloon, but what is intriguing is that the engine number is given as 8272, which is in line with the numbering of W & P engines of about 1915 but with no other engines used by Morris.

Morris stated that the E-type was purely experimental and the next stage in the development of a six cylinder model was the production of a prototype in October, 1921 which W. R. Morris reserved for his personal use. It was fitted with an elegant coupe body of exquisite luxury; in fact it is the most luxurious coachwork that the authors have seen fitted to any Bullnose, with its West of England cloth upholstery, deep pile carpets, braided side panels and railway carriage type windows with heavily embroidered straps for raising and lowering them. The chassis of this prototype was almost identical to that of the E-type but for the engine, which had reverted from overhead valves to side valves and explains why W. R. Morris, on the introduction of the car to the public, judged it an opportune moment to state that in his view overhead valves had no advantages over side valves unless a multiplicity of them were used and that this had been borne out by racing practice. The reversion to side valves was the most significant difference between the new prototype and the E-type car, but the side valve engine, which was rated at 17·9 h.p., also had the slightly different cylinder dimensions of 69·5 m.m. bore and 102 m.m. stroke (the same as the 11·9 h.p. four cylinder Cowleys and Oxfords) giving a capacity of 2,320 c.c. and at 2,800 r.p.m. this engine developed about 39 b.h.p. Fortunately the prototype still survives and is preserved at Cowley in excellent original condition.

The prototype was promising and therefore put into production. The prototype had been allotted a chassis and engine number from the 11·9 h.p. series, but the production versions had the engine and chassis prefix F, the numbering in both cases commencing at F 101. In the case of the four cylinder engines selective assembly was used for the timing gears, but even so they could become noisy after a little use. To overcome this the prototype and first few production F-type sixes had a magneto driven by a chain from the nose of the crankshaft, but this did not provide the answer and so the later F-type engines reverted to the practice of the four cylinder 11·9 h.p. engines of having the magneto driven by skew gears. Some of the F-type engines were also fitted with an unusual air intake. The air intake was cast with the exhaust manifold and the warm air was piped round the back of the cylinder block to the Smith carburettor; in all the incoming air bent through 450° before entering the cylinder!

The first production F-type, a china white carbriolet, was finished in time for the 1922 Olympia Motor Show and also on the stand was an engine, F 104, brought up to exhibition finish and now preserved in the apprentice school at Cowley. At the 1922 Motor Show the F-type was priced at £375 as a

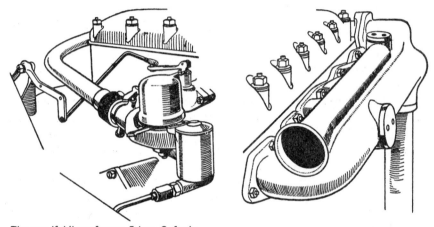

The manifolding of some F-type Oxfords

chassis and at £575 with cabriolet body. The motor show cabriolet was kept at Cowley until August 1924 and the first F-type six to be sold was an open four-seater delivered to Lord Reedesdale in February, 1923. Other recipients of the Morris Oxford Silent Six were Mr Pratt of Hollick and Pratt, who in March, 1923 had his own special sports body fitted, the Earl of Macclesfield, Morris's financial backer, who took delivery of a two-seater also in March, 1923 and Mr (now Sir Miles) Thomas, who took delivery of a two-seater with sample springs in July, 1924. A cabriolet was delivered to Fodens in February, 1924 and another to Associated Newspapers in June, 1924. W. R. Morris seemed to have a soft spot for the six, because (including the prototype) he had four of them. One had sports bodywork, but the most unusual was the one supplied in 1925 and which differed from previous F-types in that it had four-wheel brakes and artillery instead of wire wheels. The Hollick and Pratt body, which was designed by Mr Pratt himself, was a most striking coupe with the upper decking in polished aluminium, the lower part in polished and lacquered copper and with mudguards and valances painted maroon. This body was later transferred to a 1928 ohc Six chassis and the ensemble in this latter guise still survives.

The F-type was not displayed at the 1923 Olympia Motor Show through lack of stand space but the public were assured that the model was still available. A few in fact were being offered by dealers and three were exported, one to Shanghai in July, 1924 and the other two to Australia in April, 1924, one being destined for the Melbourne show. According to Landstad, who designed the car, Morris wanted to order parts for 10,000 but parts for only 500 were purchased, which made Morris furious. Production and development of the "Six" then became very slow because the four cylinder cars were in such demand. With the exception of the car assembled from parts in February and tested in May, 1925 for W. R. Morris, production ceased in July, 1924 after only forty-nine cars, including the prototype, had been built. From 1925 to 1927 M.G.s were assembled in part of the Morris-owned Osberton Radiator Co. premises at Bainton Road, Oxford, and an M.G. employee recalled how the lads in their mid-day break used to watch the ladies from the radiator factory bathe in the lake. All good things come to an end. The site was taken over for a new radiator factory and the numerous left over parts for the 500 F-types which were planned but never built were used to fill in the lake. Why did the "Six" meet with such an ignominious end?

An F-type six cylinder coupe was road tested by *The Motor* in December, 1922 and the car showed promise, particularly as the petrol consumption recorded was 36·4 m.p.g. at an average speed of 34 m.p.h. and 60 m.p.h. was easily attainable in top gear. The high axle ratio of 3·5 : 1 must have partly accounted for these excellent figures and this performance allied with realistic prices should have made the car a winner. However, the road test did not tell all the story. The authors have corresponded with two people who actually ran these F-type Morrises. One remembers that the engine of his particular car was so tightly assembled that it had to be started with a crowbar and that the engine seized up on more than one occasion. The main thing another owner remembers about his car was that he was jolly pleased to get rid of it! He remembers that the suspension gave a very rough ride, and, possibly due to the lightness of the flywheel and clutch assembly, the low speed pulling power was not much better than that of the four cylinder Morris; the advantage of the six cylinders could only be felt at high revs, when the engine seemed to wake up. This particular car, however, did make a successful journey from Manchester to the Great Exhibition at Wembley in 1924. These two owners were lucky as their cars did not suffer from the F-type's most serious weakness, about which there is a most interesting story.

Neville Minchin, in his excellent book *Under My Bonnet*, recalls a trip he made to France in convoy with W. R. Morris, who was driving his F-type "Six". At this time Sir Henry Royce, for the sake of his health, was winter-

ing at his villa at Le Canadel and Mi͏   great
motor car manufacturers, who ha   had
respect for the work of Royce, as "F   *Motor
Sport* of April, 1958, which discus   oyce
"Twenty". Of the Rolls-Royce "?   t his
"impression was one of disappointment" to ..   lied:
"If I were Mr Northcott I should not criticise the work of a firm which has
for so many years held the reputation of designing and manufacturing the
best car in the world." Minchin introduced Morris to Royce on the 27th
February, 1925 at the Beau Rivage Hotel, St. Raphael, and the two manufacturers disappeared into the hotel garage to inspect the Bullnose Oxford Six.
When Minchin found them they were deep in conversation. Royce had
spotted the car's weakness: the crankshaft.

The wheelbase of the F-type Oxford Six was 9 in. longer than that of the
11·9 h.p. four cylinder Morrises, but the extra space was taken up by the
F-type engine which was also 9 in. longer than the 11·9 h.p. engine and so
the F-type provided no extra body space. Landstad maintained that this
lack of extra body space was the doom of the "Six", but what really sealed
the car's fate was its gluttony for crankshafts. The F-type engine was so to
speak an 11·9 h.p. engine with two extra cylinders tacked on and the engines
were so similar that even the dimensions of the crankpins and webs were the
same. There were two natural periods of the crankshaft in the speed range of
the "Six" and its slim proportions allowed these periodic vibrations to build
up to an appalling level. The vibration was so bad that one motoring
journalist refused to road test the car and indeed the best "Six" of them all,
the prototype, once fractured its centre main bearing. This vibration inevitably led to frequent crankshaft breakage. That it was the engine at fault in
the "Six" is proved by the fact that at least nine cars had to have the engine
changed before leaving the works; three different engines were tested in one
car before a satisfactory one was found. Efforts to make the engine smoother
included fitting a small flywheel on the camshaft and fitting Aerolite split
skirt pistons with two compression and one scraper ring. However, these
features could not compensate for the bad crankshaft design. Even for the
11·9 h.p. engine the crankpins and webs were on the small side and hopelessly
so in the case of the longer and less well supported six throw crankshaft of the
F-type. It may have simplified the spares situation to have big-end and
main bearings of the two engines interchangeable, but interchangeability
had in this instance been carried too far. Royce, with his gift for engineering,
deduced that there was something amiss with the bottom end.

The chassis prefix F was given to the overhead camshaft 2,468 c.c. six
cylinder cars introduced at the 1927 Olympia Motor Show. The first ten
car built had a 48 in. track and their chassis numbers were F 201 to F 211.
Seven of these ten cars were dismantled at Cowley, two were sold and one,

chassis F 210, was sent to the Morris Garages where it was modified into the first 18/80 M.G., a black fabric saloon with chassis number 6251. Production of the Morris Six with the JA-type overhead camshaft engine, but with the track increased to 56 in., was resumed in March, 1928 and the chassis numbering of the revised cars started at F-251.

The Bullnose Six was a bad car, but had little effect on the fortunes of Cowley. Morris quickly saw that it would never sell well and on realising this put no more money or effort into the car.

In 1925 the number of Cowleys being built in one day was three times the number of Bullnose Sixes built altogether.

Morris Leon Bollees

W. R. Morris was always eager to develop the export market and a measure of his early success is the number of surviving Bullnoses, including W & P engined models, in New Zealand and Australia. France and the French colonies did not have the sales potential of the British colonies for cars but provided nevertheless a market which could not be ignored by anyone seriously interested in exporting.

In October, 1924, the Societe Francaise des Automobiles Morris was formed to handle French sales of the Bullnose. They had showrooms in Paris, but sales were disappointing. French import duties were largely responsible, and to overcome them Morris started to look for a factory so that he could manufacture there. After all, if Citroen were manufacturing in England, why shouldn't Morris manufacture in France? On the 10th December, 1924 Morris signed a preliminary contract to purchase the factory and assets of Automobiles Leon Bollee.

Amedee Bollee had a bell foundry and engineering shop at Le Mans, and is chiefly remembered today for his steam road vehicles. The first of these, "L'Obeissante", was built in 1873 (before the advent of the petrol-engined car) and is preserved in the Musee des Arts et Metiers in Paris. Amedee Bollee had three sons, Amedee, Leon and Camille. Amedee fils and Leon became motor car manufacturers, but their firms were entirely separate and the cars completely different. Amedee Bollees were beautifully built luxury cars of advanced design, but expensive, and remained in production until 1927. The fortunes of Automobiles Leon Bollee were founded on their speedy tri-car of 1895, of which a large number survive, and the British rights of which were purchased for £20,000 by H. J. Lawson. At the turn of the century Leon Bollee sold the design of a four wheeled car to the hard headed businessman, Alexandre Darracq for £10,000. Leon Bollee then made £42,000 in dealings with a British syndicate. He was a rich man, but in 1913, at the age of forty-two, he died before he had had time to enjoy his wealth.

Madame Bollee took over the management of his business interests and ran them with remarkable competence. However, with the death of their founder Automobiles Leon Bollee had lost their guiding light and by 1924 their fortunes were waning.

On acquiring the firm Morris re-organised the management. Wallis, who had twenty years service with Rolls-Royce to his credit and who, during this time had risen to be their service manager, was appointed managing director. Five of the other senior posts were filled by Cowley men; Harry Smith was appointed works manager, Westby made chief draughtsman and Carl Kingerlee, who later became Lord Nuffield's private secretary, was appointed chief tester. One important post which was not filled by a Cowley man was that of sales manager. This job was filled by a Frenchman who had been general manager prior to the take-over. The sales manager had the very important and responsible task of recommending to the Board the type of car which would best suit the French home and colonial market. He was probably justified in not recommending a direct copy of the Oxford and Cowley because import duties may not have been the sole reason that they had not sold well in France. He recommended the manufacture of a large saloon. Hans Landstad, by then technical director of Morris Motors, and Westby, formerly chief draughtsman at Cowley, settled in at Le Mans and set to work on the design of such a car, which was to become known as the MLB Normal. In March, 1925 1,000 sets of chassis parts were ordered. In July, 1925 Van Vestrant joined Morris Leon Bollee on the technical side, but on his arrival no parts for the new design had yet arrived and so after a further three weeks of waiting he was sent all over France chasing them up. The first MLB Normal chassis was finished in the first week of September, 1925, and soon production reached fifty cars per week. Surprisingly enough, the cars were sold at this rate despite the sales manager's unfortunate knack of accepting orders for cars with body styles which were not in stock.

During the design stages of the MLB Normal, production of the established 2-litre Leon Bollee was continued under the new name of Morris Leon Bollee type M. The type M had a 72 m.m. × 120 m.m. 1,954·3 c.c. four cylinder pushrod overhead valve engine with a three bearing crankshaft. In unit with this engine was a four-speed and reverse gearbox with central control. The MLB Normal was a larger car than the type M and had an 80 m.m. × 120 m.m. 2,412·7 c.c. four cylinder overhead valve Hotchkiss engine in unit with a four-speed gearbox (ratios 4·5, 7·42, 10·08 and 19·48). The MLB Normal and type M not only differed completely from the British Morris but also differed from each other.

For example, the smaller car had left-hand steering, a dynamotor, magneto and water pump driven by a cross shaft at the front of the engine, and wood artillery wheels, although steel artillery wheels were available to order. In contrast, the larger car had right-hand steering, a separate dynamo and starter, the dynamo and magneto driven in tandem on the nearside of the engine, and steel artillery wheels. On the smaller car the carburettor was on the nearside and the exhaust manifold on the offside. On the larger car the arrangement was the opposite. An unusual feature common to both cars was full cantilever rear springs, which were reported to give an excellent ride. More usual features of the specification common to both were torque tube transmission, a Zenith or Solex carburettor fed by an Autovac from a rear-mounted tank and four-wheel brakes.

With the MLB Normal in production the design staff of Morris Leon Bollee were side-tracked by the small multi-cylinder fad. The easiest and cheapest solution to the problem was to try and fit an overhead camshaft six cylinder Wolseley engine into the MLB Normal chassis by reducing the body space a bit, and about twenty-five or so of these cars, known as the 15 CV, were built. But if one was going to squeeze a Wolseley "Six" into the MLB Normal chassis, why not go the whole hog and try and squeeze a Wolseley straight eight engine into it, which should prove a really potent combination? It wasn't! The straight eight 65 m.m. × 101 m.m. Wolseley engine lacked power and so Wolseleys sent out a new set of drawings together with a full set of patterns for a larger 70 m.m. × 100 m.m. straight eight engine, and the design features which this engine and its predecessor had in common were a camshaft and crankshaft supported in ten main bearings and built up in two pieces with the overhead camshaft drive taken from the centre. Morris Leon Bollees played around with this little lot for about eighteen months but only about half a dozen straight eights, known as the 8D, were built. The 8D was described in *The Motor* of the 14th August, 1928 and a photograph of the car shows that they looked just what they were: Gallic Wolseleys.

The production of the 8D had been left a little late. By the 30th September, 1928, Leon Bollee had made a loss of £150,000 since its acquisition by Morris. Morris was not a man to throw good money after bad so production was stopped. Finally in 1931 the assets were sold to a triumvirate consisting of Mr Dunlop Mackenzie, Mr Harry Smith (the works manager) and a large supplier of pressings. None of this syndicate made much money out of the deal. It's uncertain if they made any cars, although three models of Leon Bollee were listed for 1932. They were the 20 h.p., 8 cyl., the 15 h.p., 6 cyl., and what was described as a new 12 h.p., 4 cyl. The latter had a 72·8 m.m. × 120 m.m. four cylinder, two litre Hotchkiss engine (slightly smaller than the MLB Normal) with overhead valves, a four-speed gearbox and Bendix brakes, which were presumably as ineffective as any other Bendix brakes when the car was going backwards. A Hotchkiss engined light lorry was also in the range.

What went wrong? The type M, which was listed in 1926 at 28,500 francs and in 1927, the last year of its production, at 29,000 francs was only a stop

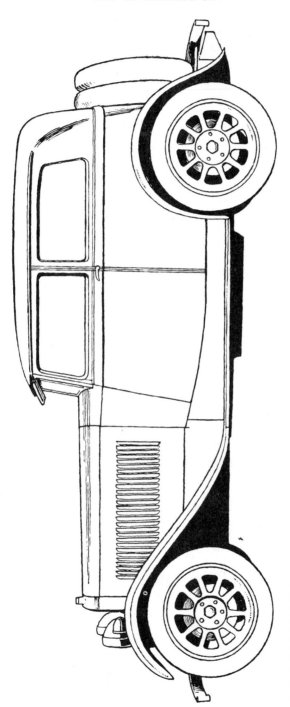

1928 straight-eight M.L.B.

gap measure until the production of the MLB Normal got under way. Neither multi-cylinder Gallic Wolseleys merits serious consideration, as they were produced in such small quantities. The car which decided the firm's fortune was the MLB Normal and when assessing this model it must be compared with other French bread and butter cars and not with Bugattis or Hispano-Suizas. In a letter to the authors Michael Sedgwick, the Curator of the Montagu Motor Museum, really drove this point home. To quote:—

"The Morris Leon Bollee was surely no worse than any other typical French family saloon of the period – immensely heavy, rustic carosserie, a whacking great stroke, and detachable wood wheels. The Bugatti cum Hispano-Suiza mentality that afflicts British enthusiasts when they think of Vintage of France seems to blind them to the fact that Delage built some awful dull s.v. sixes, while the smaller Delahayes, Panhards, Theophile Schneiders, and the like, were irredeemably dull, and all looked alike until you opened the bonnet, Mr Schneider favouring o.h.v., Delahaye i.o.e., and Panhard Mr Knight's sleeve valves. Incidentally the Imperia was indistinguishable from the 11/15 Panhard, except that it had slide valves and the added glamour of a plate on the scuttle with the magic address of 'Cordwallis Works, Maidenhead'."

The Morris Leon Bollees were big strong cars and one motoring journalist at the 1926 Paris Salon was inspired to describe them as having "a solid success, that owes nothing to curiosity, being due to British solidarity and comfort combined with the best French characteristics". The weight problem was given attention. Originally 1,000 sets of chassis parts for the MLB Normals were ordered, but before parts for another 1,500 cars were commissioned a certain amount of redesign was undertaken by Van Vestrant to reduce weight mostly by substituting aluminium castings for cast-iron ones, which saved 56 lb. Despite its weight the MLB Normal could really motor. Hotchkiss had once again turned up trumps and provided Morris with a top notch power unit. Although of French manufacture, the design of this 80 m.m. × 120 m.m., 2,412·7 c.c. four cylinder Hotchkiss engine/gearbox unit had actually been worked out at the firm's Coventry branch before its acquisition by Morris in May, 1923. This surprisingly powerful engine saw to it that the MLB Normal kept up with its competitors in performance.

Morris Leon Bollees had good showrooms, which from March, 1926 were a few doors away from the Paris Rolls-Royce showrooms in Avenue Malakoff, between the Avenue du Bois de Boulogne and the Porte Maillot. Not only were the sales facilities good but also the cars were freely available, in France at any rate if not in Britain. In Britain the cars were only available to special order as W. R. Morris firmly believed that it would be wrong to jeopardize the jobs of British car workers during a depression by importing foreign cars. Under Morris ownership output at the Le Mans factory rose from about 25 cars per week to a peak of 150 cars per week. The latter output was not maintained, however, due to the lack of demand and in two years the production was only 25,000 cars whereas production of twice that number had been planned. To encourage sales, price reductions were made in 1927. The MLB Normal in chassis form for the 1928 season cost 26,900 francs, which was 2,500 francs cheaper than the type M of the previous year, but the result was disappointing. To widen the car's appeal it was produced in de luxe form for the 1928 season, and in this guise was known as the MLB Luxe, but all was to no avail.

There was only one thing seriously wrong with the MLB Normal: so few Frenchmen wanted one.

Incidentally, it was Morris Leon Bollees who provided the Le Mans winning Bentleys with workshop facilities.

The Empire Oxford

American cars had been the favourites for colonial use from about 1909 and it is not hard to see why. American roads outside the cities were usually potholed, unsurfaced dirt, which made them dusty in summer and quagmires in winter. To cater for these conditions, American manufacturers made their domestic models strong, simple, light and powerful and consequently the cars could as easily withstand the worst colonial conditions as the equally bad American ones. This gave the American manufacturers an enormous advantage over their European rivals in competing for colonial markets because they did not have to design a special export model. The majority of European cars of comparable price were underpowered and altogether too delicate; an 8/18 Humber may have been a real little charmer in its native land but was not the thing for central Africa.

As a result of the depression in 1921 British manufacturers started to give overseas markets serious consideration and the scope provided was made quite clear in a paper presented before the Institution of Automobile Engineers by Captain E. A. Rouch at a conference at the Empire Exhibition at Wembley on 23rd June, 1924. Some South American countries, such as Argentina with 90,000 vehicles registered in 1923, imported cars in large numbers and that they were mostly American was to be expected from geography alone, but the greatest number of American exports of vehicles were to the British colonies. Some of the colonial markets were really large and for example Captain E. A. Rouch in his paper stated that in 1923 the number of vehicles operating in Australia was 97,189, in India 54,415, in South Africa 35,500 and in New Zealand 34,500. Even in the Malay States there were 13,750 vehicles, which was about the same number as registered in European countries such as Holland, Norway, Poland and indeed Russia.

Indian national sentiments were bitterly opposed to preferential tariffs, so Maharajas gained no tax advantages in importing half a dozen Rolls-Royces at a time instead of Hispano-Suizas or Packards, but custom duties strongly favoured British manufacturers in countries such as Australia, New Zealand and South Africa, but even so the total export of British vehicles was a paltry 3,041 in 1922 and 6,254 in 1923. The large American exporters got round Empire preference by setting up assembly plants in Canada, but this was not the sole explanation of American success, and considering the case of New Zealand, in 1923 they imported 8,305 vehicles from Canada, and 4,746 from the United States at the full duty rate, but only 713 from Britain. British manufacturers could not excuse their poor performance by making sly jibes that the American cars were cheap and shoddy and only sold on price. The cruel fact was that United States factories (excluding Canadian and Ford foreign assembly plants) gained most of their income from exports in 1923 from cars in the fairly expensive 800 dollars to 2,000 dollars class (the exchange rate was about 4 dollars 40 cents to the £1), which included the Buick four and six, Chandler, Hupmobile, Studebaker, Dodge, Essex, Hudson, Moon, Nash and Willys Knight. In this class they exported 41,988 cars in comparison with 29,708 cars in the 500 dollars to 800 dollars category, which included the Gray, Maxwell and Oldsmobile. Highest sales, no less than 52,536 cars were in the under 500 dollars class, which included Ford, Chevrolet, Overland and Durant Rugby, but the cash return was lower than in the 800 dollars to 2,000 dollars class. The prices quoted are of course ex-works and were much higher in foreign countries after agents fees, freights and duty had been paid. The inescapable fact was that American cars sold so well because technically they were superior to their European rivals where the going was really rough.

Exports of British vehicles rose rapidly and from the mere 3,041 in 1922 and 6,254 in 1923, they climbed to 15,659 in 1924, next to 29,050 in 1925 and then to 32,399 in 1926, which was higher than the 1930 and 1931 export sales. Morris had made his contribution to this increase and he decided to redouble his efforts by designing a car specially suited to colonial markets. The task of designing such a vehicle was allotted to Morris Commercial Cars Ltd.

The new Morris was allotted the chassis prefix EO, and chassis numbering commenced at EO 101. On the home market the cars were offered as the 15·9 h.p. Oxford for the 1927 and 1928 seasons and renamed the 16/40 Oxford for the 1929 season. For the export market the car was unashamedly called the Empire Oxford, these words, for example, being boldly stamped on the hub caps, which would have warmed the heart of the late Lord Beaverbrook and ensured a good write-up in the *Daily Express*.

The EO model was exhibited at the 1926 Olympia and Edinburgh shows, but production versions were not available until December, when one car was despatched. A further seven were despatched in January, 1927 and in February production really got under way. The 1927 season Morris catalogue describes the EO as a model which "while specially suited to cope with overseas conditions, shall at the same time make an equal appeal to the motorist at home who requires a car, larger, more powerful and capable of accommodating still more roomy coachwork than that which is normally mounted on the 14/28 Oxford chassis. "It should", continues the catalogue, "be a car universally acceptable the world over." It was an altogether larger car than the 11·9 h.p. and 13·9 h.p. models and differed from them almost entirely. The EO was the first Morris to feature a rear mounted petrol tank and Autovac, separate starter motor with Bendix pinion, four-speed gearbox and pressure fed big-ends, although a plunger type oil pump was retained. A four-speed gearbox was a big improvement, but it was six years before another Morris had four speeds. The engine was a four cylinder side valve of 80 m.m. bore and 125 m.m. stroke with a three bearing crankshaft, and like the 13·9 h.p. Oxford the pistons were aluminium and the connecting rods duralumin. The grand oil clutch had given way to a single dry plate type and this was possible because there was no dynamotor drive which needed lubrication. A separate 12-volt starter motor was fitted and the dynamo was driven from the front end of the crankshaft through a chain. The magneto was driven in tandem with the dynamo through a Simms vernier coupling. The overhead worm and wheel drive and torque tube recalled White and Poppe days and closely followed the design of the Morris Commercial. Another Morris Commercial touch was the fitment of an engine driven Maxfield tyre inflator. Two features were aimed at increasing the ground clearance; the Perrot brake operating rods were positioned above the axle instead of below as on the other Morris models and 21 in. wheels were standardised. Another feature which pointed to the car being designed for colonial use was the choice of 4 ft 8 in. for the track (8 in. greater than the 13·9 h.p. Oxford) as it coincided with the track of many railways and the car could be used on them by changing the wheels for flanged ones.

For the 1927 season the EO was offered on the home market as a chassis at £245, as a four-seater at £325 and in saloon form at £375. Sales started well in both the home and export markets. The name "Empire Oxford" seemed in no way to offend Argentinian pride and of the first sixty-one made thirteen of them, all four-seaters, twelve of them in grey and one in blue, were shipped to Buenos Aires. Many more were shipped to Australia, usually in chassis form in view of the import duties, which were designed to protect the local body builders. The Australian duties on British assembled chassis was $7\frac{1}{2}$ per cent compared with the general tariff of $12\frac{1}{2}$ per cent. The British preferential tariff on bodies was £30, £50 or £65 each or 40 per cent, whichever was the greater, and the corresponding general tariff on bodies was £40, £60 or £75 each or 55 per cent, whichever was the greater. Unfortunately of the Empire Oxfords exported to Australia at least 205 of them, which was the vast majority, were returned to Cowley and dismantled. The cars would not sell.

To try and find out why EOs were unsaleable Bob Knox sampled one of the few survivors in Britain, but was left none the wiser. In the Magazine of the Bullnose Morris Club he wrote:—

"I was delighted to accept an invitation to inspect and drive a 15·9 h.p. Oxford which has been purchased by one of our members, Mr R. J. C. Hildyard. This car, originally registered in Southampton, must have been bought in chassis form as it is fitted with a very smart two-seater body with dickey built by R. Rowdon & Son of Lyndhurst.

As I entered the car by the driver's door I felt a twinge of disappointment due to the fact that the Barker dipper lever did not enter my trouser leg as it so often does when entering my own Bullnose Oxford. However, I guess one gets used to these refinements in time! It is positioned at the side of the seat and so is very much out of harm's way. All it can do is gradually rub a hole in the seat cushion. The dashboard is devoid of instruments that would remind one of the Bullnose and is very similar to that of the flat radiator type of Cowley.

The engine burst into life at the touch of the starter and as I drove the car on to the road I discovered a very smooth operating clutch and the same delightful gearbox which Bullnose owners know so well, but another gear thrown in. This is definitely an improvement. On top of the gearbox a permanent gate is fitted with safety catch for reverse and selection of the gears is the opposite way round to normal Bullnose practice. Performance was quite good and a fairly high final drive soon lifted speed to 35 m.p.h. with only medium throttle opening. Unfortunately speed was governed by the steering which insisted on making the car proceed in a series of gradual spirals rather than a straight line. I have no doubt that this peculiarity, which is only appreciated by some, can soon be rectified.

By now I was beginning to feel at home with this Oxford and a couple of hill starts proved the smoothness of the clutch and the usual pleasant and easy gear change. An about turn in a narrow lane was negotiated quite easily thanks to a good lock. The engine seemed to be adequately cooled, as the

Calormeter needle settled at one o'clock. I returned the car feeling that I would have really enjoyed a longer run but AFTER the steering had been corrected.

An interesting car would be my verdict which caused me to wonder why it did not sell overseas in its thousands as I presume was intended. Maybe it was that steering!"

Between the beginning of February and the end of June, 1927 739 EO chassis and complete cars were produced and this rate of production was never approached again. Finally production petered out in July, 1929 when chassis EO 1841 was despatched. In two-and-a-half years 1,740 EOs had been made and quite a few of them subsequently dismantled. The model was a failure. In horsepower conscious Britain the cars were never intended to sell in large numbers because the vogue for sixes had begun and it was a car of this type rather than the big four that the customer wanted in the 16 h.p. range. Proof of this is that for the 1928 season Morris introduced the successful 17·7 h.p. o.h.c. Morris Six, which was renamed the Isis in 1930. The volume sales were expected overseas, but the "Empire Oxford" was not a success. It is hard to see why because they had an attractive specification on paper. It is suggested that they suffered from minor defects due to hurried design, although a surviving example in Australia does not support this contention. It is also rumoured that the cars were under powered for their size for colonial use and this is probably nearer the truth, but whatever the reason, they did not sell well. The Empire Oxford was Morris's answer to the Bean long Fourteen!

All the work on the 15·9 h.p. four cylinder 80 m.m. × 125 m.m. EO model was not completely wasted as many of the major components were used as a basis for the type G Morris Commercial International taxi-cab. The type G taxi-cabs were introduced in 1929, but even so had no front wheel brakes; some 840 were built. The engine was also used in the Morris Commercial 25 cwt. type R and 30 cwt. type TX.

9

Sporting aspects and early M.G.s

"Although no great performer the Bullnose was never so 'aunty' as an Austin Twelve."

D. B. Tubbs in Vintage Cars in Colour.

Shortly after production started Morris entered his cars in the gentler sporting events to demonstrate their capabilities. The first time a Morris was seen in competition was in the 1913 London–Edinburgh–London trial, and in May of that year Stewart and Ardern proudly advertised that the competing car, which was absolutely standard and delivered only twenty-four hours prior to the event, had finished to schedule and thereby gained a gold medal. In June, 1913 a Morris Oxford, with W. R. Morris himself at the wheel, took part in the Caerphilly hill climb. Morris hoped for success in the class based on formula for four cylinder cars not exceeding 70 m.m. bore but this was not to be as his car was placed fifth out of six entrants, climbing the hill in a time of 2 minutes 24 3/5 seconds in comparison with the class winning climb in 1 minute 32 3/5 seconds by J. Thomas on the 11·9 h.p. Arrol-Johnston.

Also in 1913 a Morris came first in the Dutch six-day reliability trials with full marks, no adjustments to the car having been necessary. In the Oxford-shire Motor Club annual hill climb in 1913 Morris Oxfords gained first, second and third places. Morris Oxfords also did well in the 1913 annual hill climb of the Coventry and Warwickshire Motor Club held at Irondown Hill, gaining first and second places. It must be admitted that these latter two hill climbs were only minor events.

1914 started well with two Morris Oxfords completing the course to scheduled time and gaining gold medals in the London–Exeter trial in

44. One of the first: The 1924 M.G.

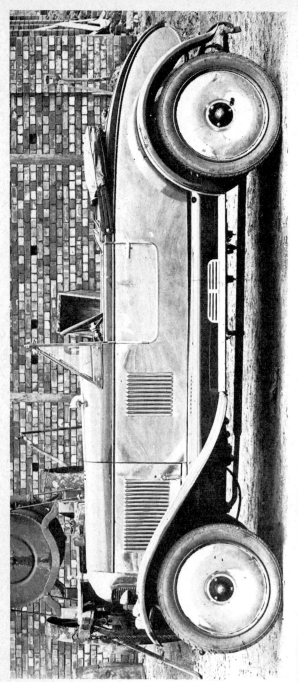

45. 1925 14/28 M.G.

46. 1925 14/28 M.G.

7. Dashboard layout of the 1925 14/28 M.G.

8. Last of the 14/28 M.G.'s: A 1927 model.

49. A 1926 Cowley: There are no doors on the other side of the body.

January. *The Light Car and Cyclecar* said of the hill climbs: "The best performances . . . were made by the Morris Oxfords . . . the fastest ascent probably by Mr W. H. Bashall on his Morris Oxford car."

At Whitsun 1914 six W & P engined Morris Oxfords competed in the London–Edinburgh–London reliability trial. W. R. Morris, in a coupé, Gordon Stewart and L. P. Kent had trouble free runs, but of the others E. Channon lost his way at one stage, S. J. Prevost had to fit a new valve and Harry Bashall's magneto gave out. In July, 1914 Mrs R. Wilkey entered her Morris Oxford in the lady driver's handicap race at the Saltburn speed trials and took second place to Miss Laura B. Starkey on a 12/16 Sunbeam. By the time the event took place the "Sporting Model" was available at £220 on the 1914 De Luxe W & P engined Oxford chassis, which according to the catalogue was "specially picked and tuned up". The specification included mudguards and acetylene headlamps but no hood or windscreen and, most notable of all, the body was only a single seater. This was the only Morris monocar ever offered to the public. At least one "Sporting Model" W & P engined Oxford was produced as the *Motor* of 23rd June, 1914 shows a photograph of one in full flight at Craig-ne-Baa on the Isle of Man T.T. course with the members of the T.T. Adler team cheering it on.

There was no sports version of the Continental engined Cowley, but a frequent and successful competitor in reliability trials when motoring sport recommenced after the Armistice was a Mr William Cooper in his Continental engined two-seater Cowley. Billie Cooper had made his name on motorcycles, favouring makes such as Triumphs, Harley Davidsons and Bradbury and in 1912 he captained the English motorcycle trials team on his Bradbury when they competed in Holland. After motorcycles Billie Cooper graduated to cars and his choice for the reliability trials of 1913 and 1914 was a V-twin Humberette. During one of these pre-war events he met an old friend, Harry Bashall, who had won the 1912 Junior T.T. on a B.A.T. and whose exploits with a W & P engined Morris Oxford have been mentioned. Bashall spoke most highly of his Oxford and after World War I Billie Cooper, on Bashall's enthusiastic recommendation of the Morris, bought a Continental engined Cowley as a replacement for his Humberette.

In April, 1919 *The Autocar* reporting on the Junior Car Club's reunion at Burford Bridge stated that Mr Cooper was "now about to possess a sporting Morris Cowley", but in fact the Sports Cowley was not introduced until March, 1921 when it was priced at £398 10s. 0d. The chassis of the Sports Cowley differed but slightly from that of the standard Cowley touring cars; the engine was reputedly "specially tuned", a delightfully vague term, and what was referred to as a "free exhaust" was used. The special tuning consisted of fitting "Aerolite" aluminium pistons and the "free exhaust" was merely a larger bore exhaust pipe; the standard Bullnose silencer needed no modification because it contained no baffles at all and was therefore in all conscience "free" enough in any case. Despite this, the standard Bullnose had a very quiet exhaust indeed because the exhaust pipe was of very small diameter. The silencers were of very thick gauge metal and consequently some have lasted for a quarter of a century or more in comparison with the couple of years or so of a modern counterpart. The other notable difference between the Sports Cowley chassis and standard Cowley chassis was that the former, like the Continental engined Cowley, had the higher 4·4 : 1 (53/12) final drive ratio instead of the 4·75 : 1 (57/12) standard final drive ratio. The Sports Cowley was at a great disadvantage in competitions because its Hotchkiss engine had a slightly longer stroke than the Continental engine which it superseded, and this increased its capacity from 1,498 c.c. to 1,548 c.c. which just put it outside the light car limit of 1,500 c.c. This handicap did not deter Billie Cooper from buying one and achieving success. Billie Cooper was an ideal owner as apart from competing in trials he also officiated at Brooklands meetings and so his Sports Cowley was frequently in full view of the motor racing public which was good free publicity for Morris. For example, at the end-of-season Brooklands meeting in 1921 Billie Cooper's Sports Cowley transported Sir Julian Orde and "Ebby" about their business. In the 1922 London–Land's End trial Billie Cooper gained a silver medal with his Cowley and only missed a gold medal because unfortunately he stopped inadvertently on a non-stop section. In the 1923 London–Land's End he made no mistakes and gained a gold medal, as did the general manager of Morris Garages, Mr Cecil Kimber with a Morris "Chummy". The Sports Cowley was discontinued towards the end of 1922, although the odd one or two were produced later for special orders, and Cooper was lamenting over this to Kimber because his Sports Cowley was becoming a little tired and needed replacing. Kimber thought he had just the car for him, a sports version of the Morris Oxford built by the Morris Garages, or, more briefly, an M.G.

Before discussing M.G.s mention must be made of the Morris Oxford Sports of the early 'twenties. The Sports Cowley was commoner than is nowadays supposed but everything about the rare Morris Oxford Sports was always obscure. The 11·9 h.p. Morris Oxford Sports was offered in chassis form only and once again the delightfully vague term "specially tuned" was used to describe it. For the 1923 season the Morris Oxford Sports chassis was offered with the 11·9 h.p. engine at £195 and with the 13·9 h.p. engine without starter at £220, which was the same price as the standard 13·9 h.p. Oxford chassis with starter. The authors must admit that they have never so much as seen a photograph of an Oxford Sports, but the Morris Motors record book shows that one or two did leave the factory in early 1924 and that they had a 4·07 : 1 rear axle ratio. A Bradford garage advertised a new one for sale in May, 1924.

The history of the Morris Garages has been given briefly in Chapter 1.

1922 was a most important year for them as Cecil Kimber was appointed their general manager. The main business of the Morris Garages was that of a normal garage, namely, selling new and second hand motor cars (mostly Morris, of course!) and motorcycles and servicing and repairing them. A small but none the less decidedly interesting sideline was, however, the marketing of Morris Oxford and Cowley cars fitted with a wide variety of coachwork of their own design, and usually built by coachbuilders such as Raworths of Oxford or Carbodies of Coventry. Of the special body styles, by far the most popular was the "Chummy" (built by Carbodies) on the Cowley and Oxford chassis. It was in one of these Cowley "Chummies" that Kimber won a gold medal in the 1923 M.C.C. London–Land's End trial. A Cowley "Chummy" was introduced as a standard model in the 1924 Morris range, and was officially known as the "Occasional Four". The introduction of this model to the standard Morris range must have caused a certain amount of displeasure at the Morris Garages as it was substantially the same as their own "Chummy", only very much cheaper. Another feature of the 1924 Morris programme was that the Sports Cowley was no longer listed. Clearly there was now no market for a Morris with a specially built "Chummy" body, but there might be one for a slightly tuned Morris chassis fitted with special sporting coachwork.

Early in 1924 The Morris Garages ordered six sporting two-seater bodies of their own designs from Raworths of Oxford for mounting on 11·9 h.p. Cowley (not Oxford) chassis which had been modified by fitting a special carburettor, specially cambered springs, slightly raked steering, etc. A photograph of one of these 11·9 h.p. sports cars appeared in an advertisement of The Morris Garages in the *Morris Owner* of May, 1924, the text of which read as follows:—

"The M.G. (in large letters enclosed by an octagon) Super Sports Morris will climb the famous Porlock Hill at 25 miles per hour. The gradient of this noted aclivity is one in five and the Treasury Rating of the car is only 11·9 h.p. It will be seen therefore that the inherent possibilities of the famous Morris engine can be brought out by those who know how.

The result is an exceptionally fast touring car capable of 60 miles per hour on the flat, and wonderful acceleration. The modified steering gives a glued-to-the-road effect producing finger light steering at high road speeds.

Mounted on this out-of-the-ordinary chassis is the most delightful two-seater body imaginable. Beautifully comfortable, with adjustable seat and single dickey, the finish is of the highest class and the style irreproachable.

The 'Tout ensemble' is one of the finest productions we have ever turned out from our famous Queen Street Showrooms. For a car of such distinction the price, £350, is extraordinarily modest."

The Morris Garages' advertisements never matched their prices for modesty!

Before these half dozen or so 11·9 h.p. two-seaters were completed orders were received for two Morris Oxford based sports cars with four-seater aluminium bodies. The first, which was registered on 13th March, 1924, was delivered to Jack Gardiner, a Morris Garages salesman who had just come into some money on his twenty-first birthday and the second, which was registered on 31st May, 1924 was delivered to Billie Cooper. These cars had such pleasing lines and met with so much admiration that it was decided to put them into limited production and market them as 14/28 M.G. Super Sports Morris Oxfords, or more simply 14/28 M.G.s.

Queen Street showrooms.

The first models of the 14/28 M.G. were built in Alfred Lane, Oxford (later renamed Pusey Lane) and towards the end of 1925 production was transferred again to Bainton Road. Complete Morris Oxford chassis were bought in from Morris Motors by The Morris Garages, who stripped them and then carefully re-assembled them, incorporating their modifications in the process. The chassis modifications consisted of increased steering rake, raised rear axle ratio (53/12 instead of 57/12) and a different carburettor. The flattening of the road springs necessitated two further modifications. Firstly, the brake rods had now to pass below the rear axle to avoid damage to them. Secondly, it was no longer possible to use Gabriel Snubbers at the rear because the Snubber straps would have been nearly horizontal. Therefore Hartfords were chosen. During the building of the early M.G.s Hartfords were about the only component in plentiful supply. The Morris Garages had over 1,500 of them. They were left overs from the production of the ill-fated F-type "Six" of which only one prototype and forty-nine production versions were built although supplies for 500 had been bought. Polished aluminium open two-seater and four-seater coachwork by Carbodies was standardised on the 14/28 M.G. chassis and usually polished aluminium Ace discs covered the beaded edge artillery wheels. The mudguards were either polished aluminium or painted smoke blue, claret or to choice with upholstery, hood, hood bag and carpets to match. The cars were terrifically handsome and the accompanying photographs do far more justice than words to their graceful lines. The M.G. was faster than the standard Oxford and to convince the front seat passenger of this a Smith 80 m.p.h. speedometer was situated immediately in front of him instead of the standard Morris 60 m.p.g. instrument of the same make. Only a few 1924 models were built and the Morris Garages considered them a model of direct appeal to the motorist with "sporting proclivities and cultivated taste"!

The earliest M.G.s were merely modified Oxfords and not wholly of M.G. design, so consequently the annual changes made to the Morris Oxford chassis were usually also to be seen on the corresponding M.G. For example, the 1925 season Morris Oxford differed from the 1924 season model in having a larger radiator, a chassis which was six inches longer and really effective rod operated brakes on all four wheels with 12 in. diameter drums as standard, although customers who considered them dangerous were given the option of rear wheel brakes only for £10 less. The 1925 season M.G.s consequently also differed from their 1924 counterparts in these respects. The upper part of the bodies of 1925 M.G.s were now painted steel and only the lower part was polished aluminium. Other changes to the bodywork were only minor such as the fitting of exterior door handles and the provision of eighteen flutes on each side of the bonnet instead of ten and eleven flutes on each side of the scuttle whereas before there were none. Open hub bolt-on wire wheels steadily ousted artillery wheels with discs, although 710 × 90 beaded edge tyres remained standard, and indeed continued to do so in 1926, whereas well-base balloon tyres were standardised on the Morris for the 1925 season. Many sporting motorists preferred to use beaded edge tyres.

The 1926 Morris Oxford was little changed from the previous year's model. The water temperature was now measured by the "Day and Night" Calormeter instead of by the Boyce MotoMeter, and Barker dipping headlamps were standardised. The 1926 model of The Morris Garages sports cars naturally also showed these alterations, but specific M.G. changes were an increase in the body width by some 2 in. and the fitting of a B-type Dewandre vacuum servo into the braking system. If the servo failed for any reason, such as an air leak, the foot brake was rendered inoperative, so in many cases owners removed the servo to preserve their peace of mind. There is no positive information available on the carburettors fitted to the 1924 season or 1925 season M.G.s, but the 1925 M.G. road tested by the *Brooklands Gazette* in October, 1925 and a 1925 model which the late W. H. Charnock once owned were both fitted with S.U. "Slopers". However, from late 1925 the Solex 30 m.m. type MHD carburettor was standardised. For the 1926 season an additional body style, the Salonette, was introduced. Two versions of the Salonette were available which only differed in rear-end treatment, but both versions fell well below the M.G. standards of appearance, and neither was particularly popular. One version had a smooth back in typical vintage fashion, whereas the other one had a small boat-shaped boot, which at least made for distinction if not for beauty.

M.G.s are always associated with their world famous trade mark, the octagon, so mention must be made of it. It was on the 1928 flat fronted 14/40 M.G. that the famous octagon, without any mention of the Morris Oxford was used as the radiator badge for the first time. In fact on the 1928 season cars octagons appeared everywhere possible; the newly introduced Watford instruments had octagonal faces, the Calormeter was octagonal and even the ships type scuttle ventilators had an octagonal outline to mention but a few instances. Such excessive use of the octagon rather spoilt the cars! At Abingdon the works clocks and many of the light switches are octagonal, while at Board Room meals octagonal napkin rings are used. Even the works typewriters used to have special keys for typing the trade mark. Kimber went in for octagons in a big way! However, it helped him to achieve his aim of giving his cars an identity separate from Morris, but it must have caused him some irritation when *The Autocar* announced the M-type M.G. in September, 1928 as "The Morris Midget". Without exaggeration the octagon must rank as one of the world's finest trade marks, being so simple and yet so distinctive, but it's worth remembering that this trade mark was virtually unused for at least four years. The reason for this excessive use of the Octagon trade mark in 1928 was that Kimber was anxious to establish M.G.s as a separate marque from Morris. Initially, it was obviously to the Morris Garages' advantage to have their product associated with a respected and reliable motor car such as the Morris Oxford, but by 1928 the Morris Oxford's popularity was on the wane, so Kimber wanted to dissociate his M.G.s from them. Octagons appeared on M.G.s prior to 1928, but it must be admitted that their presence was not conspicuous. For example, on the 1925 Bullnose M.G. there is a total of four octagons, two octagons on each body nameplate under the two doors, while 1926 M.G.s had an additional one etched on to the front glass of the Calormeter.

Some 1924 14/28 M.G.s were fitted with standard Morris Oxford radiator badges. However, they had an additional badge screwed on to the fascia board and this consisted essentially of two shields, one being the coat of arms of Oxford City and the other of Oxford University, and on the orange coloured background were simply the words "The Morris Garages Oxford". Kimber's famous special, FC 7900, has a radiator badge of this type, which

also may have appeared on the radiators of one or two production M.G.s, but there is no evidence to support or refute this. To confuse matters this badge is shown in the 1914 Morris catalogue as the trade mark of W.R.M. Motors Ltd., although it was not used on the cars.

The radiator badge used on the 1925 and 1926 Bullnose 14/28 M.G.s consisted of a normal Morris Oxford radiator badge surrounded by a pale blue (Cambridge blue!) garter bearing the inscription "The M.G. Super Sports". Some of the 1927 flat fronted 14/28 M.G.s also used this radiator badge, although a few were fitted with standard Morris Oxford radiator badges with the City of Oxford arms (an ox crossing a ford) in the centre, replaced by a small octagon enclosing the initials M.G. A St. Christopher badge surrounded by an Oxford blue garter which once again carried the inscription "The M.G. Super Sports" was fitted to the dashboard of most 14/28 M.G.s; a delightful touch.

Bullnose M.G.s took part in many of the reliability trials of the time and the marque did well with their three entries in the 1925 M.C.C. London–Land's End trial gaining three gold medals. A four-seater Bullnose M.G. was accorded the honour of opening and closing the Isle of Man mountain course for the 1925 T.T. races. Although in a non-competitive role, the car carrying four people covered the 37¾ mile course in 50 minutes, an average of 45·3 m.p.h. Maybe it was on this occasion that Alec Bennett was introduced to the marque. At any rate, he was sufficiently impressed to try one of the cars and be photographed doing so shortly after his victory on an o.h.c. Velocette in the 1926 Junior T.T.

King Alfonso normally showed discrimination in choosing motor cars, but for some reason, in common with H.R.H. Prince Purachatra and H.H. Prince Habib Lotfallah, he bought a most unregal 1921 £100 Carden. Maybe these royal personages were collectors of the bizarre, which the Carden most certainly was with its chassisless construction and rear mounted parallel twin two stroke air cooled engine in unit with the gearbox, the main shaft of which was extended to serve as the rear axle. With his father having set the precedent of buying British, in 1926 the Prince of Asturias, Heir Apparant to the Spanish Throne, took delivery of a four-seater M.G. finished in the Spanish Royal colours. The upper portion was purple with a broad gold band outlined in bright red, the mudguards were also purple and the chassis lined with gold. The world-famous model maker Rex Hayes worked on this car and refers to it in his book *Tribute by Trophy*:

"I recall that it was painted specially in the King's royal colour scheme, and when the body was finished I collected it from Carbodies in Coventry. I remember, too, that Cecil Cousins, who was then our Works Manager, threatened Frank and me with instant destruction if any harm befell this car; and I recall quite clearly working all night on it, and my good friend and boss, the late Cecil Kimber, bringing us relays of coffee and sandwiches on trays from his house at intervals throughout the night."

Sir Miles Thomas also ran a Bullnose M.G. for a year, and recorded his impressions in *The Morris Owner* of March, 1926. However, as he was the editor of *The Morris Owner*, his choice of car must have been rather more limited than that of most people.

The 17·9 h.p. six cylinder F-type Oxford was available with a number of body styles including a "Sports" in 1924, although the authors must admit that the only reference to this car that they have seen is in a table, "Weights of Morris Cars", given in the Morris Service Manual of July, 1928. It weighed 19 cwt. 1 qtr.! The F-type Six was also available in chassis form, priced at £375 in 1923 and £50 less in 1924, and the Morris Garages acquired three of these in February, 1924. They admittedly fitted landaulette coachwork to at least one of these but the others received the full M.G. treatment by having the steering raked, springs flattened, etc. Possibly the F-type "Sports" just referred to, the weight of which if little else is known, was really an M.G. all the time. The six-cylinder M.G.s were built at Alfred Lane, and are of particular interest as they were the very first six-cylinder M.G.s made. They were, if anything, even prettier than the 14/28 Bullnose M.G.s, which were undoubtedly amongst the most beautiful vintage cars made.

During 1921 a play, "Six Cylinder Love", by the American Wm. Anthony McGuire enjoyed a successful run in New York City. In the play a six cylinder motor car served as a catalyst to trigger off various comedy situations. An English version was produced by Ralph Lynn and starred Edna Best and Bobby Howes. It had a pre-London run at The New Theatre, Oxford, throughout the week commencing Monday, 10th November, 1924. Appropriately enough, during the play's Oxford run the car which appeared nightly on the stage was one of the beautiful Bullnose M.G.s based on the six cylinder F-type Morris Oxford. In London for its run of only two months (December, 1924 and January, 1925) at the Garrick Theatre, a 12/30 h.p. six cylinder Talbot loaned by Messrs. Warwick Wright Ltd., usurped the M.G.'s glamorous role. The play was not a success in England and received poor reviews. The reviewer in *Punch* described it as "one of those rather naive things that occasionally slip through from the other side of the Atlantic". He considered that "It was a great error of tactics that the only attempt made by the author or adaptor to translate the work into English was to dump down his puppets in Golders Green instead of Greenwich Village or wherever these particular commuters led their curiously odd lives". He continued "Strange things no doubt are done and said in our Golders Green, but not quite the strange things of 'Six Cylinder Love'. The motor salesman, for instance, does not hold so conspicuous a place in the local society, or at any rate is not let loose so readily upon unarmed private citizens; nor is there so much talk of 'lounge-lizards', or 'loose-jointed tea-hounds' or 'dancing-grasshoppers' – excellent terms as they may be for the type intended." In the opinion of the *Punch* theatre critic "The general idea of the play seemed to be that if a man has a six cylinder car he makes friends; if, through stress of circumstances, he has to sell this car to you, his neighbour, then all his friends will desert him forthwith and, without any pretence of regret for him, settle on you and your car like leeches, be entertained at your expense and cause you eventually to rob your employer in order the pay the second mortgage on your house." In view of these remarks it is scarcely surprising that the *Punch* critic should admit to being "left wondering why anybody thought that 'Six Cylinder Love' would amuse the town".

In the 1923 M.C.C. London–Land's End trial Kimber won a gold medal driving a Cowley with a Morris Garages "Chummy" body. In the same event in March, 1925 he once again won a gold medal, but on this occasion he was driving an M.G. special with the registration number FC 7900. The front half of the chassis frame was a standard Bullnose type with a tie bar between the foremost front spring shackles, but the rear half of the chassis frame was specially evolved to carry half elliptic rear springs. The gearbox, transmission and rear axle were standard Morris and the front axle was a 1925 Oxford with 12 in. diameter brakes, although these were later changed for the smaller 9 in. Cowley brakes. The footbrake operated the front brakes only, and the outside handbrake operated the rear wheel brakes only. Morris rear brakes contained four shoes per drum and on the standard cars two of these shoes are operated by the footbrake and two by the handbrake, but on his special Kimber coupled the normal handbrake and footbrake cam levers together so that the handbrake operated all four shoes. This provided two leading shoes per drum, which sounds very advanced, but there were also two trailing shoes per drum which nullified the advantage gained. The narrow two-seater body was of steel and originally painted grey.

The power unit was an old 1921 overhead valve Hotchkiss of the type supplied to the small Scots firm of Gilchrist Cars Ltd. This engine was obviously based on the Cowley engine and like the latter had a 69·5 m.m. bore and 102 m.m. stroke in standard form giving a capacity of 1,548 c.c., which put it just outside the light car class. One or two wondered why Kimber had competed with his "Special", FC 7900, in the light car class in the 1925 London–Land's End if his engine had exceeded the 1,500 c.c. limit. In reply the following statement appeared in *The Motor*:

"We are informed by Mr Cecil Kimber that the M.G. super-sports which he drove in the London–Land's End Trial was neither a Morris Oxford nor a Morris Cowley, but a car built by the Morris Garages and fitted with an overhead-valve engine of under 1,500 c.c. It therefore comes in the light car class as originally entered."

Kimber did not state what modifications he made to reduce the engine's capacity, but it could have been that he fitted a shorter throw crankshaft from a Continental "Red Seal" engine for the event. It's unlikely that the bore was altered as the car still has its original cast-iron pistons. If the original pistons had been replaced in 1925 they would almost certainly have been replaced by aluminium alloy ones.

Kimber's "Special" was registered as FC 7900 on the 27th March, 1925, which was twelve years to the day from the delivery of the first Morris Oxford. The car was completed just before the London–Land's End Trial. Reputedly on the eve of the event the chassis cracked, but however, all-night work got the car to the start on time and the only trouble with which Kimber and his passenger Wilf Mathews had to contend thereafter was occasional plug oiling. The *Brooklands Gazette* reported that this was the car's first road trip and the same magazine (by August, 1925 renamed *Motor Sport*) also carried Morris Garages advertisements proclaiming that two "M.G. Super Sports" driven by C. R. B. Chiesman and R. V. Saltmarsh had gained gold medals in the London–Land's End Trial. This is all evidence that Kimber's "Special" FC 7900 was not the very first M.G. to be built, but it was of course the first car of M.G. design as opposed to a slightly hotted up Morris Oxford.

FC 7900 is variously reported as having cost £250, £279 and £285 to build and after the 1925 London–Land's End Kimber was offered £300 for it. In 1930 it was sold by Turners of Stockport for £50 to Norman Davidson, who lived in the town, and after passing through various hands its end seemed near when it landed up in a scrap yard in White City, Manchester. Fortunately an employee of the M.G. Car Company spotted it there and persuaded his company to buy it back. It was seriously damaged in a road accident on the 12th December, 1932, but was rebuilt and now spends a well earned retirement at Abingdon. Mr Boddy, editor of *Motor Sport*, has aptly described it as an "Excellent 'early morning' car". Further he wrote that:—

"It is completely devoid of weather protection and with wings which would upset the present-day policeman. But to drive it provides the rare satisfaction of wind howling past one's face, the 'feel' of the engine working, a responsive gear change, which can also be felt, the intimacy and terrific visibility afforded by the narrow racing body and extremely positive steering which no modern sports car can convey."

How heartily the authors agree; FC 7900 is a real sports car and a true delight to drive.

M.G.s were tremendously successful and after a decade of sports car manufacture the firm had built more sports cars than any other manufacturer in the world. How had Kimber done it? He gave a clue to his success in a paper, "Making Modest Production Pay in Motor Car Manufacture", which he read before The Institution of Automobile Engineers in March, 1934. In this paper he expressed his conviction that a market existed for a car costing 50 per cent more the standard product on which it was based provided it was 10 per cent better. Ten per cent extra performance alone was not enough. After all, as far back as 1914 W.R.M. Motors Ltd. had offered a sporting version of the Oxford and the Sports Cowley which was current from 1921 until towards the end of 1923 most certainly offered 10 per cent extra performance at very little extra cost and yet did not sell very well. An even cheaper way of obtaining extra performance was undoubtedly by the use of one the proprietary light alloy cylinder heads (e.g. Pope Ricardo at £8 15s. 0d.) or o.h.v. conversions, such as the Lap at £24 or Chesterfield at £25 10s. 0d. in conjunction with a higher rear axle ratio. Kimber's success was obviously not obtained by offering only extra performance. In the authors' opinion Kimber's success was due to offering a combination of improvements, which transformed his cars. What was more notable than the performance increase of his early cars was their very much better handling characteristics and infinitely superior appearance to the standard product. To copy Kimber and describe the various characteristics of a car in terms of arbitary percentage figures, the authors consider that Kimber's earliest M.G.s offered 10 per cent better performance, 50 per cent better handling and 80 per cent better appearance than the standard Morris Oxford on which they were based. Kimber's real success lay in being able to offer the combination of all these improvements and not enhanced performance alone, at only 37 per cent extra cost. Good value indeed!

It must not be thought that other concerns did not attempt to market sports cars based on the Morris chassis. Maudes Motor Mart had attempted as early as 1918 to market a sports car based on the 60 × 90 × 4 White and Poppe engined Morris Oxford. The specially tuned White and Poppe carburettor was supplied from a rear mounted forty gallon fuel tank; handy for a non-stop run in a twenty-four hour race! In December, 1926 the motoring press gave details of another Maudes Motor Mart project, the Dragonfly. The Dragonfly was based on the Cowley chassis and the engine was fitted with Laystall forced feed crankshaft, aluminium pistons, Solex carburettor and raised compression. The price of £250 included an aneroid barometer as a standard fitting! The thing in common with both these Maudes Motor Mart projects was that they were both based on obsolete chassis.

In 1924 Stewart & Ardern produced quite an eye-catching Cowley-based sporting model, with a boat tail in either mahogany or aluminium, and this two-seater was priced at £225. There was also a four-seater at £260, but neither model sold in very large numbers.

A concern which might have beaten the Morris Garages at their own game was the Swallow Sidecar & Coachbuilding Company, who fitted quite striking two-seater sports bodywork to the 11·9 h.p. flat radiator Cowley in 1927. This attractive motor car was priced at £210 when the comparable M.G. cost £340. However, The Swallow Sidecar & Coachbuilding Company turned their attention to chassis other than Morris and an account of their success in this direction is well told in Lord Montagu's *Jaguar – A Biography*.

There have been some outstanding M.G. competition cars such as the Q-types and K 3s. M.G.s also have the proud record that each of their road going sports cars is better than its predecessor. But maybe it is the 14/28 Bullnose M.G. which showed Kimber's genius better than any other M.G. He made so few modifications to the standard Oxford chassis, and yet provided a different class of car. Appearance was undoubtedly a most important point in favour of the earliest M.G.s. If anything they looked rather better than they were. Mr John Stanford in his excellent book *The Sports Car – Its Design and Development*, ascribes the lack of success of the fairly advanced Model A Duesenberg largely to the fact that it did not look as good as its was. Kimber never made a mistake like this. On the road the 14/28 M.G. seems an entirely different car from the Morris Oxford which it so closely resembles and the only thing the two appear to have in common is the same design of gearbox with its characteristic Morris noises. Michael Sedgwick, Curator of the Montagu Motor Museum, after trying a Bullnose M.G. was puzzled and left asking:—

"Did Kimber really transform the Oxford, or was it all a gargantuan confidence trick which came off?"

Bullnoses *by W. Boddy*
(*Reprinted from* Motor Sport *of February*, 1947)

Driving through Oxford in a "T.C." M.G. "Midget" we espied in the Morris showrooms a particularly stark vintage motor car. It was, of course, none other than the M.G. which the late Cecil Kimber had built in Longwall,

Oxford, in 1925, and which became the product around which the now famous M.G. Car Company Ltd. was formed. This M.G. had taken its rightful place in the 1946 Cavalcades and we had known of it long before that, having published its photograph in *Motor Sport* over twenty-two years ago. But somehow we had always thought of this car as just a rather special-ised Morris-Cowley with queer mudguards and sports body. Seeing it "in the flesh" for the first time we were struck by its very stark, business-like appearance – as our passenger observed, it could be taken for one of the better Continental small sports cars of this period.

Kimber built this M.G. as any other enthusiast constructs a "special". The engine was an 11·9 h.p. o.h.v. Hotchkiss. Head and ports were polished, the crankshaft balanced and the white-metal run directly on to the connecting rods. Cast-iron pistons were retained, but the carburettor was special and the oil pump was increased in size to give maximum pressure of 60 lb/sq. in. Magneto ignition and wet plate clutch figured in Kimber's specification. The normal Morris three-speed gearbox and back axle were used, but the chassis frame was special, so that the normal Morris three-quarter elliptic springs of that time could be replaced by flattened half elliptics. Fuel was carried in a twelve gallon tank, pressurised from a hand pump in the business-like cockpit. The two-seater body was light and very suited to the car. That, then, was Kimber's M.G. It would do 82 m.p.h. and gained its first success in the 1925 M.C.C. Land's End Trial, winning a gold medal.

At Brooklands in 1922 Summers raced an aluminium-bodied Morris-Cowley, but does not seem to have had much success with it, although it did do a standing lap at over 60 m.p.h. Then, about a year later, Mr A. E. Keen, a director of Morris Motors Ltd., had built for him a special single-seater Morris Cowley. It was timed to do over 90 m.p.h. on the road and at the 1924 Thetford Speed Trials made f.t.d., covering the standing kilometre in 35·52 seconds, a very fine performance indeed, equal to 63·5 m.p.h. This car had a slightly modified cylinder block with ports opened out to 41 m.m. diameter, and the valve seats reduced to a width of 1/16 in. The valves had stems reduced to a diameter of 5/16 in., which reduced the weight of each valve by one ounce, and the tappet feet were also lightened. Steel connecting rods were used, liberally drilled until they weighed about 18½ ounces each. These rods were not only carefully matched but they carried oil scoops to aid general engine lubrication. The Ricardo slipper pistons, also drilled, turned the scales at a mere 6½ ounces complete with gudgeon pin; they had one ring only and were naturally noisy at low r.p.m.

Although various experiments were conducted, standard valve timing was found to give the best results. Ignition was looked after by a G.D.4 Lucas magneto and carburation by a 1 3/16 in. bore S.U. "Sloper". The compres-sion ratio was increased to 5·7 : 1 and the flywheel was reduced in weight to 31 lb. The standard thermo-syphon cooling system was retained, with the fan removed, but a large bore, straight-through exhaust system was fitted. Otherwise, production components were used and not only was the engine comparatively silent at full throttle, but F.12 K.L.G. plugs stood up quite satisfactorily. The engine ran up to 4,000 r.p.m. comfortably and the normal lubrication system sufficed. The engine was put into a chassis in which the quarter elliptics of the three-quarter elliptic rear suspension assembly were replaced by solid forgings, enabling flattened half elliptics to be used. The front half elliptics were also flattened and Hartford shock absorbers used all round. The engine was set 3 in. lower and 9 in. further back in the chassis than normal, the torque tube being shortened to suit, while the front dumb irons were braced by a cross tube and the tie bolt. To accommodate the single-seater body, which blended nicely with the Bullnose radiator, the steering was raised and carried on a special bracket to centralise the wheel and the clutch pedal was moved to the nearside of the gearbox. Gearboxes, axles, etc., were standard, and artillery wheels were retained.

Another Morris, which ran at Brooklands in 1926–28, was the late H. R. Wellsteed's 1,802 c.c. Morris Oxford, which was also driven by Cyril Paul. It could do a standing lap at over 78 m.p.h. It is still in existence and ran in the 1946 Cardiff Cavalcade.

At the same time J. Crickmay raced a Morris Cowley which lapped at over 78 m.p.h. and did a standing lap at all but 69 m.p.h.

This car was built to satisfy a bet that a fairly standard Cowley would do 75 m.p.h. A 1926 "Chummy" with 30,000 miles to its credit was stripped down and rebuilt. Dumb irons cut from another chassis were bolted at the rear to convert the three-quarter elliptic rear suspension to half elliptic, and a plate welded between the front dumb irons, and a bar between the front shackles in addition, to stiffen up the chassis. Belting was used as a sling to hold the front axle in place should a spring break. To lower the steering the box was mounted upside down, with the drop arm inside instead of outside, the frame and a bracket held the box to the side members as well as to the engine. The steering wheel was increased in size, but normal three stud road wheels were used. The axle ratio was increased from 4·58 to 1 to 4 to 1 and drilled con-rods, aluminium drilled skirt pistons in rebored cylinders and opened out oilways gave the engine new life. Double valve springs and a flywheel turned down very appreciably by Laystalls, assisted to this end. A long-tailed two-seater body was made of ash covered in aluminium strips with a streamlined undershield. New Andre shock-absorbers were used and further tuning consisted of fitting a 40 m.m. Solex carburettor and Marelli magneto, also a four branch copper exhaust system. The ports had already been widened and polished. Timed by six stop watches, the car now did 93 m.p.h. over the half mile at 4,800 r.p.m. After some racing successes an R.A.C. observed six hours run was made at Brooklands, during which 387 miles were covered at 64·58 m.p.h. including three depot stops, during one of which the sump was drained and refilled. This gallant Morris came to a full stop in a subsequent five-lap race by reason of doing nearly 5,000 r.p.m. for a far longer distance than it was accustomed to, and in a following wind, which defeated the lubrication oil.

Some idea of how comparatively fast these cars were is gained by comparing their speed with that of Webster's 1926 "Chummy" which was able to win a special Morris Cowley handicap held at Brooklands in 1930 by averaging 48·83 m.p.h. its best lap being at under 51 m.p.h. whilst the fastest car entered, a 1927 two-seater, lapped at just under 53 m.p.h. – admittedly fully equipped. Actually much earlier than this, Morris Motors Ltd. admitted that 60 m.p.h. was fairly easily obtained without drastic alteration from standard, and many special Morris cars were built by enthusiasts.

Racing a Bullnose Cowley *by N. D. Routledge*

I think that some readers may be interested in the trials and tribulations experienced on the track with a Bullnose, hence this screed.

Obviously, if one is going to compete, one picks one's weight, so all events apart from the V.S.C.C. ones are barred. As the Hour High Speed Trial requires the most preparation, and is the toughest test, I propose to describe the run my Cowley did in 1955.

It had long been my ambition to qualify for the "Hour Blind" as it is described. To do this, the car had to complete a prescribed number of laps of the Silverstone Club circuit, including a Le Mans type start, and a plug and wheel change carried out on different laps. Thus there were three standing start laps, and two with a standing finish. My Cowley had lapped at nearly 52 m.p.h. in various five-lap races, but my time for a standing lap was as long as two minutes four seconds. As the Cowley is 1,550 c.c. she had to do the same number of laps as a two-litre car, and two more than a one-and-a-half-litre – twenty-nine in all. Allowing two minutes per lap, and two minutes for the two pit stops, this left two minutes to play with: not a lot!

The car was known to be reliable. Split cotters had been fitted to the valves, the compression ratio raised to 6½ : 1 and she had a top speed of 65 m.p.h. down the back leg of the track, using the standard gear ratio.

Before the event she was given a "top overhaul" and a good check-over. All possible nuts, etc., were wire locked, including the petrol pipe unions. The axle ratio was changed to 4·42 : 1 to keep the revs down, and a rich needle was fitted to the S.U. carburettor. Quick release plug terminals were already in use, as the car had been used in driving tests.

Arriving at the track, the hood, spare wheel, screen and rear seats were removed, a tonneau cover fitted over the rear seat compartment, and the regulation driving mirror fitted. Standard 4·50 × 19 in. tyres were used running at 35 lb/sq. in. in the front and 32 in the rear. The Hartford shock absorbers were taken up fairly hard to help stability.

After scrutineering, we did the minimum number of practice laps, checking times, and then waited patiently for zero hour, biting nails and worrying about silly little things.

Lap scoring is most important. You must have a team manager who knows how you are running so a graph was made up. The hour was divided into twenty-nine divisions, and every lap was to be marked by a cross. Thus, by referring to the time below the cross the "boss" could tell just how far in front, or behind schedule we were.

Half an hour before the start we went to the allocated pit, and made the final preparations. This kept us busy, and we did not have time to worry. The jack had to be raised so that it would JUST go under the front axle, remember we would be changing an inflated wheel, and not too much lift would be required. The car was run to keep her warm, and with five minutes to go, she was left in first gear, switched on with the handbrake off. A last minute check of the pit stop arrangements was discussed; the pit staff had done lots of rehearsals and were "spanner perfect".

The driver walked across the track, fidgeted with his crash hat, took his place with the other hopefuls and waited for the flag to drop.

The moment this happened it was every man for himself, streaking across the track on my vintage pins, I stepped on to the running board with my right foot, swung myself into the car and finished up, just as intended, with my left foot on the clutch and my thumb on the starter.

The engine started right away as usual, and we were off with the milling throng. Due to our good start we were the third car to reach the Copse, which was taken at about 50 m.p.h., on we went round Maggotts and Becketts, which as you know is very tight. Here we nearly had it! A Lagonda hit the marker drums and sent them across the track right in front of the Cowley. More by luck than judgement they missed us. Up the straight we fled, and then down to Woodcote. Lap number one completed – O.K. thumbs up from the pit, and so to lap two.

This was to be our first pit stop, which was to change the plug while it was still cool, so at the end of the straight we pulled over to the right and pulled up at the pit. The staff were wonderful. Out came Les, bonnet up, then Harry whipped out the plug, put it on the bonnet board and screwed in the replacement Les had popped in the head meantime. Bonnet down, O.K. away you go. Just 25 seconds, over a minute gained. Good!

For the next few laps we really tried. As time went on I found it was possible to go into Woodcote flat out, which cut down lap times more than somewhat. Speed down the back leg was slower than with the lower ratio, but I could use second gear to pull away from Becketts which was a new experience.

0. Anti-Red: 1927 Cowley thirsting for Shell petrol. The Daily
Mail poster proclaims "No Soviet Petrol Sold Here".

. Bedsitter: 1928 Cowley.

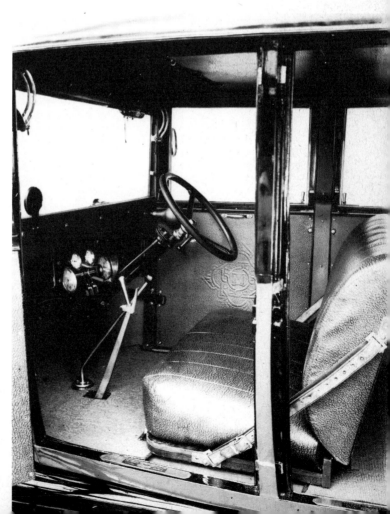

52. *Faithful servant: Des Measures' 1931 Cowley.*

53. *From small beginnings: Part of W. J. Cooke's museum which has grown from a solitary 1924 Oxford coupé to 19 Bullnoses and 5 Flatnoses.*

About half way through my pit gave me the signal that I must come in for a wheel change, so next lap, in we went to pull up just short of Les, who had the jack in his hand ready. As the wheel went up I held the footbrake on and Harry undid the nuts. The wheel was taken off, laid on the pit counter and replaced, the jack driven over to save time and we were off again in 53 seconds. Meanwhile my daughter, who was scoring, told me that we had things well in hand and had according to the tannoy lapped at 53 m.p.h.

So back to the track and round and round we went. Soon frantic signals were given by the pit, they held up the wheelbrace – the sign for a wheel change – and I was perturbed more than a little. So I put in a series of quick laps and went in to see what the bother was, feeling VERY cross.

It appeared that, to save time the spring washers had been left off the hub nuts, and the R.A.C. steward insisted on them being replaced. More time lost, and now it was "touch and go". Off into the fray once more, rather desparate now with one eye on the clock ticking the vital minutes away, minutes that I needed so badly. I tried to calculate how things were going. I tried to get round those corners just that little bit quicker, to brake later, and to get every ounce out of the willing Cowley that I could. You can imagine my relief, when with over a minute to spare, I rounded Woodcote to get the thumbs up and be shown a board with twenty-nine chalked on it. During the next lap the hour was up and next time round I was flagged off the course, having "done it" with half a lap to spare.

Even so, it was very pleasant to hear that number nineteen had qualified when the results were given out, as a lap can easily be missed by either pit staff or officials. Pleasing too, to look round and see several very sporting vehicles that had failed where my great-hearted little Cowley had triumphed.

The cost? Petrol worked out at about 24 m.p.g., oil negligible, but about a third of the tread on the front tyres had disappeared. Wear and tear on the driver was rather heavy as a four-seater Cowley is not the MOST comfortable of cars to drive.

10

The Flatnose — 4 cylinder Cowleys and Oxfords

The face lift

From February, 1921 until the end of 1925 Morris had swept all before him with cars which became increasingly cheaper but better equipped. However, during 1926 Morris sales declined by over 20,000 cars. In part, this could be attributed to the coal strike and the General Strike but of greater significance Morris's share of the market had also been reduced. Morris was losing out to his competitors because he had no model smaller than the Cowley. However, another reason for a loss of sales was that the Bullnose was too old fashioned for those with social pretentions. A face lift was needed.

Retention of the same basic design from 1915 to 1926 had enabled Morris to introduce continuous production methods and thereby reduce costs. The Flatnose was planned to retain as many Bullnose chassis parts as possible to keep costs down in conjunction with new features to make it an up to the minute model. The most noticeable difference between the Flatnose and its predecessor was, of course, the shape of the radiator. The radiator shells of the 1927 cars were a difficult pressing because the front and sides formed a sharp edge and this distinguishes them from the radiator shells of the post 1927 Flatnose which had rounded corners. The Morris Garages added a false bottom to the radiators of 1927 M.G.'s to give lower lines but omitted this deception from the 1928 and 1929 models.

The capacity of the new radiator was reduced from 18 pints to $11\frac{1}{4}$ pints in the case of the Cowley and from $26\frac{1}{4}$ pints to $19\frac{1}{2}$ pints for the Oxford but nevertheless the cooling area was claimed to be 60% greater. The new radiator followed the then current fashion of being taller to create the delusion that the larger bonnet housed an engine of equally impressive size. Cars such as 14/40 Humbers and Austin 12/4's were well cooled and it merely spoilt their appearance to fit a taller radiator. However, in the case of the Morris, the change in radiator was more than a whim of fashion and overcame the tendency of the Bullnose to boil. Indeed, to give their cars sleeker lines the Morris Garages fitted the smaller Cowley radiator without detriment to the modified Morris Oxford chassis of the open two-seater 14/28 and 14/20 Flatnose M.G.'s. The Salonettes retained the larger Oxford radiator. In the author's experience the combination of a Cowley radiator with an Oxford engine is not practical with a Bullnose. They once owned a 1926 Morris Oxford chassis which had been fitted during the early 'thirties with a Bullnose Cowley radiator and body and, let it be added, registered as 11·9 h.p. instead of 13·9 h.p. However, the saving in horsepower tax was accompanied by furious boiling, although without ill effect.

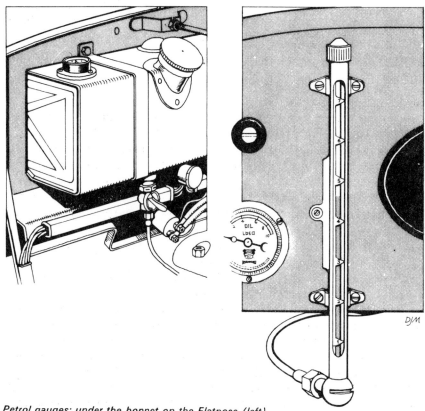

Petrol gauges: under the bonnet on the Flatnose (left), dashboard mounted on the Bullnose (right).

Because Morris had a gravity fuel feed, the capacity of the petrol tank was governed by the scuttle dimensions above the level of the carburettor. Although the taller bonnet line of the Flatnose gave poorer vision, it permitted the use of the larger 7 gallon tank on the Cowley 14/28 and 14/40 M.G. which is the same size as the 13·9 h.p. Bullnose and Flatnose Oxfords. The new tank was of much stronger design and incorporated a reserve tap, but Morris Motors felt the latter fitment justification enough for stopping the supply of a full two gallon can of petrol as standard equipment. Possibly Shell were no longer willing to supply them free of charge, as in Bullnose days. The inexplicably fine screw thread of the narrow diameter Bullnose filler cap and neck was inevitably crossed by heavy handed garage men and its replacement by a large diameter quick action threadless filler was a sensible change. Another improvement was the float operated Wilmot dial petrol gauge mounted on the tank under the bonnet. The latter was far less vulnerable than the dashboard mounted tubular glass gauge of the Bullnose, which suffered from frequent barrages of blows from the knees of front seat passengers. However, in contrast to modern instruments, both types of gauge were paragons of accuracy. Undoubtedly the Flatnose petrol tank had been given careful thought and was a big improvement.

The Flatnose chassis

Front wheel brakes were fitted to the 13·9 h.p. Oxford in 1925 and to the Cowley in the following year. To resist the front wheel braking torque, the Bullnose chassis was of slightly deeper section, a tie bar fitted between the dumb irons and stiffer front springs were used but these palliatives could not disguise the fact that the light and flexible Bullnose chassis was an Edwardian design intended for rear wheel brakes only. The much more substantial chassis frame of the Flatnose with wide front springs was specifically designed to withstand the stresses of four wheel braking, although it was seldom called upon to do so because the wierd compensating mechanisms on the pre-1930 models reduced braking efficiency to a very low level. However, the stronger chassis frame and better cooling of the Flatnose made it far better suited to Colonial conditions than the Bullnose.

The four wheel brakes of the Bullnose were much above average but instead of leaving well alone, the Flatnose had a most extraordinary brake compensating system incorporating a peg working in a slot for the 1927 season and sprockets and short lengths of bicycle chain for the 1928 and 1929 seasons. These systems were bad enough but the men at Morris Garages inflicted the 1927 14/28 M.G. with a braking system which was even more diabolical. It had no less than six shafts, two of them with sleeves operating independently of them, 13 rods and 15 levers, two of which were double ended. These were distorted and twisted by the "C-type" Dewandre vacuum servo, which unlike the "B-type" fitted to the 1926 cars, had a mechanical by-pass in the event of failure. In retrospect it is easy to poke fun at the designers of these systems who lost sight of the effect of friction and lost motion in their desire for good compensation. However, only a few years previously front wheel brakes were condemned by many as dangerous, and a zealous if misguided approach to compensation was understandable. The Morris Garages quickly saw the error of their ways and for the 1928 and 1929 season dispensed with compensating systems or servo assistance. The result was superb braking. Morris achieved similar standards from February, 1930 by imitating the M.G. non-compensating layout combined with drums which were ribbed like those of the M.G., but of traditional Cowley diameter of 9″ in comparison with 12″ of the M.G. and 14/28 Oxford. Diagrams of the various brake layouts are given in Appendix 3.

The battery was moved from the running board to underneath the driver's seat, which increased the risk of neglect. Half elliptic rear springs modernised the back end of the Flatnose chassis and those of the Oxford, which were 47″ long, should have given a smoother ride than those of the Cowley which

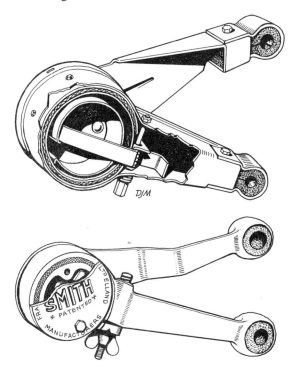

Shock absorbers: Armstrong (upper), Smith (lower).

were three inches shorter. However, the Flatnose was less comfortable than the Bullnose with its old fashioned three quarter elliptic rear suspension. The springs of pre-1930 Flatnoses were damped with Smith shock absorbers, instead of the American made Gabriels, and therefore Morris could at last claim that his cars were British throughout, and truthfully advertise "Buy British and Be Proud Of It". A change to Armstrong shock absorbers was made for the 1930 season for the Cowley and 1931 season for the van.

The engine and transmission of the Flatnose differed only in minor respects from that of the Bullnose, which helped to keep costs down. For example for the 1929 season the speedometer was driven from the gearbox. A minor alteration for 1929 was the adoption of a longer gearlever of smaller and hollow section, and this introduced a springy feel to the change. The Bullnose engine could not be lifted out of the frame with the sump in place because the starting handle fouled the foremost chassis cross member. (This did not present production problems because the chassis frame was lowered onto the engine). The Flatnose was fitted with a detachable starting handle housing to make overhauls easier, but even so the fan pulley had to be removed before the starting handle housing could be detached. The engine mountings of the Flatnose were also changed.

Credit must go to Chryslers for coining the term "floating power" for their copy of the long established Lanchester practice of flexibly mounting the engine on rubber blocks. Floating power was in vogue and therefore adopted for the Flatnose. Its chassis was designed to be sufficiently stiff without the bracing of a rigidly mounted engine, which the whippy chassis frame of the Bullnose was most certainly not. The flexibly mounted engine of the Flatnose certainly made for greater smoothness and handling characteristics should not have been adversely affected, due to the lack of bracing from the engine, because the stiffer chassis had been redesigned to cater for this. However, prior to 1930, the merits of the Flatnose chassis were largely lost, because the steering box was mounted on the engine and therefore floated with it. For 1929 matters were a stage worse because the steering box was rubber mounted on the engine, which in turn was rubber mounted on the chassis. It is a definite art to steer a straight course in a Flatnose when the rubber has perished and the steering box has worn.

Fortunately, the steering was vastly improved on the Cowley for the 1930 season and the van for the 1931 season. A Bishop cam type steering box rigidly bolted to the chassis frame replaced the engine mounted worm and wheel Morris box and earlier Flatnoses could be brought up to this specification with a conversion kit which was offered by the Works from March 1931 for £6. 5s. 1d.

Very few chassis changes were made between 1927 and the middle of the 1930 season. Early in 1927 the throttle pedal was repositioned on the right of the footbrake, although a central throttle pedal was re-adopted on some subsequent Morris models ranging from the Minor at one end of the scale to the Isis at the other. For the 1929 season a baffle was fitted to the silencer, the front axle was modified to lower the chassis and an S.U. carburettor replaced the Smiths. The already quiet car was no more silent and regrettably neither steered nor stopped any better. In contrast the changes to the brakes and steering of the Cowley in February, 1930 resulted in a much improved motor car. The 1930 Cowley did not stop or steer as well as a 14/40 M.G., but nevertheless was a great advance on earlier Flatnoses. The last of the Flatnoses were the best.

All steel bodies

A 13·9 h.p. Flatnose Oxford four-seater or saloon merits a place in any museum on account of the bodywork. The novelty of the bodies lay not in their appearance, which was typical of the period, but in the all-steel construction under Budd patents.

Morris had managed radically to reduce the cost of producing Bullnose chassis by the application of continuous methods of large scale production. There was less scope for the application of these techniques to the production of traditional coachwork, which consequently remained relatively expensive. In September, 1925 Morris visited America and met Edward G. Budd of the Edward G. Budd Manufacturing Company of Philadelphia. This company had completely revolutionised the American motor car industry with their all-steel bodies. Other companies such as B.S.A. as early as 1912 and Austin for his "Seven" in 1922 produced all-steel bodies which offered the advantages of lightness combined with strength and freedom from the hazards of splintered wood in an accident. However, Budd all-steel bodies had another advantage: they were cheap if made in large quantities. Morris realised that the all-steel body had come to stay where the initial high tooling costs could be offset against large production runs. Budd revolutionised the car body and his contribution to the motor industry, although usually underestimated, was nevertheless probably the greatest of the 'twenties.

Edward Budd was born in Delaware in 1870, but in 1888 left for Philadelphia. In 1899 he joined the American Pulley Company, and during the next few years he saw this Philadelphia firm build up a big business with pulleys stamped out of sheet steel, which were stronger, lighter and more flexible than those of cast iron or wood. In 1902 Budd took a job with Hale & Kilburn Manufacturing Co., and this confidence in the future of the pressing industry was strengthened. Following discussions with the Pullman Car Co. in 1904 Hale & Kilburn received a contract to make pressings to replace many cast-iron components for thousands of sleeping cars. In 1909 Hale & Kilburn collaborated with Emil Nelson, chief engineer of the Hupp Motor Company, to produce steel panels as a substitute for hand formed ones for clothing wooden framework.

Unlike his employers Budd was enthusiastic over the prospects offered by the motor industry, and so at the age of forty-two he set up on his own with only twelve employees and a capital of £15,000 which he raised by selling the shares he had bought out of his salary during the previous ten years. In 1913 John and Horace Dodge approached Budd for pressed steel body panels, but Budd fired with the enthusiasm of one of his dozen employees, the exceptional Joseph Ledwinka, persuaded the Dodge brothers that the all-steel body was not only technically practical, but preferable. The first bodies had to be welded up from no less than 1,200 separate pressings, but radical improvements to production techniques came quickly and for example some saloon bodies were made from only eight pressings. Other significant advances pioneered by Budd after the war were the early adoption of electrical spot welding to replace oxyacetylene welding and the installation of Keller machines for making metal copies of patterns. The all-steel body was established thanks to Budd and Ledwinka.

Morris returned to England with an agreement with the Edward G. Budd Manufacturing Company. The immediate consequence was that a Cowley saloon was loaned to Budd's in February, 1926 for their inspection and recommendations, but the main outcome of Morris's visit was the formation of the Pressed Steel Company at Cowley which came into production in 1927 and was financed by the Edward G. Budd Manufacturing Company, Morris Motors Ltd., and J. Henry Schroeder, the American bankers. Budds had the controlling interest and Morris Motors Ltd. put up £500,000 in cash; they bought £200,000 worth of 6 per cent debentures and 300 7 per cent cumulative participating preference shares of £100 each and were issued with £20,000 ordinary shares of £10 each credited as fully paid.

The Morris management received a nasty shock when confronted with the appalling quality of the first production from pressed steel; the panels were rippled, the doors hung badly and the windscreen was a poor fit. Although two Budd technicians, Mueller and Deisley, had supervised the start up of the plant, teething troubles were only to be expected from raw dies and labour unfamiliar with the new American welding techniques. Another problem was the poor quality of the sheet steel. It had a poor surface, which made finishing difficult and its ductility was so low and so variable that designs had to be of limited draw. The quality of sheet steel improved rapidly but Pressed Steel had to pay the price of being a pioneer. There were long delays before Pressed Steel overcame their problems and this must have been especially irritating to Morris because it was to avoid delays that he had purchased the designs and dies of the Oxford body for £120,000 from Budd. Consequently many 1927 Oxford saloons and tourers had to be fitted with coachwork bodies instead of all-steel ones, as originally intended. Morris was caused considerable anguish by the lack of production from Pressed Steel, in which he invested so heavily, but 1927 also had its brighter side. In February of that year he bought himself Wolseleys and remained in sole ownership until July, 1935. Then on 20th May, 1927 the 200,000th Morris, a Cowley four-door tourer, left the works.

All Flatnoses were spray painted, but at first air drying spray paints were used on the wood framed models and cellulose based finishes only on the all steel bodies, which suffered no ill effects in the drying ovens. From the 1929 season all Flatnoses, wood framed or not, were finished in oven dried "Bripal" cellulose supplied by the British Paint and Lacquer Company, which had been set up by Morris Motors, Pressed Steel and the Cleveland Varnish Company of Ohio.

It was planned that the Pressed Steel Company would supply Morris Motors on a cost plus basis and in addition obtain orders from other motor manufacturers, but these proved unwilling to deal with a firm in which their chief competitor had such a close interest. Another difficulty was that other pressing firms no longer gave Morris realistic quotations, because they considered that such quotations were not requested with the serious intention of placing orders but only to check the costs achieved by the Pressed Steel Co. Consequently Morris Motors sold their shares in the latter in 1930 (Budd followed suit in 1936). However, Morris must get the credit for introducing the all-steel body to Britain.

The sight of the 1,600 ton Hamilton press at work at Cowley led the reporter from the *Autocar* to prophesy in November 1927; ". . . . . the imagination naturally flies to the day when the whole car may be stamped out by huge presses, and separate chassis frames rendered a relic of the past".

The 11·9 h.p. Cowley range 1927–1930

1927 season Flatnoses were available officially from the 11th September, 1926. The range consisted of a two-seater at £160 the four-seater tourer at £170 10s. 0d. the coupé at £180 10s. 0d. and the saloon at £195. The "Chummy" was no longer available, but two commercial versions of the chassis continued to be listed, namely the Commercial Traveller's Car and 8 cwt. van.

The mudguards and accessories such as the lamps for the 1927 and 1928 season were similar to those for the previous year's Bullnose models. However, the bodies were considerably re-styled, and not necessarily for the better. It must be admitted that the new, wide, high sided dickey of the open two-seater and coupé had practical advantages, but these were at the expense of appearance and contrast with the dainty rear end of a pre-1923 Bullnose two-seater. The 1927 four-seater has the dubious distinction of being amongst the ugliest Morrises made. Like the saloon, there were two very wide doors, one on each side of the body, and the front seats tipped forward to give access to the rear seats. In February, 1927 Morris added a much more handsome four-door tourer to the range at £177 10s. 0d. and little more was heard of the ugly wide door design, which was only £5 cheaper. The open models were available in blue or grey, but the closed cars came in the former colour only.

1928 models were available officially from the 1st September, 1927, and were similar to the previous season's range with the addition of a new saloon. 1928 features were a single panel windscreen on the closed models, a tool box mounted on the running board and, on the four-seaters and saloons, a bench front seat, the back of which could be lowered to form an uncomfortable bed. This mobile bedroom was described as being suitable for camping and doubtless saw much interesting service. The new saloon at £185 was a much better looking four door model, although the previous season's version with two very wide doors was still officially listed at £177 10s. 0d. However, one suspects that the latter, which was remarkably good value, was only available as long as unsold stocks lasted. The standard colours for 1928 were blue or beige, except for the two-door saloon, which was available in the former only.

The 1929 Cowley designs celebrated the fact that Pressed Steel had overcome their teething troubles. The rear panels were more deeply drawn to give what was proudly called a "dome back" body, and also new were the single piece domed front mudguards, which were braced with a cross bar on which the headlamps were mounted. More of a true dome was the pressed steel roof of the Cowley coupé that superseded the previous fabric covered design. Smaller items of new presswork were the visor over the windscreen and a nasty and unnecessary apron over the dumb irons. "Duotone" cellulose finishes were introduced and standard colours were stone and brown with brown Karhyde upholstery. Other 1929 features were separate adjustable front seats, Lucas suction operated headlamp dippers, an electric horn instead of a bulb horn, a Calormeter with wings and bumpers fore and aft. Economics included hollow nickel door handles and "earth" return for the lights which didn't always. Triplex glass was a worthwhile extra at the small additional cost of only £2 10s. 0d. for the windscreen of the open cars and £7 10s. 0d. for the windscreen and all the windows of the saloon. By 1929, saloons had ousted the open types as the best selling Cowley and many survive.

The innovation for 1930 was the sunshine roof, which was standard on the coupé, and fitted to a special version of the saloon, known as the "Folding Head", which also differed from the standard model in having a luggage grid. The "Folding Head" differed in that the latter wore a visor. A third version of the saloon, the "Commercial Traveller", was copied from the previous season's special body by Stewart & Ardern and had a detachable rear seat and door, rather like that of a hearse, in the rear panel of the body, in addition to the four side doors. Otherwise, this model was identical to the standard saloon and superseded the Commercial Traveller's Car, which was a two-seater with a large box instead of a dickey. Triplex was standard in anticipation of forthcoming legislation, and colours were Niagara blue or Morris brown on all models, except the folding head saloon, which was available in Morris maroon only. Chromium plating was standardised and was of excellent quality and free from the maladies that inflict the plating of modern cars.

The 13·9 h.p. Oxford range

It was intended that the 1927 type Oxford four/five seater tourers and saloons should be of all steel construction but it appears that the majority had conventional wooden framed bodies due to the troubles at Pressed Steel. The saloon and tourer were four door designs and very much more handsome than the Cowley models with two very wide doors. However, Oxford luxury was expensive and at £265 the saloon cost £70 more than the comparable Cowley. The luxury features which distinguished the Oxford from the Cowley were Barker dippers in 1927 and 1928, a speedometer with trip mechanism, leather upholstery, nickel hub cap centres, door pockets, an internally illuminated instrument board and a luggage grid. Other models in the Oxford range were a two-seater, a folding head coupé, a cabriolet and the rare Vee-windscreen saloon landaulet, of which at least one survives. The saloon landaulet was available only in brown with upholstery in furniture hide, whereas there was a choice of blue, grey, brown or claret for the remainder of the range. The open two-seater and folding head coupé had the same wide, high sided design of dickey as the Cowley and it is interesting to note that this ugly, if practical, style was also fitted to the last few Bullnose Oxford chassis. In July, 1927 the Prince of Wales took delivery of a coupé upholstered in grey velvet calf hide.

For the 1928 season the tourer and saloon had bodies of all-steel construction but the only detailed changes were the addition of a tool box to the running board, the adoption of a single panel windscreen on the saloon and a choice of blue, maroon, brown or beige on all models except the Vee-windscreen saloon landaulet, which once again was available in brown only.

Bumpers fore and aft, a tie bar between the mudguards carrying the headlamps and the absence of Barker dippers or a bulb horn readily distinguishes the 1929 season cars from the earlier Flatnose Oxfords. Two entirely new models were the fixed head coupé and fabric saloon and the landaulet was replaced by the Vee-windscreen De-Luxe saloon. The introduction of the then fashionable fabric saloon as a standard model must have hurt the feelings of the people at Pressed Steel and must have been regarded with resignation by concerns already offering fabric bodies on Morris chassis, such as Stewart & Ardern, The South-Western Motor Co., and Gordon England. The all-steel Oxford saloons were available with cloth or leather upholstery to choice but the fabric saloon was available only in grey fabric with blue upholstery and what is offered is described as "Period interior furniture". At the end of 1929, the faithful four cylinder Oxford was dropped from the Morris range.

The Simplified or Plain Cowley

Morris reverted in 1927 to the policy he had abandoned in 1923 of offering open bodied Cowley's in simplified or plain form at a reduction in price of £11 10s. 0d. for the two-seater and £14 for the four-seater.

The Simplified Cowley differed from the standard model in having no front wheel brakes, speedometer, clock, spring gaiters, Calormeter, windscreen wiper or driving mirror and a three lamp set instead of the five lamp set. A lack of windscreen wiper or driving mirror may sound like economy carried to extremes but hand wipers serve their purpose at reasonable speeds and just a glance over the shoulder sufficed on the less congested roads of 1927. Of equal surprise to the modern reader is that, even in advertising, adjectives had not become completely debased and the Simplified and Standard models were not called Standard and De-Luxe respectively. Only the two-seater was available in simplified form in 1928. Standard colours were grey only in 1927 and blue only in 1928. The Simplified model was dropped in 1929 because Morris was purchasing such large quantities of accessories that he obtained low prices and the austerity of the Plain version saved little in cost.

The authors have never encountered a Simplified Flatnose but the official Morris records show that they were built in quite large numbers.

The 11·9 h.p. Oxford

The Flatnose 11·9 h.p. Oxford, which was introduced in 1928, differed in concept from the Bullnose 11·9 h.p. Oxford, which had been available until the end of 1924. The latter was a luxury version of the Cowley with, for example, leather upholstery whereas the Flatnose model was intended for those who wanted Oxford roominess with Cowley running costs. It was available as a tourer or saloon finished in blue or maroon cellulose and was more austere than the 14/28 h.p. model in having Karhyde upholstery and simpler instruments such as a speedometer without a trip mechanism. Winston Churchill introduced a tax of 4d. a gallon on petrol in his 1928 budget, but this did not prove the salvation of the smaller engined Oxford. It was no more economical than the 14/28 model because its axle ratio had been lowered from the standard 4·75:1 to 5:1 so that the 11·9 h.p. engine could cope with the weight of the Oxford.

The sacrifice in performance and equipment was not justified by the saving in price, which in the case of the tourer at £205 was only £20 less than the 13·9 h.p. model. Sensibly, the 11·9 h.p. Oxford was not on offer for the 1929 season.

Export models

Morris, a keen Empire loyalist, offered special export only versions of the Flatnose saloons and 4/5 seater tourers which primarily differed from the home models in having the same axles as the Empire Oxford with a 56″ track, which was 8″ wider than the standard and the front brake cross shafts above rather than below the axles for greater ground clearance. For 1928 both the 14/28 Oxford and 11·9 h.p. Cowley were available in this export form, but both were displaced in 1929 by the 14/28 h.p. Cowley with cloth upholstery as an optional extra. The larger engined Cowley was a far better proposition than the under powered home market 11·9 h.p. Oxford of the previous year.

New Designs

Production at Cowley during 1925 was confined to a basically ten year old design, the Cowley, and variations of it, the 14/28 Oxford, but nevertheless Morris output accounted for 45% of all private cars manufactured in the U.K. During the second half of the 'twenties one model was no longer enough to obtain a large share of the market.

The first new design was the Empire Oxford, which is discussed in chapter 8. The Morris Commercial one ton truck, which went into production in 1924, was fitted with the 13·9 h.p. Morris Oxford engine. However, Morris Commercial Cars Ltd. had to produce a 15·9 h.p. four cylinder engine of their own design at Soho, Birmingham, to power the 30 cwt. truck, because no suitable engine was available from Morris Engines Ltd. The Empire Oxford was designed around this 15·9 h.p. commercial engine and introduced for the 1927 season. Morris had great expectations for the car export markets, but it was rough and noisy and a total failure in competition with cheap, but good, American cars.

Next came the very fine 2468 c.c. ohc six cylindered engine designed by Wollard and Pendrell of Morris Engines in Coventry. Kimber and Wollard had worked together at E. G. Wrigley & Co., and Wilson McComb records in *The Story of the M.G. Sports Car* that Kimber persuaded Wollard to embark on the JA six cylinder engine project. Unfortunately Wollard and Pendrell designed an engine only and its first home was in an elongated Oxford chassis, with the standard 48" track. A bad omen was that the chassis serial "F" was the same as that allotted to the six cylinder Bullnose. A batch of only eleven of these "JA" engined Morris Sixes was built, the assembly of the first with chassis number F 201 and engine number JA 6003 (later changed to JA 6004) being commenced on the 27th October, 1927 and the last with chassis number F 211 and engine number JA 6017 on the 17th November, 1927. The performance of these narrow track Morris Sixes was sparkling due to the low weight but handling was impossible. Of the eleven built eight were dismantled subsequently by the works. Morris was not above using the aforementioned engine number JA 6004 in a later type Morris Oxford Six chassis number F 255. Of the other three, one with a fabric body designed by Douglas Clease of the *Autocar* was sold to Morris Garages on the 29th December, 1927, and formed the basis of the first 18/80 M.G. Most interestingly another took the road because Michael Sedgwick claims to have seen one of these narrow track rarities. A revised JA-type Morris Six with chassis numbering re-commencing at F 251 was despatched on the 13th March, 1928, with a roomier body and wider track to improve the handling. Precisely 3,500 were completed by the 23rd July, 1929 when the JA engine found its final resting place in the all-steel Isis, which was current until 1935. The Isis was well constructed and thoroughly reliable, but in his autobiography, *Out On A Wing*, Sir Miles Thomas claims that the model was grossly overweight, which killed all performance. Wilson McComb supports this view in his M.G. history by quoting contemporary road test data. However, Michael Sedgwick recalls the Isis as a very fast car for its day and his father bought one because he thought it offered the best performance for its price. The car would certainly do 70 m.p.h. but Michael Sedgwick admits that 80 m.p.h. on the Twyford by-pass is probably family legend. But for a Series III Morris 25, Michael's father considered the Isis the best of the many Morris models that he owned. We incline to the Sedgwick assessment of the Isis from our experience of an Isis tourer, which was purchased by its owner in the mid-thirties and which he found so satisfactory that he retained it until his death a few years ago.

Next followed a crash programme. Since 1927, Sir Miles Thomas had been advocating, without result, the production of a small Morris to compete with Sir Herbert Austin's miniature, which had been introduced in 1922 and could no longer be dismissed as a joke. It was rapidly increasing its market share because it was practical, reliable and commendably economical, which was of particular importance with the re-introduction of the petrol tax in 1927. The Austin 7 could no longer be ignored and the motoring journals were eagerly awaiting Morris to join the "battle of the babies". The *Motor* of the 29th May, 1928 gave "Some details of the New 7 h.p. Morris" and

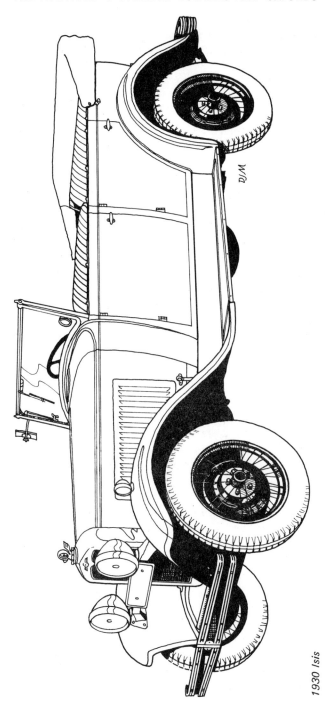

1930 Isis

claimed that only one prototype had been built to date, which had a Cowley radiator and a small four cylinder ohc engine on Wolseley lines, which was rather coarse running but sufficiently powerful to enable it to climb hills in top which the Oxford could only manage in second. The Minor was officially unveiled in August, 1928 and the *Motor*'s references to Wolseley in the previous May proved well founded. The purchase of Wolseley by W. R. Morris in the autumn of 1926 was particularly fortuitous because it not only provided him with a design staff but also spare production capacity for the Minor. The Minor was like a miniature Flatnose in appearance but the body was fabric to save tooling costs and time. The engine was two thirds of the six cylinder unit which Wolseleys were developing for their new car, which was subsequently christened the Hornet, and it certainly gave the Minor a brisk performance. Its merits were fully exploited by the Morris Garages but it was altogether too fussy for an economical vehicle. The overhead camshaft drive was transmitted through the dynamo armature, which became saturated in oil unless the engine was serviced with skill and care. Of more fundamental importance, on early engines this layout restricted the dynamo dimensions and its consequent output and therefore discharged batteries were common in winter. This was annoying, although not the disaster that it is with a modern vehicle with an automatic transmission. To overcome this, from engine number U 15135 (i.e. after 15,034 engines had been built) the block casting was modified with a concave portion to accommodate the larger diameter Lucas DEL 24 dynamo as a replacement for the earlier Lucas DELS and DEL 19 dynamos. In 1931 the ohc Minor engine was supplemented by a side valve unit which, according to Sir Miles Thomas, was a scaled down Ford. The authors have always considered the Minor a much better proposition than the similarly priced Austin Seven.

The staff of Morris Commercial, Morris Engines and Wolseley had tried their hand at design and now it was the turn of the team at Cowley. The result was the LA-type, 1938 c.c., 15·9 h.p., six cylinder, side valve Morris Oxford, but unfortunately its advanced design was better in theory than in practice. It was a well founded car with a deep, stiff chassis frame equipped with Lockheed hydraulic brakes and useful refinements such as thermostatically operated radiator shutters and the famous fume consumer which gave the side valve engine the appearance of an overhead valve unit. Another refinement was a disc type oil cleaner operated by the clutch pedal, but it was far from a happy arrangement because it was a major source of oil leakage. Allegedly, the engine could run on paraffin and was very sensitive to ignition setting. The Autocar recorded that on moving the ignition control from full retard at 35 m.p.h. to full advance, the car's speed increased by nearly 10 m.p.h. However, the engine was notable for its compactness, but there was insufficient water space around the bores and most of the heat was transferred to the oil, which disintegrated the cork linings of the clutch.

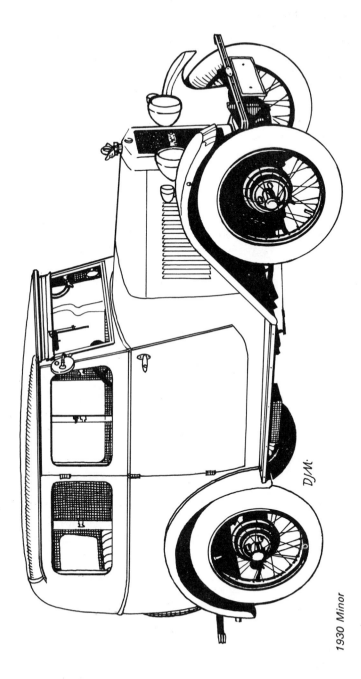

1930 Minor

The Last Flatnose

The LA-type six cylinder engine was so compact that it would fit into a Cowley chassis and this inspired Morris to produce a cheaper "Six" for the 1931 season, the "Major". The decision that the Major and Cowley should share the same chassis and running gear justified the cost of modifying the latter, although sales were falling.

The 1931 Cowley appears similar to the earlier Flatnose Cowley at a casual glance, but many of the parts had been changed so that they were also common to the Major. For example, the 1931 Cowley chassis frame differed dimensionally from those of the earlier Flatnoses and was the same as that of the Major but for the engine mountings. Innovations for the Cowley, which were common to the Major, included grouped chassis lubrication and a new design of Armstrong shock absorbers. The radiator of the 1931 Cowley was taller than the previous year's model and of the same size as the Major, but the latter was distinguished by "calorstat" operated shutters. Despite the taller radiator some export Cowley's were fitted with a water impeller. Professor Whatmough was consulted about providing the 11·9 h.p. engine with greater torque at low speeds and on his recommendation the cylinder head was modified and the engine block was modified to take smaller and equally spaced valves. On the road the authors cannot detect the extra punch from Whatmough's modifications. The body styles available were the same as in 1930, namely, the two-seater, four-seater, coupé, saloon and fixed-head saloon, with Triplex glass and chromium plating as standard. The Cowley's retention of its basic appearance owed much to artillery wheels remaining standard equipment. At first wire wheels, as fitted to the Major, were only available as an extra at £3 10s. 0d. but were standardised on the sliding head saloon by July, 1931.

The 1931 Cowley was the last and the best, of the Flatnoses. For 1932, "eddy free" bodies, a new rounded radiator shell, and wire wheels changed the Cowley shape. For 1933 a four speed gearbox and engine with chain driven coil ignition system were new features and in its last year, 1934, the Cowley was also available with six cylinders. The marine and industrial engines provided the last true link with the Continental engine of 1915.

Marine and Industrial

Morris marine and industrial engines, based on the 14/28 Oxford unit, were introduced in late 1926. The petrol version was rated at 12/24 h.p. and the paraffin model at 11/18 h.p. The first figure in the rating is mysterious, but it cannot be the RAC horsepower, because the bore was the same in all cases.

In service the Morris Navigator Mark I would be accessible from above but not from underneath and therefore it was fitted with overhead starting

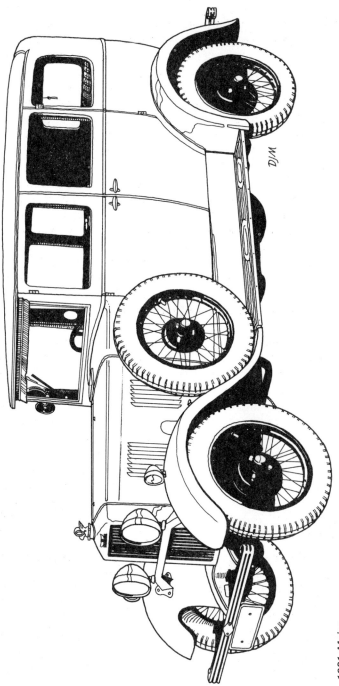

1931 Major

gear, a crankcase draining pump and a longer oil filler neck. The detachable starting handle of the Flatnose sump was replaced by a support bracket to carry a water pump driven from the end of the camshaft. Unlike the 14/28 h.p. car engines, the con-rods were steel and the Smiths carburettor was a single jet model, but later versions used a Solex.

Not every Morris engine in a boat was a genuine Navigator, for they were expensive at £100 for the petrol model and £110 for the paraffin burner. A second-hand Oxford or Cowley engine was cheaper by far and firms such as Wrotham-Blake & Co., for example, offered marine conversions. The "W.B. celebrated ½ inch No-Trouble Pump" for direct camshaft drive cost a modest thirty shillings. Wrotham-Blake suggested:

"Where the extra length of the Morris gearbox is not inconvenient we recommend that it be retained and the reversible propellor shaft be machined to fit the Morris standard universal joint. This we can do for 7/6d. extra. A separate clutch is available and by using the normal second speed manouvering in and out of locks is much easier and for fishermen attending to lobster pots, etc., the temporary slow speed is invaluable." It was claimed that the Cowley usually required a 13-inch three-bladed propeller and the Oxford a 14-inch and sometimes a 15-inch.

The "Morris Industrial Engine" incorporated most of the modifications of the Navigator with a few exceptions. The cylinder head was suitable for carrying a water-pump and on the front of the sump was fitted either the usual detachable starting handle of the Flatnose or a mechanical governor. These engines were used in welding sets by Murex Welding Processes Ltd., portable air compressors by Broom & Wade of High Wycombe, Sigmund trailer fire fighting pumps with a delivery capacity of 180 gallons per minute, road rollers by Wallis Stevens Ltd., of Basingstoke (these were fitted with either 12/24 h.p. or 11/18 h.p. engines) and portable welding sets marketed by Holmes & Co. of Hepburn on Tyne. In the days when the Claughton 4–6–0 locomotives used to run into Euston station one could see on the platforms small tractors made by Lansing, Bagnall & Co. and powered by the

12/24 h.p. engine. The Reliance Tool & Engineering Company of Heck-mondwike also chose the Morris engine for their small trucks. They had to change to Ford engines during World War II but switched back to the Morris when they became available again after the war. This is a tremendous tribute to the much older Morris design. Morris themselves could have chosen more modern alternatives on which to base their marine and industrial units but until 1952 kept the basic Continental "Red Seal" in production. The design had served for 37 years.

Light vans

On its introduction in 1923 (see Chapter 7), the chassis of the 8 cwt. light van was similar to the 11·9 h.p. Cowley but the radiator was a "sawn off" or "squashed" version and directly interchangeable with the Bullnose Cowley radiator and its badge carried the inscription "Morris Commercial". From 1927 to 1931 the light van radiator was larger and interchangeable with the Bullnose Oxford and the "sawn off" shape was retained. The legend on the badge now read "Morris Light Van". The bonnet had an uncomfortable curve so that it could marry up the rounded radiator with the square shaped scuttle. In 1931 rationalisation at last won the day and the same radiator was used on the light vans as the cars but the badge was the same as those of earlier Flatnose vans.

During Bullnose days the axle ratio of the Cowley and the Light Van was the same at 4·75:1 but from the 1927 season, although the 4·75:1 ratio was retained for the Cowley a lower ratio of 5:1 was standard on the van. At first the van was rated at 8 cwt. but from the 1928 to 1930 season inclusive this was increased to 10 cwt. From the 1931 season onwards the Light Van was fitted with the 13·9 h.p. engine but its official load carrying capacity was the compromise of 8/10 cwt.

Although 1931 was the last year for the Flatnose cars, according to the author's definition, the Light Vans were a suitable sink for obsolete parts and for 1932 were unchanged in appearance.

Morris value

The Flatnose, like the Bullnose, offered outstanding value for money. In 1927 the Singer Junior was introduced at the same price as a two-seater "Plain" Cowley at £148 10s. 0d. and the only cars that were cheaper were the Austin Seven at £145, the short chassis two-seater Jowett at £139, the Trojan at £130 on solid tyres or £145 on pneumatics and of course the Model-T Ford. In comparison, an Austin 12 or Bean 12 was £275 and a Humber 14/40 no less than £460. At £485, admittedly the 12/50 TG Alvis offered an entirely different level of performance. Low prices enabled Morris sales to reach a peak of 61,632 vehicles in 1927, which was only fractionally exceeded in 1929 and then not again until 1935.

Low prices helped, but the most important reason for the Flatnose's success was that it was a thoroughly good car, combining reliability, average performance and a far greater degree of refinement than its cheaper rivals. The Flatnose inherited the Bullnose's outstanding characteristics of being extremely simple to drive; indeed it must be the easiest vintage car to drive. The Morris cork clutch running in oil was beautifully smooth and light in operation and silent gear changes were the rule rather than the exception. Sound design, low prices and simplicity of control enabled the Flatnose in its first year or two of production to compete successfully against its most serious rival the Clyno. (See page 71). Despite a fantastically heavy clutch Clyno advertised their cars as being particularly well suited to the lady driver. Clyno's descent to bankruptcy in 1929 was not reflected in radically increased sales of the Flatnose because U.K. sales of cars in the 11 to 14 h.p. class fell from 55% of the total in 1927 to 22% in 1931, whereas for the same years the home sales of cars in the 8 to 9 h.p. class rose from 16% of the total to 28% of the total. Furthermore, it was not merely a question of price and Humber and Talbot proved that many people bought small cars for preference, although they could afford something larger.

The Flatnose was a cheap, but excellent motor car. The great pity was that the minor faults in the braking and steering layout were not rectified before halfway through the 1930 season.

D/M

11

Bargaining for Bullnoses

How I got my Bullnose Morris *by N. D. Routledge*

"Well my third book was serialised in a newspaper, and they gave me a whole £500 for that. It was wonderful. I bought a thing that I thought I would never have, a car, a Bullnose Morris. That is one of the big thrills of my life, having a Bullnose Morris." – *Agatha Christie in the* Sunday Times *of 15th October*, 1961

Years ago, when I served my time as an apprentice, Bullnose Morris cars were very popular among the Yorkshire folk, who know a good thing when they see one. Naturally, I did a great deal of work on them, and I got to know their innards quite well – the cars not the folk!

It was therefore only to be expected that some years ago, when I was seeking an old car to rebuild my choice was a Bullnose.

A friend of mine who represented an agricultural concern, and whose work entailed visiting farms was asked to help find one. Calling on the local farmers, as he did, he often found the odd laid up and forgotten vintage model.

One day while discussing business with a Harrogate man, he asked casually "How many old cars have you tucked away in your barn?" and nearly fell through the floor when he was told "I got an old Morris and two or three old motor bikes". Alan, that's my friend's name, asked to see them. He was taken to a small door in a very large barn, and after holding back the overgrown creeper managed to get in and have a look.

Just behind the door was an old Lea Francis motor bike, and further in the gloom he could discern yet another. "Where's the Morris?" he enquired. "Oh, that's way back under all that rammel" was the reply. "It's been there since 1935 when we modernised this farm." When he found the owner might sell it, Alan contacted me, and I was briefed to approach with great care.

The following Sunday was the first chance I had to follow it up, so off we went to Harrogate. The old man was very polite, he enquired as to my business, but told me to "Go away, and come back any day but the Sabbath, we don't do business on the Lord's day young man." I was of course much younger then, and he was very old! Somewhat taken aback, I did just that, and the next Saturday there I was once more with Alan and another friend as moral support. This time he actually did get to telling us all about the Morris, how he and his wife had used it years ago, and how it had been entombed in the barn "way back in 1935, fifteen years ago when the old farm had been extensively rebuilt." "Yes, it had a Hotchkiss engine, and only two wheel brakes."

"Would he sell it?"

"Well, what is it worth, and what use is it anyway?" he countered.

I made him an offer, he was sceptical. "You'll only laugh when you get it out of there, and then we'll have to put it back," he said.

"Look," said I, "if you'll guarantee it has a Hotchkiss engine and no front wheel brakes, I'll pay you for it now, and then we'll get it out."

Sadly he shook his head, he clearly thought me mad, "Seems fair enough" he mused, "yes, that's fair enough" he said and the deal was clinched. 'Twas too late to extract it then, so we made a promise to collect the following week, and made our various ways home.

Next Saturday, well prepared with tow rope, jack, spare tyres and tubes we journeyed yet again to Harrogate. Creeper had overgrown the door, the old man would not let us cut it! We had to coil it up and tuck it out of the way before we un-nailed the big doors. A tree had grown part of the way over the door, but not too much. Had it been in the way, the car must have stayed there for ever, for I am sure no axe would have been permitted to attack it!

Soon the doors swung open, and a hoard of junk greeted our eyes. The car could not be seen, it lay behind old window frames, farm machinery, wooden beams, and the two old motorcycles. Three of us worked like Trojans (all right I know, but vintage Trojans then) to gain access to the Morris. At last we had cleared a path, but more work lay ahead. Under the car old fall pipe and guttering had been placed, the tyres had gone flat, and the car had settled on them. Out came the jack, and at long last after two hours of really hard work, she was ready to move.

All her tyres were flat, one headlamp rim missing, she was covered in the dust and grime of decades – one-and-a-half – and looked a picture of misery. The footpump was applied to the tyres in turn, only one refused to inflate, so we made our way to the tow car for a spare. As we were returning, tube in hand, the noise of an explosion sent us back for another tube – yes, one of the inflated ones had failed to stand the strain.

The two new tubes fitted and some of the thickest dust removed, the tow car was backed up ready to lend a hand. Gently the clutch was let in, and the Morris once again breathed in good fresh air.

She was in a terrible state, mice had built nests in her, an old newspaper of '35 was found in one of the pockets, the clock had been removed, and the engine was seized solid – but it was a Bullnose and it was mine.

Proudly we towed her home, and in due course rebuilt her. When she was stripped all kinds of things were discovered, an old map, a Bass bottle opener with the vintage billposter engraved on it, and "Great Stuff this Bass"; how many of you remember those adverts?

Eventually she was mobile once more, and with no road test was taken on the Northern Trial, where, with six up, she came eighth in the general classification, and has gone from strength to strength ever since.

I believe she has a soul, I know she has a heart, the biggest any car ever had, and it's my belief she goes so well because she's so pleased to be out of that barn!

The story of "Evan-William" *by R. M. Knox and R. H. Gray*

Bob Knox starts the story:—

Whilst taking a Sunday afternoon walk during my holiday at Barmouth, North Wales, in July, 1956, I saw the roof of a van over the high stone wall which bordered the steep path. I could not resist the temptation. I climbed the wall and there it was: a 1924 Bullnose Morris Cowley. It had started life as a tourer, but at some stage had acquired a van body, on the side of which one could just discern " . . . Williams, Butcher . . . th".

That night I saw a vision in my dreams of a fully restored Morris with its original body. The damage was done. The next day I found out the owner and was soon in his butcher's shop. I recognised him as the gentleman who was precentor at the local chapel. He was over eighty when I first met him. We discussed a sale. If I was going to restore it we could do business. He picked up some wrapping paper and tore it in half. One piece he gave to me and the other he kept. I was told to write down the price I would give, and he would scribe on his paper the price he wanted. Add the two together, then divided by two and that was the price at which it would change hands. Not bad for a man over eighty!

I bought it. Plans for its collection were the next problem. However a good friend, Raymond Gray, agreed to help and within a week or so, on August Bank Holiday Saturday, we set off from Bradford for Barmouth in Raymond's 1934 10/4 Morris to tow home the van which we had already christened "William" after the butcher who was the previous owner. As time was at a premium a very careful schedule had been worked out. We arrived at our destination only twenty minutes later than planned. It was a glorious evening which made a beautiful part of Wales look even lovelier, not a cloud in the sky. Two hours had been allocated to prepare the Bullnose for its long tow home. As is always the case it took a little longer, but even so we were not more than an hour behind our target. Lights had been made to work and a tow bar fastened between the two vehicles. I made myself as comfortable as I could in the cab of the van and at 9.15 p.m. a start was made on the 150-mile return journey.

Before we had travelled 10 miles I noticed spots of rain on the windscreen, but "William" did not boast the luxury of a windscreen wiper, so they had to remain! Soon it was a deluge and then it happened – Raymond's car disappeared in a cloud of steam! This of course, brought us to a compulsory stop. A core plug had dropped out of the engine block and allowed the water to pour on the ignition system. Try as we would, we could not gets things dried out under these conditions, and so decided to retire into the van and have supper. Our appetites seemed to have developed out of proportion to our mobile pantry and only too soon we had "eaten up".

A return was made to get the towing car to start. We coasted down a long hill to try and get the engine to fire but without success and then met at the bottom of this hill two vans standing side by side. Their drivers had apparently been spending an hour at the "local". I approached one to see if he would be willing to offer us a tow but after consultation with his mate he volunteered the information that they could not help but would be willing to push. When I pondered on their reply later I thought that probably theirs was a wise decision! So push we did, and at long last the engine was coaxed into life again. Next problem was to obtain some water. It was still raining hard and I had noticed a deep square hole at the roadside. The only container was an Oxo tin, and so, armed with this, I was lowered upside down by Raymond into this hole. The water supply however was only a trickle and so this brilliant plan reluctantly had to be abandoned! One of our two acquaintances suggested a stream about two miles away with a plentiful supply, and so off we set. After allowing what seemed to be a lifetime for the engine to cool, we filled up with water and returned to the point at which we had left the Bullnose. Couplings were again connected and we continued at a fair pace, but about four hours behind our schedule. One halt for forty winks and we made Manchester about 8 a.m.

A cup of coffee at the first coffee bar to open and we were again on our way. It was now quite a task to keep awake and whilst I cannot say I have ever regarded the Bradford City boundary signs as attractive, on this occasion they took on a new look and announced that we were only half an hour from a good breakfast and a long sleep.

From here, Raymond Gray tells the story:—

During the following months Bob searched fruitlessly for a tourer body.

This search ended abruptly in December, 1956 in Bradford, for he set eyes on a 1925 Oxford coupe which had been carefully stored for twenty-five years. This was due to go to the wreckers in a matter of hours but common sense prevailed and it soon had a new owner.

I took over the 1924 Cowley, "William", which was by now completely dismantled and the parts stored at three different addresses.

On the outward trip to Barmouth to collect William we called at a farm near Corwen where there was a 1925 Cowley two-seater being used as a tractor-cum-haycart, etc. This car was in constant use and not for sale. However, the following year saw us back in North Wales, preparing to tow back the 1925 two-seater Cowley! The farmer, Evan Owen, had used the car on the farm for nearly thirty years. It had no door, dickey or hood frame, but did have half a windscreen and plenty of rotting timbers.

During the tow home the passenger had to keep wrapping the nearside body panel round her in order to stay on board the Cowley, now christened "Evan".

From the wreck of Evan I decided to combine the two, Evan and William, into one good car, "Evan-William". I proceeded to make a complete new body framework with measurements taken from the rusty panels, twisted beading, rotting uprights, etc., of "Evan".

The scuttle from the 1924 Cowley, "William", was in fairly good condition, but has a more definite curve which does not match the higher waistline and more slender curve of the 1925 model. However, the finished car would have to be a 1925 because I had a registration book for a 1925 two-seater. The mention of the 1924 Cowley's van body in the registration book had given officialdom some ideas about purchase tax, i.e., converting van to car!

The curve of the lower portion of the scuttle of the 1924 car was altered to fit the new look of 1925. A new door was made – sounds simple doesn't it? If you've nothing to do for two or three weeks just try making one!

The ash bends for the dickey lid had to be specially made to my template by a firm in Nottingham, who incidentally made the bends for the hood frame. The biggest single expense, i.e. £12 10s. 0d. was for rolling the body panels. These we cut and fitted ourselves.

We managed to get measurements and cardboard templates for the metalwork of the hood frame, and proceeded to make and assemble these parts. We thought it better to have the hood frame covered with canvas and then removed before starting on the painting of the body. A friend in the furniture trade took away the instrument and windscreen boards and worked wonders on them, bringing out the lovely grain in the wood.

In the meantime I was making a set of Gabriel Snubbers. There was one rusty broken sample from which to copy but with lengths of balata belting, brass strip, springs and the help of a blacksmith for the centre pieces, the set cost me around £5. According to records the originals cost around £5 10s. 0d., no doubt because they were made in the U.S.A. The chassis and wheels had to be shotblasted, mudguards and valances well painted underneath and then given two coasts of Rubba-seal. Endless searches in wreckers yards for suitable seats and cushions, etc. were made. By now it was June, 1958 and we were ready to start spraying. Three reds, four or five greys, four blacks or greens to finish were necessary.

The usual deficiencies on the instrument board, i.e. clock and speedo were supplied by a club member in Cambridge, and by August we were ready to put the finishing touches to the job that had taken us most of our spare time for a whole year.

During the long winter months as I laboured in a cellar making the body framework or tackled the soul destroying task of scraping paint off mudguards one thought was uppermost in my mind; the thrill I would get when I eventually sat behind the steering wheel. Since Evan-William, as my car is affectionately called, was rebuilt it has travelled well over 16,000 miles in all weathers to and from work every day with the odd jaunt at weekends.

I would pay tribute here to the help received from Bob Knox during many stages of the rebuilding, especially the mechanical, electrical and spraying sections.

For those interested in the £-s-d side of things, and who isn't? The two cars cost £11 15s. 0d. and £2 10s. 0d. respectively plus the cost of rebuilding which was around £80.

PS

After many thousands of trouble free miles I sold the two-seater Cowley and bought in its place a four-seater Oxford in excellent condition because I thought it would suit me better as a family man. Somehow I just can't take to this Oxford like I did to Evan-William. A lot of "Raymond Gray" went into that Cowley, but with the Oxford it was just a question of writing out a cheque!

12

Postscript

We sometimes wonder whether certain authors have ever driven the cars about which they write or if they are even familiar with them. Readers may well question our first hand experience and therefore we close with a summing up of our vintage motoring to date. We started out with the fatal combination of an urgent desire to go motoring with lack of funds and sheer ignorance. The penalty was terrible: Austin Seven ownership. Lytton still maintains that his atrocious 1933 saloon was even worse than Robin's appalling 1931 version. Because of this sad let-down we eye even a mint condition "Seven" with suspicion and disbelief. In contrast, we found a 1919 "Twenty" superb.

The illustrator of this second edition, Des Measures, never fell into the Austin Seven trap. His search in 1962 for the cheapest form of transport resulted in the 1931 Cowley saloon which he still owns. At first magneto problems were followed by burnt-out valves. The Morris agents obligingly refaced and refitted them, but after a very few miles the problem recurred. These disappointments lead Des to offer the car for sale but at the last moment the only potential purchaser decided on a Riley instead. This drove Des to lift the head of his unsaleable car and he found that some former owner had interchanged the inlet and exhaust valves and that the Morris agent had perpetuated the crime. Since replacing the valves correctly the car has been a model of reliability and for many years took him daily from Rugby to work in Coventry and back. Initial disappointment changed to positive enthusiasm for vintage Morrises and Des is now running-in his 1924 Cowley two-seater which he bought as a circular saw bench from a gipsy. This restoration is perfection, in infuriating contrast to ours.

Lytton Jarman at the age of seven weeks was taken to his christening in the family 1929 Oxford saloon MM 8602. However, it was much later that he thought it prudent to practice maintenance on an old chassis before he worked on the 1935 Wolseley "New Fourteen" saloon which he had been given for his twenty-first birthday. Bert Coffin of Yeovil was offering in an advertisement in *Motor Sport* a 1919 Model-T Ford in driveable condition for £10 or a 1925 Oxford chassis for £15. Which was the better choice would be an ideal subject for an essay but Lytton settled for the Bullnose, towed it to Rugby and soon had it running. He then set out to find a body, which he did quite easily in those days, in a scrapyard in Coventry. It was a coupé in very good order and fairly priced at £7. 10s. 0d. The completed car still attends Club rallies. There were no settled ideas on ergonomics at Cowley, for even a tall man needs cushions in front of the seat squab of the Oxford coupé to reach the pedals, whereas the Bullnose Cowley can be criticised for being cramped. The Flatnose provided the answer in an adjustable driving seat, adjustable pedals and adjustable steering rake, although we never bothered to adjust any of them. To find an Oxford coupé body complete shows that Messrs. Clutton and Stanford were not exaggerating when they said that at the time Bullnose spares lurked under every hedge.

Robin Barraclough has always been an enthusiast. Turning to four wheels the latest Le Mans Replica Frazer Nash would have been ideal if funds were unlimited but even the Vauxhall 30/98 at the local garage, which would have been more than acceptable, was many times too expensive at £175. The Austin Seven was appallingly bad value even at £20 and a sensible decision was to trade up to a 1929 Morris Cowley saloon at £25. A condition of the purchase was that the buyer removed it from a parking lot in Kensington. The first hour was spent in swinging the engine which engraved on the memory that one should check that the magneto is not permanently earthed as a first cause of non-starting. The 1929 Cowley was thoroughly worn out but gave over a year's service for only the cost of replacing the top radiator hose. The latter expired on being given a squeeze to test its flexibility. Convinced of the basic soundness of the Cowley design, Robin decided to blow (it is now called investing) the first of many loans on an original 1926 Cowley for £75. In his ignorance he spurned earlier but cheaper non-fwb cars as potentially dangerous! The 1926 Cowley two-seater completely lived up to every promise and expectation.

Between us we currently own a 1922 four-seater Cowley, a 1924 two-seater Cowley, a 1926 four-seater M.G. and two chassis awaiting bodywork, a 1923 11·9 h.p. Oxford and a 1925 13·9 h.p. Oxford to M.G. specifications. However, the latter two are long term projects. In addition to our first Bullnose which we have already mentioned we have also owned and disposed of the Cowford and two 1929 Cowley saloons.

We purchased the Cowford for £45 from the widow of its creator, a Rugby garage mechanic. To improve his 1924 Cowley in the early 1930's he mounted its body, bonnet and radiator onto the chassis of a 1926 Oxford saloon, which had been written off in an accident. A result of this marriage was that the 9″ extra length of the Oxford chassis protruded behind the Cowley body and the Airfix kit of the 1924 Cowley exhibits the same feature for, unknown to us, it was modelled on the Cowford. The car was registered NX 4681 as a Cowley, which defrauded the tax man, but the Cowley radiator could not cope with cooling the Oxford engine. On a long run on a hot day the Cowford boiled with great vigour. The Cowford was sold to raise funds for the Bullnosed M.G. over which we enthuse in Chapter 9. Mechanically the M.G. is fully capable of daily use but to keep the aluminium body properly polished is so laborious that we were glad to add a 1929 Cowley saloon for £40. This car possessed the vital requirements of a hack of being easy to start in any weather. The engine started invariably on half a turn of the handle even after standing for a week, although the mixture could scarcely have had time to work its way round the inlet manifold and into the cylinders. The Flatnose was abused but gave absolutely reliable daily transport.

A natural question is why do we own Bullnoses. Part of the answer is simple. We like them. Nevertheless the cars could not be mere playthings and had to provide reasonable performance and economy with reliability and simple maintenance. And most important of all, they had to be cheap. Anything sporting was too expensive.

In good condition a Bullnose or Flatnose can cruise at about 38 to 42 m.p.h. in comfort, although, if pushed, can hold nearly 50 m.p.h. without distress. One can reckon on covering 100 miles in three hours, so that most journeys in England can be covered in a day and petrol consumption works out at around 25 m.p.g. if the car is driven hard, although gentler methods readily give 30 m.p.g. On a well assembled engine it is not necessary to top up with oil between changes. We usually add a pint or two of water before starting out on a long run but this is to be on the safe side because even now we do not know how much to allow for expansion. In comparison with most vintage light cars Bullnoses and Flatnoses have good springing, a sweet clutch, an easy gearchange and a lively performance. Their least satisfactory feature is the steering, which can deteriorate to passable rather than among the finest, unless the non-adjustable box is overhauled to remove wear and the front axle carefully wedged to obtain the correct castor angle.

On the score of reliability, of overwhelming importance, a Bullnose or Flatnose has always got us home. We cover relatively modest annual mileages but in twenty two years the number of breakages have been two crownwheel and pinions, six half-shafts, a broken fan, a burnt out dynamotor and the collapse of a piston. The crownwheel and pinion failures were caused by the working loose of the nuts and bolts holding the crownwheel to the differential assembly. A sharp crack from the rear end on changing from over-run to drive or vice versa gives warning of this. If prompt action is taken no harm results but we were too lazy to heed the warning. In one case a new crown-wheel and pinion was fitted at the roadside. It is part of Morris lore that a clumsy clutch foot results in broken halfshafts but we are of the opinion that weak halfshafts were fitted for only a limited period and that these were succeeded by stronger shafts. A rule of thumb is that a car breaks its halfshafts once and there is no further trouble when they are replaced. Nevertheless we always carry a spare. We remain mystified by the fracture of a fan blade but it is the only occasion that we have heard of this occurring and the total damage was a dent in the bonnet. The burnt out dynamotor was the result of it being left on charge when a battery lead had come adrift. Indeed most of the troubles, apart from the halfshafts and the fan blade breaking, could have been avoided and can be entered in the balance sheet as learning from experience. Morris always exhorted that one should use only genuine Morris parts. This recommendation was ignored when we fitted a rebored engine with some old but unused pistons of obscure make and peculiar design which we had bought at £1 for the set. The economy was false. One piston collapsed and the other three cracked around the gudgeon pin bosses. Nevertheless the car limped about 30 miles home, admittedly making horrible noises, and the cylinder block had to be resleeved. We feel that this is a good record of reliability.

On the maintenance side, a tremendous economic advantage of owning a Bullnose or Flatnose instead of a modern car in the mid-fifties was that spare parts were thrust upon one either free of charge or at a nominal cost by garages clearing out obsolescent stocks on the advice of business efficiency experts. When we started Morris motoring we had new clutch plates fitted by the local garage and did not begrudge the standard £5 charge. This service is no longer available and we carry out the job ourselves. It is heavy work and the worst task on the Morris. The clutch is beautifully light in operation but we sacrifice some of this in the interests of long life and as a matter of course fit heavier springs from the Morris Commercial. The splash fed big-ends probably need more attention than in most cars. If they are shimmed so that they are a good tight fit they will last for years without further attention and the engine can be revved freely. Disaster is by no means imminent if a tap develops in the big-end but it is best to take remedial action at the earliest opportunity, which is only an afternoon's work for the practised hand. Bullnose front wheel brakes are excellent and if they work well, leave well alone except for adjusting them with the turnbuckle and oiling the linkages. If however the front wheel brakes are unpredictable the only answer is the expensive one of having the whole system rebushed, the shafts built up and reground and the brake drums skimmed. We have driven Flatnoses which could stop on the proverbial pre-decimal sixpence but our own examples, which were not lovingly maintained, stopped as badly as a perfectly maintained Austin Seven.

Having a Morris stable for daily transport we felt we could indulge in a vintage car for only occasional use, providing the initial cost was low. We fell for an exquisitely original 12/25 1926 Humber four-seater tourer at £12 10s. 0d. The 12/25 made way for a 1927 14/40 Humber saloon, which was a runner as one would expect at £45 but, with an oil consumption of 50 miles per pint, in need of an engine overhaul. Lytton had disposed of his Flatnose and was restoring a 1924 two-seater Cowley for daily transport. This took rather longer than planned and meanwhile the Humber had to serve. Its only rest from daily hack work was to take the Barracloughs on a honeymoon tour of Wales. We have nothing but praise for the 14/40. Despite the condition of the engine, in four years and 10,000 miles nothing went wrong with the car (other than oiled up plugs!) A wonderful record. Like the 12/25 the bodywork and fittings are of the highest quality, the suspension comfortable and the performance dignified rather than racy. Its two best features are the typically Humber steering and gear-change.

For a time for daily transport we used a 1934 10/4 Morris tourer, which was one owner from new and in a near perfect condition. We understand why the 10/4 is considered by many as the best Morris model of the 'thirties. It is a mystery how an Austin Ten could even be considered competitive for it is prone to clutch slip and has poor brakes in comparison with the Morris hydraulics.

We have made the mistake of selling a long chassis 23 h.p. Lanchester tourer which was so much more satisfying than a 20 h.p. Rolls-Royce, and currently our non-Morris stable consists of a 1905 Mass with an 8 h.p. De Dion engine and an exceptionally elegant Lancia Lambda saloon. The compact dimensions of the Mass make it look so easy to drive. However, to go from a modern automatic to a Bullnose takes less acclimatisation than changing from a Bullnose to the Mass. It would be tedious to repeat the fully justified praise of the Lambda's road-holding, steering, brakes and general road manners. At present price levels we have left it too late to buy a 30/98 or Silver Ghost but there is still plenty in store by savouring other people's cars. We hate to admit it but it was only a few months ago that for the first time we had a run in a Model-T and a G.N. Edward Riddle's ohc sporting GN is a superlative sports car. It makes no compromises and offers an unmatched combination of performance, economy and lack of needless complication. However, to return to Morrises, Edward Riddle assures us that apart from fuel economy his 1926 Cowley, the ex-Raymond Gray car "Evan William" (See pages 169–172), can do all that his touring GN can manage but in a more civilised manner with half the maintenance.

Appendix 1

The Bullnose Maintenance Manual
by N. D. Routledge

(Reprinted from the Magazine of the Bullnose Morris Club)

Tuning a Bullnose

Before getting on with the job, let us assume your Bullnose engine is in good condition and sound in wind and limb, otherwise tuning will only lead to trouble.

Now let us consider the limitations. Firstly, due to the comic inlet tract the engine cannot breath deeply enough for REALLY high r.p.m. Secondly, as neither the rods nor the crank would permit this for long, we have to concentrate on power low down the scale. The breathing can be overcome by "blowing" the motor, but if carried out at a high enough pressure to make it worthwhile would surely blow the lot up, and in any case the fitting of a "blower" closes the door on most V.S.C.C. and other club events.

So we must turn to other ways of coaxing the gas into the cylinders. The ports can, with the aid of riffler files, small emery wheels, carborundum stones and the like, be blended in to give a smooth gas flow. All steps and projections in the port must be smoothed away, remembering the gas flows into the inlet ports and out the easy way.

This is a painstaking job, on which many man-hours can be spent, but with very worthwhile results. If you feel so inclined, you can withdraw the valve guides, streamline the part which projects into the port (and so obstructs the gas flow) and replace. If any guides are worn renew them; they can still be obtained new from stockists.

Next the valves. See they are all sound and not knife edged, replace if they are or if worn on the stems. NEW ones can be obtained – not bad for forty-odd year old motor cars?

The heads of these can be machined very slightly concave with advantage, as the less they weigh, the less power is used both in lifting and returning them.

When carefully ground in, polish with a little liquid metal polish in place of grinding paste. When refitting stronger springs can be used or packing between the spring and the cylinder block if you wish to save this expense. Please use new cotters. The tappet screws must be either replaced if at all worn, as adjustment is impossible if they are pitted. The best clearance for performance is 4 thou. inlet and 6 thou. exhaust.

The cylinder head can be shaved if you have (or know someone with) the facilities. As much as an eighth of an inch can be taken off, but I would take

179

it by degrees, as once it is off, you've had it. A good finish on the face of the head is essential. A Whatmough type head is fitted to post 1929 "Flats" and this will give beneficial results, but you will have to give it clearance for the exhaust valves as they used smaller ones. This is easily done with small grinding wheels, checking with mechanic's blue for fouling. A small electric hand drill is invaluable for this operation. You can take off 2 m.m. from either type of head without the car being too choosy over petrol.

When all this has been done the car's performance will be much improved, but the ignition can be set much further advanced than the standard setting if you are prepared to use the control intelligently. Bullnoses are quite happy on the tamest of plugs and I personally use K.L.G. type ML 50, set at 20 thou. gap. The contact breaker gap should be set at 12 thou. Make sure that both cams show the same amount of lift. This is very important with the Lucas mag. Should this magneto be the "brush-wipe" type it is most important to check that the contact between the brush and the distributor is good, that there is no wear, and no carbon tracking between the contacts. The inside of the distributor can be polished with very fine sandpaper.

Next we must turn our attention to the bottom end. The increased loading on the big-ends, and here we are rather up against it. Assuming the car has been rebored (many haven't) aluminium pistons will be fitted. These can be lightened by drilling, but if in doubt, don't, or ask expert advice.

In the case of a rebored engine, if two slotted oil scraper rings are fitted, the bottom one can be left off with advantage until the car starts to use oil, when it is a simple job to fit it. Skirt rings are a well known source of power loss (due to increased drag).

The dippers on the big-ends may be improved as neither type usually fitted is satisfactory. The ones on the alloy rods can be opened out to allow more oil to enter the bearing. Scoops can be made to fit the bolts on the steel rods using 18 swg. mild steel sheet, the feed holes must be enlargened to mate these in the scoops. This will take care of any bearing troubles providing the journals are reasonably sound, 2–3 thou. ovality does not seem to matter too much All pistons and rods should be balanced before assembly.

If the engine is out of the frame, or the gearbox off, the flywheel can be lightened. It is roughly T section and either one of the webs, or both, can be removed to make it either an "inverted L" section or just a disc. As there are no teeth on it this is an easy task for a good lathe turner. If you do this remember you are sacrificing tick-over for acceleration, but one flange removed can be regarded as the "happy medium".

This coupled with the increased compression ratio, due to machining the head makes for a very much faster "change up" and much improved get-away. Easy on those half shafts.

Carburation remains – Can't do much about this, the standard carburettor with the standard settings is hard to beat.

I favour the later type S.U. for all round performance, tho' they are not as economical as the fixed jet models.

Now your Bullnose should really motor, and you may have road holding problems.

Bullnose steering gear

Before going into technicalities, let's run through the way the steering operates.

First the wheel. This is used to transmit movement to the shaft which runs down inside the column to the worm wheel inside the steering box. This worm wheel gears with another toothed gear wheel on the sector shaft, hangs down the drop arm, which gives movement to the drag link, and thence to the steering arm on the offside of the front axle. Movement is transmitted to the nearside road wheel by the track rod, which is carried on two steering arms attached to the stub axles.

Thus you will see, that there are several points which can wear and cause lost movement, and consequently play in the steering gear, which shows up as excessive movement on the steering wheel, and can cause bad handling characteristics, and in some cases very bad wobble.

The box itself was made adjustable up to a point. To do this, one removed the drop arm from the sector shaft, it fits on a square shank and is locked by a bolt, revolved the inside wheel through 180 degrees, and re-assembled the drop arm again. This was an easy way of replacing the worn teeth on the sector shaft wheel with those that had, up to that adjustment being made, not been used. BUT by now your Bullnose will have had that adjustment done times without number, so more drastic methods must be employed to eliminate wear.

New parts are almost unobtainable; we will therefore have to remove and recondition the box. To remove the box complete first undo the big nut that holds the steering wheel, and using a block of hard wood drive it up off the taper on which it fastens.

Then remove any controls which are attached to the column, on some models they are separate, take off the clip, remove the drop arm, undo the three bolts that fasten the box to the crankcase, and the box will then come down out of the chassis.

The next move is to dismantle the box. First remove the fixing clamp, and then the endplate held by three bolts. This will expose all the innards to your astonished view! The sector shaft wheel which runs in two brass bushes can be seen. This must be moved further into mesh with the worm wheel on the column to take up the wear.

To do this, remove the original bushes and have a machinist make up two about 15 thou. eccentric. These must be marked as a pair to mate the eccentricity and then assembled by trial and error until all the play is taken out but the column can still be turned easily by hand. You will not get perfection as there is still wear on the faces of the teeth but a very good compromise is obtainable. Next assemble the box with new grease, I'd suggest one with a molybdenum disulphide additive as this will minimise future wear. The box can then be replaced on the car ready for the next move.

Check that the drop arm is tight on the square and that the clamping bolt is really tight. If O.K. split pin this and attack the draglink. There is a ball pin at each end of this. They are not obtainable now but replacements can be got that are easily made to fit. If these balls are worn oval replace them. Check the assembly of the thrusts in the draglink ends; first a spring, check this for damage, then a pad then the ball pin, another pad, another spring and then the end cap. Tighten this end cap until no play remains and the ball pin can be turned with some effort, split pin the cap and fit the complete draglink. There is no adjustment needed to this component.

Now, if your car needs attention to the swivel pins and bushes, you can check this by jacking it up on the front axle, and pulling outwards at the lower extremity of the road wheel to check the amount of play. You should not be able to move the wheel more than $\frac{1}{2}$ in., if you can, replacements are called for.

To get at them, remove the road wheel, the hub nuts, the one on the nearside is a left-hand thread, and pull off the hubs. Strip the brake back plate (you are saved this job if no f.w.b.) and then take off the track rod. Ball pins here again if f.w.b. – bolts and plain bushes if not.

Drive out the cotter pin after taking off the nut of course, then you can drive out the swivel pin complete. Much force needed here, and care so you don't bash your fingers! If the pin is very tight warm the end of the axle with a blow lamp to free it off, but don't burn your fingers on it. Watch for the boiling grease that will run from the bushes too.

Non f.w.b. axles have a long bolt with nut and split pin, very much easier to take out. With these however no spares can be got, you have to make, or get made, your own.

The pre-war Morris Ten pins and bushes fit the f.w.b. axles, they are a little longer but this is a good fault. The bushes should be pressed in, reamed to suit the pin, and assembled with new thrust washers between the lower bush and axle beam to take out all the up and down movement without making the steering too stiff. Then drive in the pin, follow up with the cotter, the nut, and the job is done.

Re-assemble in reverse order to dismantling, and check the track rod as the draglink in the case of a f.w.b. model, the earlier ones have pins and plain bushes. The track rod can then be fitted and adjusted. This must "toe-in". That is, the track must be greater at the rear rims of the front wheel than the front. This is best set by your garage as a special tool is required to check it, but it can be done with a large trammel.

The car should then be tried on the road. If everything is O.K. she should steer easily and accurately, the wheel returning to the "straight ahead" position on its own after cornering. The castor angle controls this. This angle is the inclination back of the front axle, and if too much will cause heavy steering. Again, a special tool is required to check this. Should this angle be too small or negative, the car will wander at speed, and the wheel will not return after turning a corner – everything else being correct of course! To alter this a wedge is made up, and fitted between the axle and each front spring, to tilt the beam whichever way it should go. I'd leave this to the expert if I were you.

Once reconditioned your Bullnose steering should be greased regularly and keep in in clean condition, again I would suggest a Moly grease to help ward off wear. I have tried these over a long period and they do all that is claimed for them.

Bullnose steering is not light by modern standards, it is too high geared for that, but properly serviced and in good condition it is as good as anything made today.

Sumpthing about big-ends

This month, by special request, I have been asked to natter about big-ends.

Now I don't consider that amateurs should dabble with these, but in case you fancy your chances here are a few suggestions.

First, don't assume that the noise you hear is a big-end until you have checked thoroughly. A big-end will knock or emit a tapping sound when the engine is running lightly loaded. It will disappear when the car is accelerated or on the overrun, but make itself heard when the engine settles down to run evenly at anything over 20 m.p.h. If the ignition is advanced and the throttle opened up smartly with a "free" engine, a pronounced knock will be heard, and by shorting out each plug in turn with an insulated screwdriver you will be able to find the culprit. If the noise is fairly constant, and retarding the ignition does not reduce its volume, it is not a big-end, and you must look elsewhere. It may be worn timing wheels, a worn mushroom head on the oil pump or a broken valve spring.

Should your fears be confirmed, you'll have to remove the sump. The technical term for this is "to drop the sump" and should not be taken too literally. To do this first drain off all the oil by removing the big drain plug, the one with the raised rib along the centre, and also the one behind it which is a hexagon. Don't forget that the tin you drain the oil into must be capable of holding at least a gallon.

Next take off all the little clips that hold the engine trays, and remove all bolts except two handy ones which should be left loose, so you can extract them with your fingers or a screwdriver, not forgetting those in the gearbox housing. Now only two remain, and they are just behind the fan pulley, difficult to see and hard to get at. If you are lucky they will come out with a screwdriver bringing the studs with them, but you may have to use a box spanner. They may even not have nuts on, I have known that! Take out all the sparking plugs.

Next lie on your back beneath the car, loosen and withdraw the two bolts you left in the sump, lower the rear end first, and feeding the starting handle over the front axle as the sump comes away from the engine. This being done, go for a pint, have your tea or take the girl friend for a walk until all the surplus oil has dripped from the innards, or it will get in your eyes, foul your clothes and heaven knows what. You'll get covered in oil before you're finished, but there's no need to collect too much of the stuff on your person unnecessarily.

Next crawl under the car with pliers and a stout well fitting $\frac{5}{16}$ in. Whitworth box spanner, of the socket type if possible. If you do jack the car up to give more room, do please make sure that it is safe, then make yourself comfortable on your back and peer up into the internals of your Bullnose engine. You will now observe the crankshaft with the con-rods attached, the underside of the pistons, the main bearing caps, and the thing that hangs down and keeps dripping oil on you which is the oil pump.

Next check if the big-end caps are numbered and if they are not, stamp them up numbers one to four from the front. If you do not have number stamps use a centre punch, and lightly "pop" each cap at the front so that you can see which way it goes back without difficulty.

Now remove the split pins from the bolts of the bearing you wish to check. Undo the nuts and carefully take off the bearing cap noting the shims (little thin bits of packing with, usually, two thick ones on each side) which must be kept to their respective sides and neither lost nor misplaced. This is most important! Lay the bits down out of the way, but where you can easily reach them. Check on the oil dipper, if your car has steel rods, or that the hole is clear if Dural alloy rods are fitted. One of the two types of dipper was used on the steel rods, either a hollow rivet or a tab-like device with a pressed out finger. They collect the oil from the troughs and feed it to the bearings. If the finger has broken off, or the hole in the hollow rivet is bunged up, it may be the cause of the bearing failure. The only cure is to replace them.

Now examine the bearing surfaces of the two halves; they should be smooth, with oil grooves cut in them to feed the oil and possibly slightly darker in colour where they are bedding to the crankshaft. If the white metal has "run" and the bearing shell, which is brass, can be seen where white metal should be, you will either have to replace both halves of the bearing, or have the existing one re-metalled. In either case you will have to measure the journal, that is the part of the crank that the bearing fits on, with a micrometer to find out exactly the size of the bearing you need. Re-metalling is a specialist engine reconditioner's job and it may pay you to call him in to measure the job for you. The con-rod should then be "drawn" from the engine complete with the piston and the piston taken off, noting which way it was fitted, so that it can be replaced in the same position before re-assembly.

Before re-metalling the bearing the brass shell must be checked for fit in both con-rod and bearing cap. If either is worn and the shell does not fit snugly a replacement rod is called for. It is possible for the bearing to make a noise when the shells are loose in the rods, although the actual bearing surfaces are good! This is, as a rule, a rather lighter tap than a big-end proper.

When the bearing is machined after re-metalling, all the shims that were taken out on stripping should already be back in their correct positions with both nuts tight, but the re-metaller will attend to this.

When the bearing is returned to you, it should be offered up to the crank with the piston off. This saves time and you get a better "feel" of the fit. It should be tightened up on the shaft and the crank turned by grasping the webs between the big-ends and heaving it round. Should it be too tight for this, slacken off both nuts evenly until you can just turn the crank; this will mark the bearing on the "high spots" and show you where it is binding. This operation should be carried out with the journal and bearing dry, as the high spots will show up dark on the soft white metal. Next the con-rod must be removed and the high spots scraped off. This is best done with a bearing scraper, but a broken piston ring can be used with excellent results, by holding the rod in the vice and using the ring like a slice of melon, drawing it across the bearing so that the sharp edge removes a small amount of metal. When you have scraped the bearing in the rod, fit the cap on the studs to hold it, and ease off the high spots on that too. Then offer it up once more, repeating the process until the bearing surface showing dark is spread well over both cap and rod and the crank can just be turned with both nuts tight, and "to pin holes". This is correct for one bearing, but if fitting more than one, remember not to have each so tight that when all four are put up you cannot turn the crank at all. This is very important, as the dynamotor will not turn the engine if the bearings are too tight, and you may damage a half shaft if the car is towed to start it.

While the sump is off, you may wish to check the main bearings. First check for play in them by inserting a stout metal lever under the flywheel and lifting it as far as it will go, using the clutch housing as the fulcrum. Here you must be careful to distinguish between actual play and spring which you will also notice. If the play is excessive it can be minimised by removing a shim, or if very bad, more than one. Once again the bearing caps must be removed after first taking off the oil pump and oil pipes. Remove the bearing caps ONE AT A TIME! Take care to replace the shims exactly where they came from except the very thin one you remove. Check this shim for thickness so that you can take out a similar one from the other bearings. It is not advisable to remove shims from one main bearing only, as the crank sits on the bearing caps when it is whirling round, and as you will see shimming up one bearing will cause it to take more than its share of the load. Again check for movement of the crank by pulling it round using the webs, and always remembering that although you may be able to turn it with one tight bearing you'll never shift it when they are all tight. Should a main bearing have "run" and the white metal require replacement the best plan is to remove the engine complete and have it replaced by an expert, the others being checked at the same time. Bedding a crankshaft in its bearings is not a job for an amateur and in fact in these days of steel shell bearings few garages can undertake such a task.

By now you will be used to working on your back and being well soaked with dirty oil. Doesn't it sting when you get an eye full! That is due to the impurities after years of use, and one of the reasons why you should drain and refill the sump now and again. It is specially important if you are laying up a car for the winter season, as these impurities will badly corode the crankshaft if the engine is left unturned for a long period. I have seen cranks with marks of the bearings oilways etched deeply in them after they had been in store for a year or two. It is a very good plan to turn the engine of a stored car over an uneven number of times once every month, because this will give the valve springs a change of position and the same ones will not always be compressed. Also, get someone to turn the engine for you while you hold the clutch pedal out then the corks won't "weld" on to the flywheel. I've seen that happen too.

After that little interlude you'd better put the oil pump back. Not much goes wrong with these pumps. True, the seating for the ball does wear, but the engine performs quite well on two pounds of oil pressure. It may be a good idea if the mushroom head of the plunger is badly worn to have it faced up on an emery wheel. They do wear very deeply sometimes and if this occurs the only cure is to replace it. Some of the later camshafts had a four lobe cam to operate the oil pump, and it is inevitable that some of these camshafts have been fitted to Bullnoses. These shafts whilst giving better oil pressure, are rather puzzling when the oil is thick and the engine cold. You start up – bags of oil pressure, but as you drive away and speed up you lose all pressure! Bags of panic, lift your foot off the accelerator and as the engine slows down back comes the oil pressure! The only cure here is take it easy until the oil warms up and circulates freely. Often this symptom is mistaken for shortage of oil.

We've still got to put that sump back! It must be thoroughly cleaned first, both inside and out, and all the old packing material and jointing scraped off the top and rear surfaces. A new gasket has to be made for it, which is best done just before fitting, as gaskets which have been in stock for any length of time tend to shrink and are difficult to fit without damage to same. A good packing material thirty thou. thick or 1/32 in. will do best. The top gasket has to be made in one piece and this is not easy to do. Cut the sheet of the material nearly to size, larger of course, grease the face of the sump so the gasket will stick to it, remove the two front studs, unless they are obliging and came out with the nuts and lay the material on the sump. Smooth it along the face of the sump until it lies quite flat and covers all the top face. Then with a small ball pein hammer, that's one with a rounded end, tap out all the stud holes. Be careful not to miss any holes; it can be very annoying to find you've missed one when you're fitting the sump. If you haven't got a hammer small enough procure a large ball bearing and locate it on top of the gasket material above the hole in the sump. A smart tap with the hammer will cut the hole as clean as a whistle! You may not be too successful at first but why not practise on a bit of scrap material first. When this has been done tap round both the inside and outside edges of the sump, remove the gasket and trim off with scissors to complete it. The same method should be used to make one for the rear face of the sump.

Now all you have to do is replace the thing. That is not so easy. With a car of any age making an oil-tight seal of these two faces is difficult, so, reluctantly, a jointing compound must be used. The one I use is Red Hermi-tite No. 5400; it seals but never hardens, and is easily removed weeks after it was applied; a very good point as you'll agree having just cleaned that sump!

Stick the finished gasket back on the sump with grease and the one on the rear face with Hermitite, and smear both faces with jointing ready to fit to the engine. On your back again, mate! Leave the two front studs out of the sump. Have two of the sump bolts handy and away you go.

Slide the sump in position, feed the starting handle over the front axle, noting how perverse and unco-operative it can be, and raise the sump up so that it goes into position from the front. If you leave the drain plug and filter out it will help as you won't have to locate it on its way up. Bring the sump up to the rear face first watching the gasket carefully so you don't dislodge it (if you do, lower the sump, adjust the gasket and start again), and lastly bring up the front of the sump into position. Then, if you haven't lost them, screw in the two bolts, one either side, and take a breather. Don't tighten them right up, as all must be in position before any one is tightened fully. Screw in the clutch housing bolts, noting that if you have to force them into the holes either the gasket is out of place, or the sump not up far enough.

Next tighten up all the bolts from below, ignore the two at the front topside. Screw in the drain plugs, emerge, cut a slot in the top of each front stud, screw them into the sump and fit the nuts and the job is complete. Fill the sump with oil, not forgetting to put a quart through the clutch inspection plate inside the car. Start and run the engine, check for leaks, and if there are none replace the engine trays by just slackening the appropriate bolts back far enough to allow the trays to slide under their heads, retighten and fit the little spring slips.

Should you have a leak and it is a bad one you may have to take the whole wretched sump off again and have another go! You may, if you wish, pean the metal between the clutch housing and the sump (where the leak is most likely to occur) with a small hammer, but don't tell anyone I told you to do that!

Chassis tuning

I hope by now your tuned "Bullnose" engine is giving you good service, and you now wish to improve the road holding.

The long and whippy chassis is rather a problem; we must minimise this. A tie bar between the front dump irons will help greatly, but be careful not to interfere with the operating of the starting handle. The engine, too, helps, providing the mountings are not loose. If this is the case, and the rivets are slack in the frame, they must be chiselled out ONE AT A TIME, the holes are reamed out, 7/16 in. as a rule and good bolts fitted as tight as possible in the holes. This is most important as the steering is mounted on the engine, and if this is loose, then the steering is virtually "fully floating".

All steering joints should be good, and all play eliminated. The swivel pins should not be worn; new ones can be fitted to the f.w.b. models using those for the 1934–35 Morris Ten. The track must be carefully set to the regulation 3/16 in. "toe-in". This has a bearing on tyrewear, control, self-centring, and can, if far out, cause wheel wobble.

Next the wheels must be balanced. I favour the Dunlop method: this is both static and dynamic, and is effected by cementing lead strip on the rims. Believe me, it is well worth the trouble and expense. Not only does it help road holding but it cuts down tyre wear, and lessens the work required of the springs and shock absorbers.

Did someone say "shockers"? By now no "Bullnose" will have a working set, they should be worn right out! Neither type fitted as standard is repairable, so they should be replaced. Please do not fit modern hydraulics – you wouldn't fit Formica to a Chippendale table, would you? A very good compromise is a set of Hartfords; they can be obtained second-hand and are easily reconditioned. Choose the multi-disc type in preference to the thinner and less effective ones, making sure that the bushes are not worn out.

First strip them, clean off and sandpaper all the discs, replacing any damaged ones, re-assemble the units and carefully adjust them to "break" at 24 lbs using either weights or a spring balance applied to one arm while the other is held firm in a vice. They will fit straight on in place of Smith shock absorbers, but a fair amount of work is needed to replace the snubbers fitted to the early cars. Next a run on the road to set them to suit your car. If you need to adjust them, treat them as pairs; you have started with them as equal, keep them so; if one is altered a turn, alter its fellow on the same axle the same amount.

And now, tyre pressures, I find the beaded edge run best at 45 lb/sq. in., $4 \cdot 50 \times 19$ at 28 lb/sq. in., and if $5 \cdot 00 \times 19$ oversize are fitted they must be 26 lb/sq. in. If high-speed track work is contemplated an increase of 5 lb/sq. in. is desirable, more at the front if you corner really fast.

I think we should now consider the steering. Check the drop arm for play; it may be possible to eliminate most of this by removing it, turning the wheel through 180 degrees and replacing it, if of course this has not been done already. The bolt through the arm must be dead tight and well split pinned. Any end float in the column can be removed by adjusting the two nuts at the top, near the wheel, but DO NOT overdo this as if too tight damage to the ball races will ensure. Your aim should be to have it running freely without end play.

We can pass over the gearbox, as nothing can be done to improve this; the only point worthy of mention here is the dynamotor chain, which should be checked and replaced if worn; take care that the small split pin in the coupling is sound or the chain may shed altogether. At the rear end of the box is the universal; if worn this can cause endless trouble, vibration and jerky running. Spares, I regret to say, are no longer available; they can be reconditioned, but that costs an awful lot of money.

The torque tube should be a good fit in its housing, and this is adjustable by fitting or removing shims as required; these fit between the flange on the tube and the box itself.

Now the final drive unit. There are three popular ratios in use. $4 \cdot 75 : 1$ the standard one and the best for all practical purposes, $5 \cdot 0 : 1$ useful for trials only and then only really tough ones as a good "Bullnose" will tackle incredible gradients on the standard ratio. Lastly, there is the $4 \cdot 42 : 1$. This is actually the Oxford ratio and fits the large diameter propeller shaft. This is rather too high for the average Cowley but O.K. for an Oxford. In passing, it is important that the hub ball races are good and fit the housings (the brake drums) and that the hubs are tight on the axle shafts. If the shaft breaks they are easily replaced, and the car can be towed, but take it easy and not too far; the wheel will never come off as it does on some modern cars, but care is needed as the engagement of the axle shaft in the diff. is essential to the true running of the wheels.

The springs are our next interest. All the shackle bolts should be good, bushes too; new ones can be got from your local Morris dealer. They really fit a later model but if you take him a sample he will get them for you. The front spring shackles can be made out of steel strip if too worn to use. If you want to go to town you can have the springs flattened, but I don't think it worthwhile, besides you lose ground clearance. A good scheme is to bind the top quarter elliptical rear springs with either cord or tape; this makes it more rigid and helps cornering no end. The spring can be replaced with a dumb iron member but this – to my mind – spoils the car by making it too non standard.

In these articles I have outlined what can be done without materially altering the appearance of the car. Much can be done by shortening the chassis, moving the engine back in the frame, and lowering it too, but this work would make it a special.

I have purposely ignored brakes as they deserve a chapter to themselves.

Bullnose brakes

This is quite a point! Especially if they are only on the rear wheels. Make no mistake if you want them to work you've got to spend time and money on them.

First let's get the drums off. As the fronts come off with ease we'll ignore them for now. After removing the road wheels take out the three large countersunk screws, then "draw" out the hub and half shaft. You will then see a very big nut, with a locking tab, which, unless you are *very* lucky will be about ready for renewal. Having bent back the retaining lug of the locking tab proceed to remove the big nut. No doubt it will have been removed many times before, but never with a spanner. Spanners can be bought, the nuts are 2 1/16 in. across the flats, but generally the nuts are removed with the aid of a punch and a hammer. Note carefully these nuts are designed so that if bearing trouble occurs they tighten up with the action of the wheel going in a forward direction, thus the nearside is a left-hand thread and the offside the normal right-hand thread. Having done this pull off the brake drum complete with the hub bearing. This should not be very awkward as they will be worn unless you are fortunate. If the bearing is loose on the axle there's little you can do about it except replace the axle. More commonly it will be found to be a loose fit in the brake drum assembly. This must be cured, or you'll have all kinds of bothers.

The easiest way is to fit the bearing with a steel shim, but first the outer ridge will have to be removed, either by grinding, or with a scraper, a very tedious job indeed. This done, the bearing – a new one if it is at all worn – should be a force fit in the housing. This can be accomplished by cutting a shim to encompass the bearing with a butt joint, and forcing it in, care must be taken that it goes in "square" and does not tear the shim. By the way it is advisable to fit a new felt oil seal before fitting the bearing, as once in, the bearing should only come out either for renewal or the fitting of a new oil sealing washer. This having been successfully carried out (and if you get the shim in FIRST go you're lucky!) turn your attention to the brakes themselves.

If the linings are worn, or if either a brass or zinc bonded lining is fitted replace them, but not so fast!

Having removed the linings from the shoes, refit them and slack off the adjustment so the shoes sit down on the cams absolutely flat, so that they have all their lift to go at. Then measure the diameter of the shoes and make a note of it. Next measure the internal diameter of the drums, and note that down too. Half the difference of these two dimensions is the thickness of lining you need. Most likely the drums will be very badly scored, I do not advocate having them ground out, as they are thin enough as it is, they can be built up and re-machined but that will cost the earth.

The best plan is to send the shoes in to your local brake lining factor for him to fit and grind the linings to the dimensions you took previously, he will have lots of different linings to select from, and you have lots to do meanwhile.

All the cross-shaft bearings will have to be checked for wear, the shafts stripped down, machined round where worn oval, special bushes made up and fitted, the drums in position, and the pull-rods fitted the operating arms should incline towards the rear of the car. This means you will have the maximum leverage, as the arms will pull toward "top centre" and not past it. Jack up the car and equalise the brakes, care must be taken to ensure that they "free off" when the brake is released.

It may be that the linings are the correct type, that is unbonded and fairly soft die-pressed material, but still the brakes are not good. Look at the cams, and if they are well up and there is plenty of lining left on the shoes better braking can be obtained without much trouble and dismantling.

Strip the shoes and make up some striker plates to fit the heel of the shoe where the cam strikes, these must be of equal thickness, and flanged over at each end so that "stay put", about $\frac{1}{8}$ in. steel should be used. Next offer up the drum, and if it won't go on file down the plates you have just made, taking care to take the same amount off each, until you can just get the drum on. This will have the effect of bringing the cam operating arms back past the dead centre, you will have, of course, to slacken off the adjustment and set up the brakes again. This gives quite good results without undue expense or relining, but can only be tried out if the linings are fairly thick, and the cams are well up, a sure sign of worn drums.

I use linings that are made for the pre-war Vauxhall Ten, they are much thicker than the standard ones, and give very good results. It is necessary to re-drill the shoes to fit, but as the holes come in between the original ones, all is well.

My own opinion is that four-wheel brakes are well worth while, true fitting them can make the car non standard, but if you hit a wall you'll make it even more so!

They can be easily fitted to the standard two-wheel braked chassis, with very little trouble. First you must have a 1926 f.w.b. axle with the built-in speedo drive if you still want to know how fast you are going. The later types had gearbox driven speedo, so although they will fit, they are not the complete answer. Having got the axle, it is as well to check the swivel pins and bushes, as if worn both the steering and braking will suffer.

If they are worn enough to warrant replacement, get a set for the 1935 Morris Ten Four, they will fit! It's well worth while doing as they have so much bearing on the handling of the car.

Next the cross shaft must be replaced by the four-wheel brake type which you should get with the axle, and rods made up for the front wheel brakes, unless you are lucky enough to get them with the other bits. The cross shaft should be mounted with its centre line 3 in. behind the universal joint flange. Care should be taken when connecting up the cross shaft that the brake arms pull towards their top centres when the brakes are applied, this is most important.

Assuming this to be done, the brakes are ready for lining. If the axle is fitted with the cast-iron drums with a shrunk on ribbed band, they can be ground out with safety if badly worn. Vauxhall size linings fit here too.

Now jack up the car, fore and aft, DO NOT put the jack under the front brake operating rods that go from the axle to the back plate, this will bend them and impair their efficiency.

The brakes should be adjusted so that the front ones come on before the rears, this is due to the weight distribution, as application of the brakes causes weight transfer from rear to front axles, the braking is done roughly 60 per cent by the front wheels 40 per cent by the rears. This depends of course on the loading of the car but for general purposes can be taken as read.

I have done all this on both my Cowley and the Oxford, I used Telamite die pressed linings, and have had 100 per cent on the Tapley brake meter when tested by our local police. I find in practice that it is seldom necessary to adjust the rear brakes, although I often have to screw up the fronts. This is very easy to carry out, it can be done between driving tests if circumstances warrant it. The only snag with the f.w.b. axle is the universal joint linkage. This makes the brake adjustment very critical, the wheels must be straight ahead when setting and checking, when in lock the tendency is to brake harder on the inside wheel, this can be used to advantage when cornering fast.

One point I would stress, it is most important that in the case of two wheel brakes both do exactly the same amount of work, as one locked wheel detracts from the braking power, and will cause a skid. This is easily checked by applying the brakes on a cinder track or any loose surface and it will leave a telltale mark when one wheel slides. The target is maximum retardation without locking any one wheel. This goes for four-wheel brakes too.

How to re-line your Bullnose's clutch

The most important things you need to do this are the proper tools, or some you can make yourself, which amounts to the same thing.

A spring compressor is needed. I made mine out of a piece of tube about $\frac{3}{4}$ in. diameter, cutting it length ways for about $1\frac{1}{2}$ in. and then cutting through from one side to make a half round cut-away. If you could see me waving my arms about, you'd get the idea I am sure. The tube should be about 6 to 8 inches long, and fairly heavy gauge, say 18 S.W.G. or a little heavier. Next you'll need a VERY thin $\frac{5}{8}$ in. Whitworth spanner; this is 1 3/32 in. across the flats, and can be made from some $\frac{1}{2}$ in. plate if you wish.

Next you must have some means of supporting the rear end of the car, oil drums or something tall, as they have to fit under the chassis and not the axle. You will of course have all the usual spanners, etc., the average "Bull-nose" owner carries (to help repair broken down modern motor cars, you understand!)

Now, there are two ways of doing this job. Either remove the engine or the rear axle, and as the latter is the easier, we'll do it that way.

First jack up the car and place the drums or stands under the chassis frame so that they take the weight of the car, but do not obstruct the axle when it is drawn back. Disconnect all the brake rods to both hand and foot brakes, remove four spring shackles, two from the front of the rear springs, one from each side of course and a rear one from each spring. Then undo all the bolts around the universal casing at the rear of the gearbox; disconnect the handbrake rod, and withdraw the axle complete back from the gearbox. You may need some force to get it to start, but it does come aft. Next take off the gearbox top with the car in neutral, disconnect the dynamotor and remove the clutch inspection cover. Now you can see the springs, there are usually six evenly spaced out but some of the older models have only four. They are retained with a cup and pin which have to be removed, using the tube described above.

Each spring must be at the top when removing the pin, etc., and to avoid losing the bits stuff the clutch housing with rag, then using the tube with the cut-away end to the spring, compress the spring and withdraw the small pin, release the pressure with care, and catch both cup and spring before they fly out; you will have already placed the pin in a safe place. Turn the flywheel and repeat this operation until all the springs are removed. Remove the rag to turn the engine. Next loosen off the bolts round the clutch housing, removing all but the two long bolts, one at each side of the engine. Next, prepare to lift off the gearbox assembly. This with the dynamotor attached is quite heavy and I would advise getting an assistant to help. It is quite in order to have your wife help you, but NOT the girl friend if you wish to keep her, unless she has heard you swear when a half-shaft broke! If so, and she still loves you, well, you've been warned.

Having now got the gearbox on the floor, yourself off it, bandaged your damaged knuckles and got your breath back, you have to get the cork lined plates off the clutch. A small self-aligning ball race on the end of the shaft has to be removed. Ignore it. Instead remove the split pin in the nut behind it, and using the $\frac{3}{8}$ in. Whitworth spanner screw off the nut, which will force off the ball race too, and without damaging it – simple!

Now remove three split pins from the clevis pins (spring loaded) in the periphery of the plates, this will enable you to withdraw them, and remove the plates from the toothed wheel on which they sit.

If you haven't got a pair of plates ready to fit, you gotta bit of thinking to do. They can be got on a "Service Exchange" system and that is the way to do it. No use celebrating and using the corks, by the time you'd got enough you'd see so many gearboxes and clutches you'd likely sign the pledge! Actually plates can be recorked fairly quickly, but the snag is that the new corks must be allowed to dry out and consolidate before grinding, and this takes time. Storing ready corked plates is a problem too as mice like to nibble the corks! Fancy that – Mickey a Bullnose fan!

Next replace the clutch plates exactly as they came off, taking great care that they are not forced back over the edge of the aforementioned wheel on which their inner diameter fits. If this occurs, you'll have fun getting them back, but it is easy with the gearbox on the floor.

When this is done put the clevis pins, springs, etc., and splits in, screw on the nut, split pin it leaving clearance for the ball race, tap the ball race on and you're ready to fit the gearbox to the engine.

This next move is a trial of strength, patience and temper. Care must be taken that the plates do not slip back over the aforementioned wheel, as once in this position it is a hellova job to coax them back again.

Assuming that your wife hasn't left you, invoke her aid, promise you'll not swear like you did before, she'll come, then raise the box up to the engine having first lined up one of the studs in the flywheel at top dead centre, and one of the holes in the plates to suit, and gently coax it into position. Slide it gently forward, DO NOT force it, or the plates will go back over the afore-mentioned wheel, and when you're sure that all the holes have entered on all the studs ease it forward and locate if on the two long bolts you should have left ready in position. I have forgotten to mention that either a gasket should be cut, or the mating face anointed with jointing; the former makes a better job, but it is more complicated in assembling. A leak on this face joint will, however, cause oil to leak from both clutch and engine!

Bolt up the housing in position, and pack the interior with rag to catch any bits you may drop when replacing the springs. Using the tube, replace all the springs and pins, and try the clutch for operation. If O.K. adjust the pedal for clearance (remembering that as the corks wear the pedal comes back, and takes up its clearance) and assemble the rest of the car, not forgetting to pour into the clutch pit $1\frac{1}{2}$ pints of engine oil before fitting the cover plate. Don't leave the rag in!

Feeding the propeller shaft spline into the universal joint can be rather tricky. Once again line up the splines as near as you can by eye and bring up the axle gently but firmly. Rocking the engine back and forth may help to "mate up" these splines. After bolting up the universal flange give it plenty of grease through the greaser or filler plug on top of the housing.

Next, connect up the dynamotor, refit floorboards, etc., and try the car on the road. With new clutch plates, it is not uncommon for the clutch to drag at first after starting up from cold, do not worry about this, but, running the engine as slowly as possible, gently ease the gear lever into gear, with the clutch "out" of course. You will find that after the initial withdrawal it will operate easily and correctly for the rest of the day, but may drag next time you start up from cold.

This trouble is more prevalent in the colder weather when the oil is thicker and the corks tend to adhere to the running plate.

One last "tip" to prevent misplacement of the clutch plates during assembly, if the clutch pedal is kept "back", that is, pulled away from the engine, until the clutch plate is lined up, and the pins are entered in the holes, then it must be released to allow the clutch springs to be fitted.

Having relined your clutch, remember, easy does it, or I'll have to tell you how to replace a half-shaft!

The back end of your Bullnose

"Back end" is the term applied to the complete rear axle assembly of a car, and failure of any component is usually described as "back end" bother, be it just a sheared half-shaft, or the loss of teeth on the crown wheel and pinion.

Firstly we should become familiar with the axle and all its component parts. The Bullnose axle is, oddly, not the Hotchkiss type with the propeller shaft running in the open, but encloses this shaft inside a tubular member attached at one end to the rear axle casing, and at the other a ball joint enclosing the universal joint and attached to the rear of the gearbox. There is only one universal joint used in this design, a simple Hook's type which is lubricated by oil fed to it from the gearbox, plus any grease you may care to pump in through the greaser or filler plug on top of the housing. Wear on this joint causes excess play in the transmission, "snatching" at low speeds in a high gear and vibration on the overrun. The only sure cure is to renew the worn parts, or should replacements not be available have the originals built up and re-machined. Either remedy is costly but well worth the trouble and expense.

The propeller shaft fits into an internal spline in the rear half of the universal joint and runs down to the rear axle housing inside a large diameter hollow tube which is known as the "torque tube". This is riveted to the ball end at the front, which swivels in the gearbox fitting and to the differential housing at the rear. From now on we will call the differential simply – the diff. At the rear of the torque tube, just forward of the diff. housing you will find a plate held by two bolts on top of the forging which gives access to the pinion adjustment and should never be disturbed unless the meshing of the pinion has to be altered.

At the rear of the axle casing is a coverplate which carries the filler plug and is attached to the housing with ten bolts. Removal of this plate gives access to the diff. assembly proper and crown wheel adjustment. From this assembly a half-shaft goes to each wheel hub, it is splined to the diff. wheel and attached to the hub which is tapered and has a woodruffe key to locate it. The drive is taken mainly on the taper which must be a good fit and very tight, care being taken to ensure that the key is not too big causing the hub to "ride the key". The hub locates on the wheel studs and these transmit the drive to the wheels. The three large countersunk screws hold the hub on to the brake drum but do not take the drive. There is a gasket between hub and drum to prevent leakage from the axle.

The most common rear axle failure experienced with Bullnoses is half-shaft breakage, either at the hub end or worse still at the diff. end. The former is easily dealt with by removing the wheel, the hub with the broken piece of shaft in it, and using a piece of wire with a loop at one end, pulling the broken shaft out from the axle casing. Press or drive out the broken end from the hub, fit your replacement, and assemble using a new gasket unless the original is in very good condition.

Should the shaft be broken at the diff. end unless you are very lucky you may have to remove the complete diff. from the axle. In either case it is best to drain the oil and take off the coverplate at the rear of the axle casing. By using a long piece of small diameter steel rod you may be able to dislodge the broken bit of shaft by removing the other side hub and shaft and feeding the rod through the casing entering the diff. cage and forcing the broken piece out. Care must be taken to remove all the slivers of steel that you will find around the diff. where the shaft broke, or they may get in the teeth of the gears and cause further trouble. Should the offending piece have jammed tight in the diff. you will have to remove the other hub with its half-shaft to allow the diff. unit to be withdrawn from the housing. Before doing this check the diff. bearing caps for marks and note which is which, mark them if you prefer, as they must go back exactly as they were. Remove the bolts holding them in and coax the caps off the bearings, holding the diff. with your other hand so it does not fall out. Lower it into a tin and using a drift drive out the broken piece from the other side. The parts must be replaced in reverse order to stripping, and a new gasket fitted to the coverplate. Refill with oil and replace both half-shafts, etc.

If you are so unfortunate as to have the teeth on the crown wheel and/or pinion to strip, you will have a much bigger job on your hands. You will need to proceed as before but the crownwheel must be removed from the diff. and the replacement fitted in its place. To do this is easy and so obvious that it requires no instructions. Fitting the replacement too is simple but observe the marks on the diff. cage and see they "mate" when it is re-assembled. If you can't get locking tabs for the bolts use spring washers and lightly centre pop the ends of the bolts to lock them unless you care to make up a set of locking tabs from mild steel sheet.

Crownwheel and pinions must only be used in mated pairs and cannot be interchanged at all. Even if only one gear is damaged both must be replaced. While changing the crownwheel you may wish to examine the diff. and gears. This can be done by separating the halves of the diff. cage after the broken crownwheel has been removed, care being taken not to lose any of the gears inside. In case you didn't know the idea of a diff. is to allow corners to be negotiated without either of the wheels spinning due to the inside one running in a tighter circle than the outer, the diff. speeds up the outer wheel and slows the inner so that no slip takes place. To check that the diff. is working correctly jack up both rear wheels, put the car in gear with the brake off and you will see that if one wheel is turned the other revolves in the opposite direction. Generally speaking Bullnose diff. gears never require replacement. It is the action of the diff. that allows one wheel to spin in snow, mud, ice, etc., and prevents the car from moving off, but then very little is perfect and the advantages far and away outnumber the faults.

Now back to work, we have a propeller shaft to remove. To do this remove the little locking plate from the top side of the torque tube and you will see the pinion barrel nut. Note the tongue on the locking plate and see how it operates. Using a stout screwdriver inserted in the slots in the barrel nut screw the pinion assembly out towards the rear of the car. It is a right-hand thread. The propeller shaft will come with it, you haven't broken anything! As soon as the thread on the nut is clear of that in the housing the whole assembly can be withdrawn. Do this and clean it off.

Break the locking wire in the pin behind the bearings and screw off the sleeve. Remove the bearings, spacers and shims if any, noting the order for re-assembly. Next hold the shaft in your vice using some aluminium in the jaws to prevent damage, remove the split pin and the nut. Next warm the pinion by plunging it in very hot water and drive it off the shaft from behind. If it is very tight try warming it with a blow lamp, but don't beat the screwed end with your hammer or you'll not get the nut back on. Having done this if you find the taper or the keyway in the propeller shaft is damaged, replace the shaft. Broken keyways lead to trouble and I'm afraid they are rather common. Check carefully for "hair" cracks radiating from the keyway too. If a replacement shaft is needed you'll have to be sure to get one with the correct taper. Two were used and as a rule it is small size for the Cowley and big for the Oxford but after all the years that have gone by since the cars were made no doubt many will have been interchanged. The main thing is that the taper on the shaft must match that of the pinion. Again there are several different lengths of shaft but they can be adapted by jointing with a sleeve and welding.

When fitting the replacement gears it is always best to replace with the same ratio unless you have very good reason for raising or lowering it. The ratios were very well chosen, and altering can upset the characteristics of the car.

The standard ratio is 4·75 : 1 but some of the later saloon models and many of the "Flats" ran on the commercial ratio of 5 : 1 which is ideal for trials but too low for road work. The Oxford ratio is 4·42 : 1 and would be too high for the average Cowley; in any case the taper would be wrong.

To re-assemble the propeller shaft, first fit the bearings and barrel nut in the correct order. In case you have forgotten, the big bearing goes adjacent to the pinion, the two thrust races one on either side of the barrel nut with the internal spacer in between the inners of the races. Note the races must be arranged that the thrust is taken both ways, most races are marked "thrust" on one end, these should be at the outer ends of the assembly so that the rear one takes thrust towards the rear of the shaft and the front one the thrust forward. Now plunge the pinion in hot water and place it in position and tighten up the nut before it has a chance to cool off. This will ensure a good tight fit on the taper and lessen any chance of keyway damage. Split pin the nut. The races should have a clearance of about 0.002 in. to 0·003 in. when the nut is tightened up. Check this with a feeler gauge and if O.K. fit and wire lock the pin.

Next replace the assembly in the torque tube and screw it home with the barrel nut. It should be taken well into the housing care being taken to ensure that the propeller shaft enters the spline in the universal joint. Turn the pinion with fingers while the nut is being screwed home to help this. Once again make sure the pinion goes well towards the housing so that when the diff. assembly is fitted the pinion does not foul the crownwheel.

Now fit the diff. assembly, slack off the two small locking bolts in the two big nuts so they can be adjusted and offer it up to the bearing housings. Replace the caps but do not screw home the bolts fully as the two large nuts

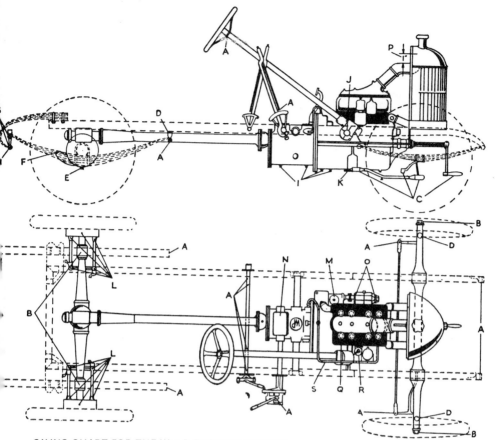

OILING CHART FOR THE W & P ENGINED OXFORD

A. Oil every week.
B. Grease every week.
C. Oil every day.
D. Grease, two turns weekly.
E. Drain oil once a month.
F. Oil every week with special heavy lubricant.
G. Oil every week, 1913 model.
H. Screw down grease cup two turns weekly, 1914 De Luxe model.
I. Empty every three months.
J. Fill steering box with special heavy oil every month.
K. Keep float stem not less than 1 in. above casing.
L. Oil brake cams and shafts every week. Brake drums (only few spots) every day in wet weather.
M. Oil here for engine and gearbox; but when empty, oil at N.
O. Oil magneto (few spots thin oil) every month.
P. Water should never be below this mark.
Q. Examine sparking plugs every month, clean and adjust points.
R. Take caburettor off to clean and empty water every month.
S. Remove pipe and clean every three months.

Other notes:

Oil more freely for touring.
The maximum revolutions at which the engine should turn is 2500 per minute.
If the back axle ratio is 4.2 :1 do not drive faster than 28 m.p.h. on second gear and 14 m.p.h. on the first gear. If the back axle ratio is 4.6 :1 26 m.p.h. on second and 13 m.p.h. on first should be the maximum speeds.
Specification of lubricating oil: The viscosity at 50°F must not exceed 1170 seconds and must not be less than 70 seconds at 158°F; flashpoint not to be less than 405°F (closed test).

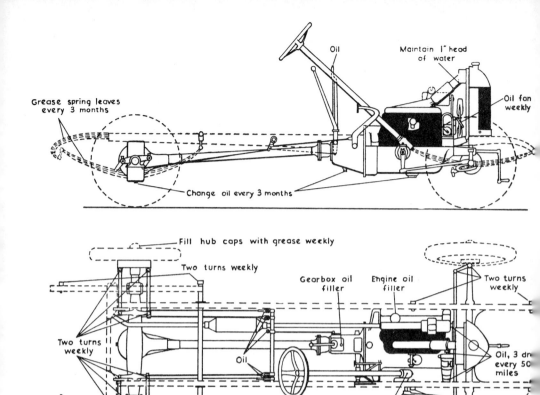

Oil
Maintain 1˝ head of water
Grease spring leaves every 3 months
Oil fan weekly
Change oil every 3 months

Fill hub caps with grease weekly
Two turns weekly
Gearbox oil filler
Engine oil filler
Two turns weekly
Two turns weekly
Oil
Oil, 3 dr every 50 miles
Two turns weekly
Oil weekly
Two turns weekly

Oiling chart for the Continental engined Cowley.

must be free to adjust the gear. Screw the two big nuts towards each other until there is no end float and the diff. can be revolved freely as far as the pinion will allow. The gear lever must be in neutral from now on. It is best to bring the crownwheel out of mesh, that is towards the left-hand side of the car before adjusting the pinion. This is done by screwing the barrel nut to bring the rear edge of the pinion (the smaller diameter) just flush with the inside edge of the crownwheel teeth and should be about right. Next moving both of the big nuts the same amount and in the same direction take the crownwheel into mesh until there is about 0·007 in. to 0·010 in. clearance when meshing should be correct. Lock the cap bolts home after tightening making sure the two locking bolts will fit in the slot and tighten them too. Fit the barrel nut locking plate after pouring in a small amount of gear oil to lubricate the pinion bearings. Replace the diff. cover, fill with oil (I use an E.P. 140 oil which is not as heavy as that used when the cars were new but is of better quality) and road test the car. If you have the "know-how" you can check the meshing of the gears with Mechanic's Blue, but if not 'tis a case of trial and error. Should the axle be noisy on drive the pinion should be eased out of mesh a slot or two on the nut, if noisy on overrun try taking it in

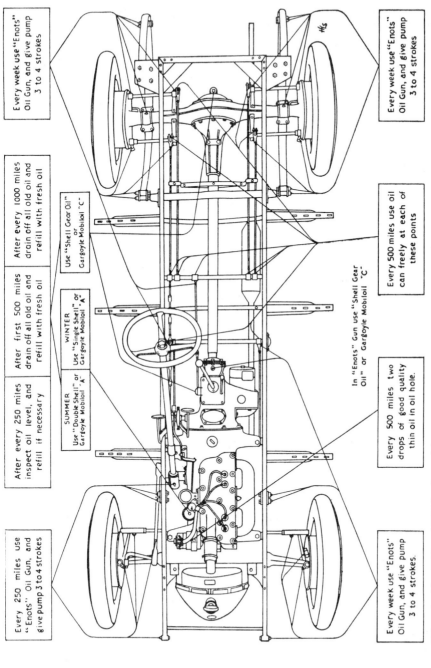

Every week use "Enots" Oil Gun, and give pump 3 to 4 strokes

Every week use "Enots" Oil Gun, and give pump 3 to 4 strokes

After every 1000 miles drain off all old oil and refill with fresh oil

After first 500 miles drain off all old oil and refill with fresh oil

Use "Shell Gear Oil" or Gargoyle Mobiloil "C"

WINTER Use "Single Shell" or Gargoyle Mobiloil "A"

After every 250 miles inspect oil level, and refill if necessary

SUMMER Use "Double Shell" or Gargoyle Mobiloil "A"

Every 500 miles use oil can freely at each of these points

In "Enots" Gun use "Shell Gear Oil" or Gargoyle Mobiloil "C"

Every 500 miles two drops of good quality thin oil in oil hole.

Every 250 miles use "Enots" Oil Gun, and give pump 3 to 4 strokes

Every week use "Enots" Oil Gun, and give pump 3 to 4 strokes.

Oiling chart for 1925 and 1926 f.w.b. models.

towards the crownwheel a little. Do give it a good run to get the oil all round all the gears.

Should you have used second-hand gears give them greater clearance as they will be worn, and used gears must be meshed to run in their original position if they are to be quiet, which is quite a job.

I find that if you wish to have two alternative ratios it is best to fix yourself up with two complete torque tube and diff. assemblies, leaving them correctly meshed and changing the whole rather than meshing the gears every time. This is an easy job, in fact it may be the best plan to fit one if you've trouble. To do this jack up the rear of the car on the chassis, undo shock absorbers (if any), brake connections to both rear brakes, remove one shackle pin from the front and rear of each road spring, take out the nuts and bolts from the universal joint housing and draw the axle back. Remove half-shafts, unbolt the torque tube from the front of the axle casing, fit the replacement torque tube assembly with a new gasket and replace all the parts in the reverse order. Getting the propeller shaft spline to enter the universal joint is a fiddling job, a little piece of bent wire like a hook may help here, as the shaft can be lined up from above. Even if you've changed the ratio the speedo will still be accurate, as driven from the front wheel it is not affected by gear ratios or wheelspin – how lucky you are!

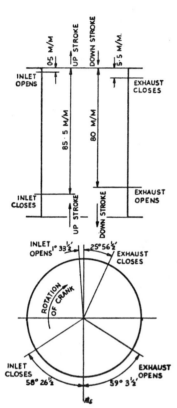

Timing diagram—single-throw oil pump cam—with 0·008" tappet clearance (top diagram) and crank position at valve openings with 0·003" tappet clearance (bottom diagram).

There is one more fault that assails Bullnose rear axles, wear on the internal diameter of the brake drums. This is rather common and difficult to cure. First jack up the car, remove wheel and half-shaft, turn back the locking tabs and unscrew the big nuts, remember the nut on the nearside is left-hand thread and the offside is a right-hand thread. Check for wear. If you can insert a feeler between race and hub divide this thickness by two and that is the thickness of the shim you need. BUT the wear is not at the outside edge, only where the bearing fits, so the ridge must be scraped away, or using rotary files and an electric drill machined until it is slightly bell-mouthed to enable the shim to be fitted. Cut the shim to a butt joint, a little wider than the bearing, grease well and force bearing and shim in together. You may spoil the first one or two, but you'll manage it in the end, and it is better to persist and get a tight fitting bearing than to make do. Re-assemble, grease the bearing, fit new locking tabs, and away we go.

Finally when fitting the diff. assembly do make sure the crown wheel goes to the left-hand side of the car otherwise you'll have three reverse speeds and one very low forward one, it can be done, I've seen it done, it's very funny, but not I imagine if you do it yourself.

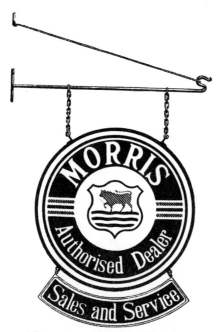

Whenever you see this hanging sign you know that it denotes an establishment where Morris Service can be obtained.

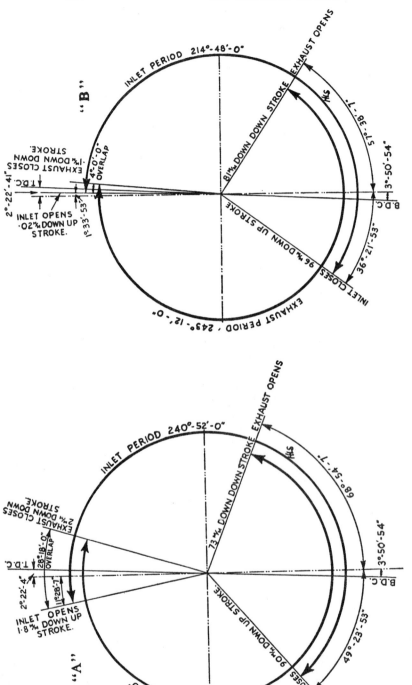

Diagram "A" shows valve periods of 11.9 h.p. and 13.9 h.p. engines numbered 191680 and above with tappets set at 0.003 in. clearance and diagram "B" the same camshaft with tappets set at 0.008 in. clearance. In both cases also, the piston movement is marked in millimetres, measured from the piston in its highest position. (This should not be confused with the vertical position of the crankshaft, because, while in a non-offset engine crank vertical is also top dead centre, in the case of offset bores the two points do not coincide, and also the piston downstroke is greater than the piston upstroke, for the same reason.)

When the large difference in the two diagrams made by so small a variation in tappet clearance is noted, it will be seen that great care is necessary in checking valve timing, and that the method and instruments used may make much more difference than actually exists in

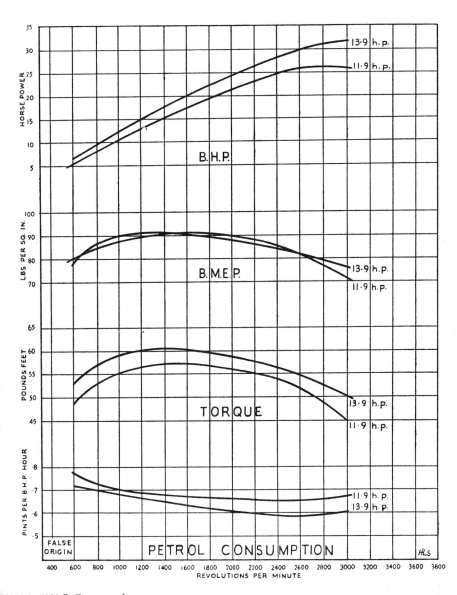

1919 to 1926 Bullnose engines.

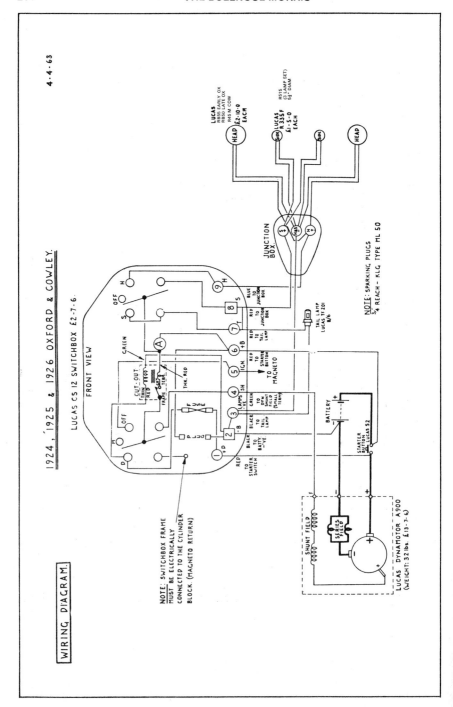

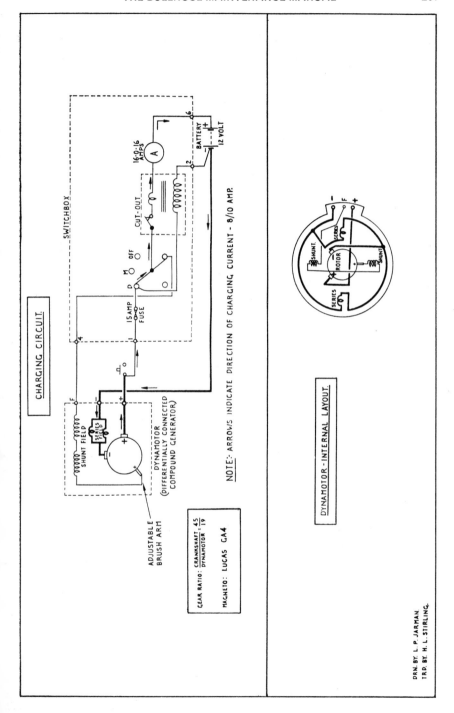

CHARGING CIRCUIT.

SWITCHBOX

16-0-16 AMPS

CUT-OUT

OFF

M

D

15 AMP FUSE

BATTERY

12 VOLT

SHUNT FIELD

SERIES FIELD

DYNAMOTOR
(DIFFERENTIALLY CONNECTED
COMPOUND GENERATOR)

ADJUSTABLE
BRUSH ARM

NOTE:- ARROWS INDICATE DIRECTION OF CHARGING CURRENT - 8/10 AMP.

GEAR RATIO: CRANKSHAFT 45
DYNAMOTOR 19

MAGNETO: LUCAS GA4

DYNAMOTOR - INTERNAL LAYOUT.

SHUNT

SHUNT

SERIES

SERIES

ROTOR

F

DRN. BY. L. P. JARMAN.
TRD. BY. H. L. STIRLING.

1919-1923 Oxford and 192

Wiring diagram

Lucas F15 switchbox £2-17s-6d

Note:-

The three switches 'H','S' and 'C'
(head, side and charge) push in
to close the circuit.
'H' operates head and tail lamp
'S' operates side and tail lamp
'C' push in for charge

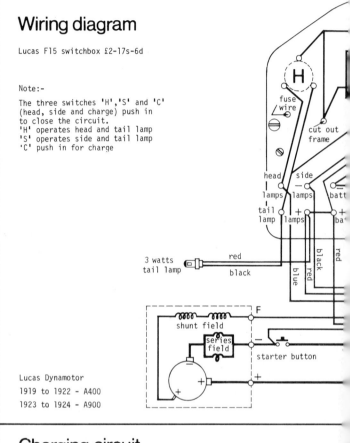

Lucas Dynamotor
1919 to 1922 - A400
1923 to 1924 - A900

Charging circuit

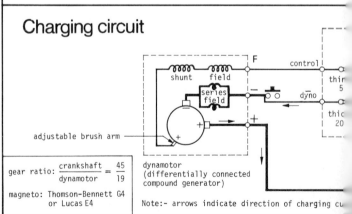

gear ratio: $\dfrac{\text{crankshaft}}{\text{dynamotor}} = \dfrac{45}{19}$

magneto: Thomson-Bennett G4
         or Lucas E4

dynamotor
(differentially connected
compound generator)

Note:- arrows indicate direction of charging cu

‚23 Cowley

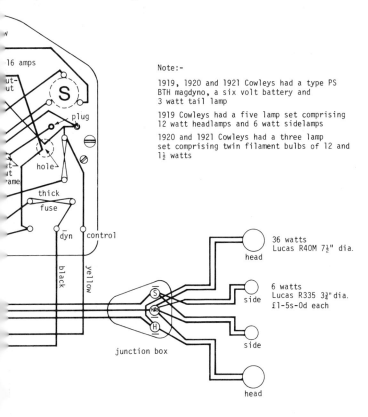

Note:-

1919, 1920 and 1921 Cowleys had a type PS
BTH magdyno, a six volt battery and
3 watt tail lamp

1919 Cowleys had a five lamp set comprising
12 watt headlamps and 6 watt sidelamps

1920 and 1921 Cowleys had a three lamp
set comprising twin filament bulbs of 12 and
1½ watts

36 watts
Lucas R40M 7½" dia.

6 watts
Lucas R335 3¾" dia.
£1-5s-0d each

junction box

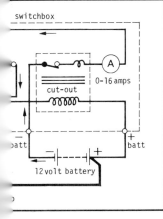

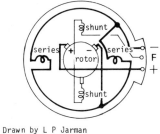

Dynamotor internal layout

Drawn by L P Jarman
Traced by D J Measures

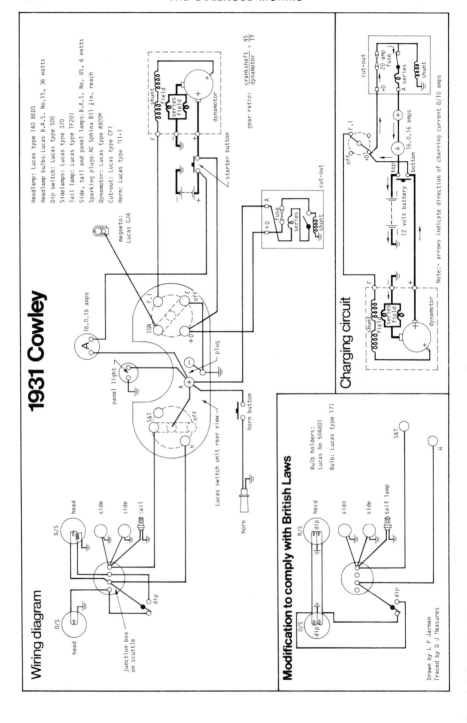

1931 Cowley

Wiring diagram

Headlamp: Lucas type 140 BEDS
Headlamp bulbs:Lucas B.A.S. No.1S, 36 watts
Dip switch: Lucas type S05
Sidelamps: Lucas type 370
Tail lamp: Lucas type TF201
Side, tail and panel lamps:B.A.S. No. 8S, 6 watts
Sparking plugs:AC Sphinx B11 ½in. reach
Dynamotor: Lucas type A900P
Cut-out: Lucas type CF1
Horn: Lucas type :11-1

magneto:
Lucas GJ4

gear ratio: crankshaft = 45
dynamotor   19

Charging circuit

Note:- arrows indicate direction of charging current 8/10 amps

Modification to comply with British Laws

Bulb holders:
Lucas No 504801
Bulb: Lucas type 171

Drawn by L P Jarman
Traced by D J Fleasures

Appendix 2

Specifications and Prices

The Morris Motor Bicycle *from a 1904 Morris catalogue*

ENGINE:	2¾ h.p. M.M.C. 1904 type, with mechanical inlet valve.
IGNITION:	Wipe, with accumulator, Basse Michel Trembler coil.
LUBRICATION:	Pump conveniently placed, so that it can be worked without dismounting.
CONTROL:	Absolute control from the handlebars, making it an ideal machine for town riding.
CARBURETTOR:	Morris Patent or Longuemare Spray.
THROTTLE GAS AND IGNITION:	These are all controlled from the handlebars by means of Bowden mechanism, instead of the usual levers on top tube of frame.
TANKS:	Nickel plated, or aluminium finish with lines, with compartments for petrol, lubricating oil and accumulator.
EXHAUST LIFTER:	Actuated from handlebar, giving complete control without releasing hold of handles.
DRIVE:	Chain drive with "Morris" clutch, giving free engine. V-shaped belt and special grip pulleys. By the use of this combination all belt troubles are avoided, there is no slip, or pulling through of belt hooks and practically no stretch. The belt rim is specially built into the back wheel and not simply attached with screws. Patent applied for.
TYRES:	We fit and strongly recommend Clincher A Won tyres, but any other make of tyre can be fitted at the option of the purchaser.
FRAME:	Registered design No. 400850, built of heavy gauge weldless steel tubing and eccentric bracket is fitted, thus enabling the chain to be adjusted without interfering with the engine drive.
FRONT FORK:	Girder pattern, extra strong, rendering breakage at this vital point practically impossible.
FINISH:	Best black enamel and gold lined, or aluminium if preferred. Usual parts plated on copper, including rims and spokes.
SILENCER:	Extra large size, preventing back pressure, and ensuring quietness in running.
BRAKES:	Front and back rim motor.
MUDGUARDS:	Wide motor pattern, front guard fitted with forward extension.
WEIGHT:	140 lbs.

PRICES: With wicker body—£70-0-0
                       With cane body —£72-10-0
                       With coach body—£73-0-0
                       Complete with two brake band brakes, Apron and
                       Lamp brackets. Upholstered in green or red.
                       Finished in black enamel and plated parts with extra
                       for lining in gold leaf 15/- and nickel plated rims
                       7/6d per pair.

W & P engined "Standard" model Oxfords

ENGINE
  Makers: White & Poppe Ltd., Lockhurst Lane, Coventry.
  Cylinders: 4 in line, cast en bloc with fixed head and detach-
                       able valve caps.
  Bore and stroke: 60 mm × 90 mm (2.362″ × 3.543″)
  R.A.C. rating: 9 h.p.
  Cubic capacity: 1017.8 cc. (62.113 cu. in.)
  Crankshaft: 0.5/0.6% carbon steel, 3 white metal main bearings
                       in bronze shells.
  Piston material: Cast iron.
  Valve gear: Side valve T-head. Exhaust and inlet valves operated
                       by separate camshafts in each side of the crankcase
                       through adjustable tappets with fibre insets.
  Carburettor: No. 25 W & P. Typical setting 450/350/350.
  Ignition: Bosch type ZF 4 magneto, or occasionally Mea
                       magnetos on later engines. Bosch sparking plugs.
  Firing order: 1, 3, 4, 2
  Lubrication: Oil flung off the flywheel fed through galleries to the
                       main bearings. Splash fed big-ends.
  Cooling: Thermo-syphon. No fan. Radiator with brass shell
                       made by Coventry Motor Fittings Ltd.
  Power output: B.H.P.:   16.4   at 2400 r.p.m.
                       B.M.E.P.: 87.2 lb/sq. in. ,, ,,   ,,
                       Torque: 35.7 lb/ft.   ,, ,,   ,,
                       (Note: The above, taken with the gearbox in position,
                         are not maximum figures).

CLUTCH AND GEARBOX
  Makers: White & Poppe Ltd.
  Clutch: Alternate hardened steel and bronze plates running
                       in oil. Initially 36 plates but later reduced to 34.
  Gearbox: 3 speeds and reverse in unit with clutch and engine.
                       Gears contained in a light cylindrical cage, carried in
                       turn in a cylindrical extension of the clutch case.

Gear box ratios:	Top —direct 1 : 1
	2nd —1.98 : 1
	Bottom—3.39 : 1
Gear-change:	Right-hand gate outside body.

TRANSMISSION

Universal joint:	Bronze centre piece with steel spiders. Totally enclosed in a housing carried on the gearbox back cover plate.
Propeller shaft:	Enclosed by torque tube.

REAR AXLE

Maker:	E. G. Wrigley & Co. Ltd., Soho, Birmingham.
Construction:	Welded single piece banjo. Overhead Wrigley worm. Splined halfshafts.
Final drive ratio:	3.5 : 1 or 4.2 : 1

CHASSIS

Chassis frame:	Pressed steel made by Rubery Owen.
Front axle:	Forged steel, girder section, reversed Elliott type made by E. G. Wrigley & Co. Ltd.
Front springs:	Semi-elliptic. 32″ long.
Rear springs:	Three-quarter elliptic. 40″ long. Slung above the rear axle.
Steering gear:	Manufactured by E. G. Wrigley & Co. Ltd. Worm and wheel in an aluminium box mounted on the main frame. 15″ diameter Xylonite covered steering wheel. Drop arm below the axle.
Brakes:	On rear wheels only. Metal-to-metal, internal expanding with four shoes per drum. Side lever inside the body operates one pair of shoes per drum and the foot pedal operates the other pair. Brake rods slung under the rear axle.
Wheels:	3 stud Sankey detachable with 4 Dunlop plain 700 mm. × 80 mm. tyres. No tyre on the spare wheel.

COACHWORK

Types available:	Standard model torpedo two seater.
	Commercial model torpedo two seater.
Differences:	The Commercial model body is narrower and of poorer finish than the Standard, but otherwise identical.
Upholstery:	Pleated and buttoned leather, usually green but red on early models.
Body colour:	Pearl grey.

ACCESSORIES
Horn:	Bulb.
Lamps:	Powell and Hanmer. 2 acetylene headlamps with Mangin lens mirrors, 2 oil side lamps and 1 oil rear lamp.
Windscreen:	Auster.
Tool kit:	Pump, jack and oil can.
Self starter:	None.
Dynamo:	None.

PRINCIPAL DIMENSIONS
Wheelbase:	7' 0"
Track:	3' 4" on chassis numbers 101 to 244, 250 to 252, 257 to 259, 267 to 269, 277, 306 to 311, 331 to 332, 351 to 354, 362, 376, 412 to 421, 429 to 431 and 460 to 465 inclusive. 3' 6" on chassis numbers 245 to 593 (except for the 43 listed above as having a 3' 4" track).
Overall length:	10' 6"
Overall width:	3' 11"
Ground clearance:	7"
Width of frame:	2' 0"
Chassis weight:	8 cwt.
Weight complete:	11 cwt.

W & P engined "De Luxe" model Oxfords

As for the Standard model with the following exceptions:—

ENGINE

Larger radiator. Radiator shells for the last few cars of German silver instead of brass.

CLUTCH AND GEARBOX

Clutches of all De Luxe cars had 34 plates.

REAR AXLE
Construction:	Bolted-up three piece banjo.
Final drive ratio:	4.6 : 1

CHASSIS
Front axle:	Elliott type.
Rear springs:	Slung below the rear axle.
Steering gear:	Drop arm above the front axle.
Wheels:	Two grooved tyres on rear wheels and three plain tyres. Disc wheels on the Sporting model.

COACHWORK
Types available:	De Luxe model torpedo two seater. Mahogany panelled delivery van.

Coachwork—*cont.*	Cabriolet coupé.
	Limousine coupé.
	Sporting model.
Upholstery:	Pleated and buttoned in green leather. Coupés in Bedford Cord.
Body colour:	Two seaters in dark green; coupés and delivery van to choice.

ACCESSORIES

The van and Sporting model had neither door nor windscreen and the Sporting model was fitted with a speedometer as standard.

PRINCIPAL DIMENSIONS

Wheelbase:	7' 6"
Track:	3' 9"
Overall length:	11' 0"
Overall width:	4' 2"
Ground clearance:	8½"
Width of frame:	2' 0"
Chassis weight:	8¼ cwt.
Weight complete:	12½ cwt.

PRICES—W & P engined Oxfords

	1913	1914
Standard model chassis		£160
Standard model		£180
Commercial model	£175	£175
De Luxe model chassis		£180
De Luxe model	£195	£199–10–0
De Luxe model coupé		£255
Delivery van		£230
Sporting model		£220

Continental engined Cowleys

ENGINE

Makers:	Continental Motors Company of Muskegon and Detroit.
Type:	"Red Seal" type U.
Cylinders:	4 in line cast en bloc. Detachable head with four priming taps. Gasket of thick sheet copper.
Bore and stroke:	69 mm. × 100 mm. (2.717" × 3.937").

R.A.C. rating: 11.9 h.p.
Cubic capacity: 1495 cc. (91.235 cu. in.).
Crankshaft: Desaxé. 3 white metal main bearings in phosphor bronze shells.
Piston material: Cast iron.
Valve gear: Side valve L-head. Helical timing gears.
                Tappet clearance: 0.004″ cold.
                Camshaft end float: 0.008″ to 0.010″.
Carburettor: Horizontal Zenith
                Jet sizes: Main 70 or 75. Compensating 75.
Ignition: Magneto: American Bosch type NU 4, Dixie type 40 A or Thomson-Bennett type AD 4 C.
                Sparkling plugs: American Bosch.
Firing order: 1, 3, 4, 2
Lubrication: Plunger type pump fitted to centre main bearing plumber block. Main bearings pressure fed. Big-ends splash fed by troughs and dippers. One oil breather at the front above the timing gears. One combined breather and oil filler on the nearside of the crankcase.
Cooling: Thermo-syphon assisted by a fan driven by a flat belt from the camshaft. Radiators by Doherty Motor Components Ltd. or Randle (both of Coventry).
Exhaust system: Three ports from the block to a ribbed manifold with rear exit.

CLUTCH AND GEARBOX

Makers: The Detroit Gear Company.
Clutch: Two Ferodo lined plates running dry.
Gearbox: Three speeds and reverse in unit with the clutch and engine. Cast aluminium housing.
Overall ratios: Top—direct—4.42 : 1
                2nd   —7.6 : 1
                Bottom   —14.13 : 1
                Reverse —17.2 : 1
Gear change: Central ball change.

TRANSMISSION

Universal joint: Bronze centre piece with steel spiders.
                Totally enclosed in a housing carried on the gearbox.
Propeller shaft: Enclosed by torque tube.

REAR AXLE

Construction $\frac{3}{4}$ floating. Welded single piece banjo.
                Spiral bevel crown wheel and pinion.

Final drive ratio:	4.42 : 1 (53/12)
	Some cars had 4.75 : 1 (57/12)

CHASSIS

Front axle:	Elliott type.
Front springs:	Half elliptic.
Rear springs:	Three quarter elliptic, slung under the rear axle.
Steering gear:	Worm and full spur wheel in a steel box mounted on the chassis frame.
Brakes:	Rear wheels only. Internal expanding with four shoes per drum of 11″ diameter. Central lever with button ratchet applies one pair of shoes per drum and right hand rectangular pedal operates the other set. Brake rods slung under the rear axle.
Wheels:	3 stud detachable pressed steel artillery.
Tyres:	700 mm. × 80 mm. Dunlop (85 mm. or 90 mm. section tyres available at extra cost).

COACHWORK

Types available:	Two seater.
	Four seater.
	Coupé.
	Cabriolet.
Upholstery:	Light chocolate-grey leather.
Body colour:	Light chocolate-grey with chassis, wheels, valances and mudguards black.

ACCESSORIES

Lamps:	Lucas electric. Two side lamps fitted to brackets on the Auster windscreen. Two head lamps. One tail lamp.
Dynamo:	6 volt Lucas mounted by a steel bracket on the cylinder head. Driven by a flat belt from the fan pulley. Fan mounted eccentrically for belt adjustment.
Battery:	6 volt.
Horn:	Bulb.
Self starter:	None.

PRINCIPAL DIMENSIONS

Wheelbase:	8′ 6″
Track:	4′ 0″
Sump capacity:	8 pints.

PRICES—Continental engined Cowleys

	Apr. 1915	Sep. 1915	Oct. 1915	Mar. 1916
Chassis			£178–10–0	
Two seater	£165–18–0	£163–16–0	£194–5–0	£199–10–0
Four seater	£194–5–0	£192–3–0	£222–12–0	£222–12–0
Coupé				£435–0–0
Cabriolet				

	Aug. 1916	Apr. 1917	Apr. 1918	Feb. 1919
Chassis			£255–0–0	
Two seater	£229–8–6	£295–0–0	£290–0–0	£295–0–0
Four seater	£255–19–9	£310–0–0	£310–0–0	£310–0–0
Coupé				£360–0–0
Cabriolet			£360–0–0	

Hotchkiss and Morris engined Cowleys

ENGINE

Makers:　Hotchkiss et Cie, Gosford Street, Coventry (Jul. 1919 to May 1923).

Morris Engines Ltd., Gosford Street, Coventry (from May 1923).

Cylinders:　4 in line cast en bloc with upper part of crankcase. Detachable cylinder head. Copper asbestos sandwich head gasket.

Composition of cast iron: 3.0% total carbon, 0.4% combined carbon, 2.1% silicon, 0.8% manganese, under 0.1% sulphur and under 0.12% phosphorus. Surface finish of bores: Burnished by rolling to 69.5 mm. +0.05 mm to −0.00 mm with a wall thickness of 5.5. mm.

Crankshaft:　S 26 steel stamping. Ground journals and pins with bronze backed white metal bearings.

Crankshaft bearing diameters: Front main 38 mm.

Centre main 39 mm.

Rear main 40 mm.

Big-ends 35 mm.

Crankshaft—*cont.*	All have tolerances − 0.045 mm. to − 0.070 mm.
	Crankshaft end float – 0.003″.
	Con-rod side clearance – 0.006″.
Flywheel:	57 lb. steel stamping machined to 43 lb.
Sump:	Cast aluminium. Filling and level indicator combined with breather. Starting handle housing cast in unit with sump.
Bore and stroke:	69.5 mm. × 102 mm. (2.914″ × 5.016″).
R.A.C. rating:	11.9 h.p.
Cubic capacity:	1548 cc. (94.470 cu. in.).
Valve gear:	Side valves in L-head. Helical timing gears. Camshaft of S 14 bright drawn steel bar supported in two plain bearings of 50 mm. diameter − 0.06 mm. to − 0.09 mm. Single valve springs. Valves of K10 steel operated by mushroom head tappets, 44 mm. diameter.
	Angle of seat: 45°.
	Stem clearance: 0.004″.
	Tappet clearance: 0.004″ inlet, 0.006″ exhaust (cold).
Ignition:	Helical bevel magneto drive. A.C. sparking plugs.
	1919 —Thomson-Bennett type G4
	1920 —B.T.H.
	1921 to 1923—Lucas E4 or B.T.H. magdyno if no self starter fitted.
	1924 to 1926—Lucas GA 4.
Firing order:	1, 3, 4, 2
Exhaust:	Non-ribbed manifold with central outlet of 1¼″ diameter.
	1919 to Feb. 1922—three port.
	From Feb. 1922 —four port.
Lubrication:	Plunger pump operated by a single lobe on the camshaft. Main bearings and camshaft gear pressure fed. Big-ends and pistons lubricated by dippers fitted to the connecting rods splashing in troughs.
Cooling:	Thermosyphon, fan assisted. 1919 radiators by Randle. Later radiators by Osberton.

GEARBOX AND CLUTCH

Clutch:	Two driven plates, each lined with 26 ¾″ diameter cork inserts, running in oil.
	Driving surfaces: Flywheel, centre ring and rear pressure plate.
	6 clutch springs.

Gearbox:	Three speeds and reverse, in unit with the clutch and engine. Cast aluminium casing. Chromium nickel case hardened gears. Splined shaft ground all over.
Gearbox ratios:	Top—direct—1 : 1 2nd —1.72 : 1 Bottom —3.18 : 1 Reverse —3.88 : 1
Gear change:	Central ball change.

TRANSMISSION

Universal joint:	Bronze ring with forks of S 11 chromium nickel steel. Totally enclosed in spherical housing.
Propeller shaft:	Enclosed by torque tube.

REAR AXLE

Construction:	¾ floating. Welded single piece banjo. Four star wheels. Spiral bevel crown wheel and pinion.
Final drive ratio:	(57/12) 4.75 : 1 Overall ratios:— Top—direct—4.75 : 1 2nd —8.17 : 1 Bottom —15.2 : 1 Reverse —18.5 : 1 Sports Cowley:— (53/12) 4.42 : 1 Overall ratios:— Top—direct—4.42 : 1 2nd —7.6 : 1 Bottom —14.13 : 1 Reverse —17.2 : 1

CHASSIS

Front axle:	Elliott type with pin and bush track rod ends on two wheel brake cars. Reversed Elliott type with ball joint track rod ends on f.w.b. cars.
Front springs:	Half elliptic. Plus 2 rebound leaves on f.w.b. cars.
Rear springs:	Three quarter elliptic slung below the rear axle.
Shock absorbers:	1919 to 1922—None. 1923 and 1924—Gabriel Snubbers £6-6-0d. extra. 1925 and 1926—Gabriel Snubbers standard.
Steering gear:	Worm and full spur wheel in a steel box mounted on the cylinder block. 16″ diameter three spoke steering wheel.
Rear wheel brakes:	9″ diameter drums. Four internal expanding shoes per drum. One set of shoes operated by the central handbrake and the other by the foot pedal. Brake rods above the rear axle.

Front wheel brakes:	1926 season only as an optional. 9″ diameter drums. 2 shoes per dum. Rod operated. Compensated.
Wheels:	Three stud detachable pressed steel artillery.
Tyres:	1919 to 1922—Two seater 700 mm. × 80 mm. Dunlop Magnum. Four seater 700 mm. × 80 mm. Dunlop Magnum Cord.
	1923—Two seater 700 mm. × 80 mm. Dunlop Clipper Cord. Four seater 28″ × 3½″ Dunlop Clipper Cord.
	1924—28″ × 3½″ Dunlop Cord.
	1925—19″ × 3½″ wheels. 27″ × 4.40″ Dunlop Cord Balloon tyres.
	1926—19″ × 3½″ wheels. 27″ × 4.40″ Dunlop Reinforced Balloon tyres.

COACHWORK

Colours:
Mudguards, valances, hub caps, chassis and lamps—Black.
Body—2 seater 1919 to 1925: Grey.
2 seater 1926: Grey or blue.
4 seater 1920 to 1925: Grey.
4 seater 1926: Grey or Blue.
Occ. 4 1924 & 1925: Grey.
Occ. 4 1926: Grey or blue.
Sports Cowley: Polished aluminium.
Fixed head coupé: Blue.
2 door saloon: Blue.
Commercial traveller's car-: Undercoat.

ACCESSORIES

Radiator thermo-Meter:	1919 to 1923—None. 1924 and 1925—Boyce MotoMeter Gem model. 1926—Wilmot Calormeter.
Windscreen:	By Auster Ltd. of Birmingham or G. Beaton & Son Ltd. of London. Two piece screen standard in 1925 & 1926.
Lamps:	1919 to 1923—Two Lucas electric lamps on the front mudguards. One Lucas electric rear lamp.
	1924 to 1926—Two Lucas electric side lamps on the front mudguards. Two Lucas headlamps on stalks on the dumb irons. One Lucas tail lamp. One Lucas dash lamp.

Electrics and self
starter: 1919 to 1921—No self starter. 6 volt B.T.H. mag-
                            dyno.
                            1922 to 1923—6 volt B.T.H. magdyno standard.
                            Lucas type E 4 magneto with 12 volt
                            Lucas dynamotor type A 900 option-
                            al extra.
                            1924 to 1926—12 volt Lucas dynamotor type A 900
                            standard.
                            Battery on nearside running board.
Horn: Bulb.
Instruments: Smith speedometer, Lucas ammeter and Eureka
                            oil pressure gauge. (0–10 lb./sq. in.).

PRINCIPAL DIMENSIONS
Wheelbase: 1919 to 1926—8'–6"
                            1927—8'–9"
Track: 4'–0"
Overall length: 2 str—12'–6"
                            4 str—12'–9"
Overall width: 4'–10"
Ground clearance: 8½"
Width of frame: 2'–0"
Turning circle: 1919 to 1926—rt. hand : 38' 6" lt. hand: 36' 0"
                            1927—rt. hand: 40' 6" lt. hand: 40' 2"
Weights (cwt.):

	chassis	2 str.	4 str.	Occ. 4	Coupé	saloon
1919 to 1922		13¾	15½			
1923		15¾	16½			
1924		17½	18	18		
1925		16½	17	16½		
1926	10¾	17	18¼	16¾		
(with fwb)1926	11¼	17½	18¾	17¼	18¼	18¾

Water capacity (pints):

	Radiator	Cylinder block	Total capacity
1926	18	$11\frac{1}{2}$	$29\frac{1}{2}$
1927	$11\frac{1}{4}$	$11\frac{1}{2}$	$22\frac{3}{4}$

Oil capacity: (pints):

Sump	Clutch	Gearbox	Rear axle
6	2	$1\frac{1}{2}$	$2\frac{1}{2}$

Petrol capacity: (gallons):

Scuttle tank	Shell can on running board
5	2

Hotchkiss and Morris engined 11.9 h.p. and 13.9 h.p. Oxfords

As for Cowleys with the following exceptions:—

ENGINE

A larger engine was offered as an alternative from January, 1923 and as standard equipment on Oxfords from September, 1924:—

Bore and stroke: 75 mm. × 102 mm. (2.953″ × 4.016″).

R.A.C. rating: 13.9 h.p.

Cubic capacity: 1802 cc. (111.070 cu. in.).

Ignition: K.L.G. type G 2 sparking plugs.

GEARBOX AND CLUTCH

Clutch: Two driven plates, each lined with 36 cork inserts $\frac{3}{4}″$ diam. running in oil.

REAR AXLE

Final drive ratio: (57/12) 4.75 : 1   Overall ratios:—

Top—direct—4.75 : 1

2nd   —8.17 : 1

Bottom   —15.2 : 1

Reverse   —18.5 : 1

Oxford Sports axle ratio—4.07 : 1

9′–0″ wheelbase cars had a pinion with a wider taper.

CHASSIS
  Shock absorbers: 1919 to 1922—None.
                     1923 to 1926—4 Gabriel Snubbers standard.
  Steering gear: 16″ diameter 4 spoke steering wheel.
  Brakes: Brake drum diameter: 12″ on f.w.b. cars.
                     1925: Four wheel brakes standard. Two wheel brakes optional.
                     1926: Four wheel brakes standard.
  Wheels: 1919 to 1922   28″ × 3½″
                         1923   28″ × 3½″ Goodyear.
                         1924   28″ × 3½″
                     1925 and 1926 19″ × 3½″ but 20″ × 4″ on saloon and cabriolet.
  Tyres: 1919 and 1920 710 × 90 Dunlop.
                     1921 to 1924   28″ × 3½″ Dunlop Magnum on 2 str.
                                    28″ × 3½″ Dunlop Magnum Cord on 4 str.
                     1925 and 1926 28″ × 4.95″ Dunlop Cord Balloon but
                                    30″ × 5.25″ Dunlop Cord Balloon on saloon and cabriolet.

ACCESSORIES
  Lamps: Barker dipping headlamps standard for 1926.
  Electrics and self starter: 1919 and 1920 Lucas dynamotor fitted above the crankcase.
                     1921 to 1926 Lucas dynamotor fitted on nearside of gearbox.
  Radiator thermometer: 1919 to 1923—None.
                     1924 and 1925—Boyce MotoMeter.
                          1926—Wilmot Calormeter.
                     1926 models had a "Thermet" thermostatic water-flow controller in the top hose.

PRINCIPAL DIMENSIONS
  Wheelbase: 1919 to 1924   8′ 6″
                     1925 and 1926 9′ 0″
                         1927   8′ 10½″
  Turning circle: 1926—rt. hand 40′ 6″   lt. hand 39′ 0″
                     1927—rt. hand 40′ 4″   lt. hand 41′ 4″

COACHWORK
COLOURS OF OXFORDS

	1919 to 1921	1922	1923	1924	1925	1926
2 seater	Sage Green Elephant Grey	Green Elephant Grey Blue Bronze	Green Grey Blue Claret	Bronze Green Grey Dark Blue Claret	Bronze Green Grey Blue Claret	Brown Grey Blue Claret
4 seater	Ditto	Ditto	Ditto	Ditto	Ditto	Ditto
Coupé	Ditto	Green Elephant Grey Blue	Ditto	Green Grey Dark Blue Claret Saxe Blue	Ditto	Ditto
Cabriolet			Ditto	Bronze Green Grey Dark Blue Claret	Ditto	Ditto
Saloon				Ditto	Ditto	Ditto
Landaulet						Blue
¾ Coupé						Brown Grey Blue Claret
Saloon Landaulet						Brown

Weight (cwt.):

	Chassis	2 str.	4 str.	coupé	saloon	cabrio-let	land.
1919 to 1921	10½	15½	16¾	16½			
1922	10½	17	17½	17¼			
1923	11¼	17½	18¼	18¼			
1924	11¼	17½	19	18½	19½	19¾	
(with fwb) 1925	12½	19¾	21	21	23	22	23¼
(with fwb) 1926	12½	19¼	20¼	21¼	21¾	22¼	23¼
1927	14½	19¼	20¼	21¼			

Water capacity (pints):

	Radiator	Cylinder block	Total capacity
1926	26¼	10¼	36½
1927	19½	10¼	29¾
Empire model	20	13	33

Petrol capacity (gallons):

	Scuttle tank	Can on running board.
1919 to 1923—	6	None
1924 to 1926—	7	2

The M.G. Super Sports Morris Oxford (1924, 1925 & 1926)

As for the 13.9 h.p. Oxfords with the following exceptions:—

ENGINE

Cooling: Radiator badge as illustrated on page 140.

Carburettor: 1924 and 1925—S.U.
1926—Solex type MHD 30 mm.
Jet sizes: Main—115 MC
Choke—23
Pilot—None fitted

Compression ratio: 5 : 1

CLUTCH AND GEARBOX

Gear change: Gear lever bent down to clear the low dashboard

BULLNOSE PRICES   Note: Blanks indicate model not available.

		Aug 1919	Dec 1919	Mar 1920	Oct 1920	(1st price cut) 9 Feb 1921
Cowley	2 seater	£315	£330	£390	£465	£375
	4 seater				£525	£425
	Sports					£398-10-0
	Chassis					
	Occ. Four					
	Fixed Head Coupé					
	Two door Saloon					
	Commercial Traveller's Car					
Oxford (4 cyl.)	2 seater	£360	£380	£450	£535	£510
	4 seater	£390	£415	£495	£590	£565
	Coupé	£450	£475	£560	£675	£595
	Chassis	£335	Not quoted	£385	Not quoted	Not quoted
	Cabriolet					
	Sports chassis (No starter)					
	Saloon					
	Landaulet					
	¾ Coupé (4 side windows)					
	Saloon Landaulet					

Oct 1921	Sep 1922	22 Oct 1922	Oct 1923	Sep 1924	Sep 1925	Jan 1926
£299-5-0[1]	£278-5-0	£225[2]	£198	£175	£162-10-0[7]	£162-10-0[7]
£341-5-0	£315	£255[3]	£225	£195	£182-10-0[7]	£182-10-0[7]
£351-15-0	£315					
£282-9-0	£252	£175[3]	£160[5]	£145	£135[7]	£135[7]
			£215	£185	£172-10-0	£172-10-0
					£195	£195
		[2] £30 extra for starter, dickey seat and instruments [3] £20 extra for starter and instruments			£235	£235
[1] £14-14-0 extra for starter and single dickey		[4] £25 extra for 13.9 h.p.	[5] £5 extra for 4 str.	[6] £10 less for no F.W.B.	[8] £10 extra for saloon and cabriolet chassis [7] £7-10-0 extra for F.W.B.	£177-10-0[7]
£414-15-0	£383-5-0	£330[4]	£300	£260[6]	£240	£240
£446-5-0	£409-10-0	£355[4]	£320	£285[6]	£260	£260
£500	£446-5-0	£390[4]	£255	£305[6]	£285 Leather £15 extra	
£304-10-0	£273-5-0	£220[4]	£195	£185[6]	£172-10-0[8]	£172-10-0[8]
		£425[4]	£385	£365[6]	£330	£330
		£195[4]				
			£395	£385[6]	£350 Leather £20 extra	£350
					£360	£360
					£295	£295
						£385

REAR AXLE

Final drive ratio: (53/12) 4.42 : 1 standard.   Overall ratios:—
Top—direct—4.42 : 1
2nd   —7.6 : 1
Bottom   —14.13 : 1
Reverse   —17.2 : 1

CHASSIS

Shock absorbers: Front—Gabriel Snubbers
Rear —Duplex Hartfords

Steering gear: Steering box mounted on a special bracket on the cylinder block above the chassis frame to give a sharply raked steering column, with a special 17″ diameter steering wheel.

Brakes: 1926—Clayton Wagons Ltd., Lincoln
Dewandre B-type vacuum servo.
Handbrake on the right.

Springs: Number of leaves: Front—8
Rear —7 (8 on Salonette)
Length: Front—31½″
Rear —47″
Width: 1¾″

Wheels: Three stud detachable Dunlop wire or artillery with Ace aluminium discs. Two spares on the salonette.

Tyres: 710 mm. × 90 mm. Dunlop Cord (60 lb/sq.in.) or 28″ × 4.95″ balloon on the salonette.

Accelerator pedal: To the right of the brake pedal.

COACHWORK

Makers: Carbodies Ltd. of Coventry.

Construction: 1924—Panelled in aluminium throughout.
1925 and 1926—Usually lower portion of the body panelled in aluminium and upper part of bonnet and scuttle and mudguards in steel. A few were steel throughout.

Standard colours: 1924—Polished aluminium or smoke blue.
1925 and 1926—Smoke blue or claret.
Special colours available to order.
Cellulose £18 extra on salonette.

Bodies available: 1924—2 seater (11.9 h.p.)
4 seater.
1925—2 seater.
4 seater.
4 seater Salonette with vertical back portion to the body.

Bodies available   1926—2 seater.
—*cont.*   4 seater.
                          4 seater Salonette with vertical back portion
                          to the body.
                          Salonette with a tail compartment.

ACCESSORIES
Horn: Klaxette.
  Speedometer: Smith 0-80 m.p.h.
  Ventilators: Two cowl type "Cruiser" on scuttle.
  Lamps: Two round dashlamps made by Homa Eng. Co. of
                          Whetstone, Leicester.
  Battery: 12 volt, 63 amp. hr. under driver's seat.
  Windscreen: Sloping two or three piece with triangular side sup-
                          ports.

PRINCIPAL DIMENSIONS
  Overall length: 2 and 4 seater—12' 8"
                          Salonette—12' 10"
  Overall width: 2 and 4 seater—5' 0"
                          and Salonette
  Height (hood up):   5' 5"
  Weight: chassis—13¼ cwt.
                          2 seater—18 cwt.
                          4 seater—18½ cwt.
                          Salonette—21 cwt.
  Petrol capacity: 5 gallons (Cowley tank).
  Body width: 1925 and 1926 models 2" wider than 1924 models.

PRICES—
The M.G. Super Sports Morris Oxford (1924, 1925 and 1926).

	2 str.	4 str.	4-seater salonette	Salonette with tail compartment
1924	*£350	£395	—	—
1925	£350	£375	£475	—
1926	£345	£360	£495	£450

*11.9 h.p. "M.G. Super Sports Morris" with adjustable seat and single dickey.

For the 1926 season—extras available:—
  Extra spare wheel, tyre and carrier, 710 × 90 Dunlop Cord, £8 18s. 9d.
Painted number plates, 15s. 0d. Aluminium number plates, £1 10s. 0d.
Tonneau cover, £2 10s. 0d. Special upholstery, £3 0s. 0d. Special paintwork,

£2 10s. 0d., excluding the more expensive lake colours and bronze finishes, for which special quotation were given. Dunlop re-inforced Balloon tyres, 27 × 4.4, cover and tube per set of five, £25 7s. 6d. Dunlop wire wheels to suit, per set of five, £11 18s. 9d. (no allowance was made for the 710 × 90 wheels and tyres fitted as standard). Steel artillery type wheels, per set of five, £7 15s. 0d. Ace discs, per set of five, £4 10s. 0d. Revolution counter, £7 10s. 0d., plus fitting. Gradient meter, £3 15s. 0d. Aluminium wings, £4 10s. 0d. Fibre mats, front £1 5s. 0d.; rear 10s. 0d. Right hand gear change, £12 0s. 0d. Spot lights from £2 7s. 0d. Three-fold luggage carrier, £3 15s. 0d. Eural steering wheel horn switch, £1 1s. 0d. Pyrene fire extinguisher, nickel, £3 0s. 0d.; brass, £2 15s. 0d.

The F-type "Silent" Six (1921 to 1926)

ENGINE

Makers:	Hotchkiss et Cie, Gosford Street, Coventry.
Cylinders:	6 in line, cast en bloc with a detachable head.
Bore and stroke:	69.5 mm. × 102 mm. (2.914″ × 4.016″).
R.A.C. rating:	17.9 h.p.
Cubic capacity:	2320 cc. (141.583 cu.in.).
Crankshaft:	Desaxé, 3 white metal main bearings in bronze shells.
Connecting rods:	Steel forgings.
Pistons:	Aerolite with two compression rings and one expander ring inside the skirt. Gudgeon pins clamped by the little ends.
Auxiliary drives:	Either—Twin inverted toothed chain in a V formation driven from the front of the crankshaft, one chain to the magneto on the offside and the other chain to the camshaft on the nearside of the cylinder block.
	Or —Camshaft driven by helical timing gears from the front of the crankshaft and the magneto by a skew gear and cross-shaft.
Valve gear:	Side valve L-head. Four bearing camshaft with a small flywheel at the extremity remote from the driving gear to damp vibrations.
Ignition:	Lucas magneto on the offside.
Carburettor:	Smith five-jet. Some cars were fitted with exhaust heated aluminium inlet manifold (see page 115).
Lubrication:	Main bearings, the four camshaft bearings and auxiliary drives supplied by oil from a plunger type pump driven by a single lobe on the camshaft. Splash feed to big-ends with sheet steel dippers.
Cooling:	Thermo-syphon assisted by a three bladed fan.

CLUTCH AND GEARBOX

Clutch:
: Two driven plates, each lined with 26 ¾" diameter cork inserts, running in oil.
Driving surfaces: Flywheel, centre ring and rear pressure plate.

Gearbox:
: Three speeds and reverse, in unit with clutch and engine. Cast aluminium casing. Chromium nickel case hardened gears. Splined shaft ground all over.

Gearbox ratios:
: Top—direct—1 : 1
2nd   —1.72 : 1
Bottom   —3.18 : 1
Reverse   —3.88 : 1

Gear change:
: Central ball change.

TRANSMISSION

Universal joint:
: Bronze ring with forks of S 11 chromium nickel steel. Totally enclosed in spherical housing.

Propeller shaft:
: Enclosed by torque tube.

REAR AXLE

Construction:
: ¾ floating. Welded single piece banjo. Four star wheels. Spiral bevel crown wheel and pinion.

Final drive ratio:
: 3.5 : 1   Overall ratios:—
Top—direct—3. 5 : 1
2nd   —6.02 : 1
Bottom   —11.1 : 1
Reverse   —13.6 : 1

CHASSIS

Front axle:
: Elliott type with pin and bush track rod ends. Forged steel, girder section.

Front springs:
: Half elliptic.

Rear springs:
: Half elliptic fitted above the rear axle.

Steering gear:
: Worm and full wheel in a steel box mounted on the cylinder block.

Shock absorbers:
: Four Hartfords.

Brakes:
: On rear wheels only. 9" diameter drums. Four internal expanding shoes per drum. One set of shoes operated by a central hand lever and the other by the round foot pedal. Brake rods fitted above the rear axle.

Wheels:
: 765 mm. × 105 mm. Dunlop R.A.F. type detachable wire spoked.

Tyres:
: 765 mm. × 105 mm. Dunlop Cord.

ACCESSORIES

Horn:
: Bulb and electric.

Lamps: Two electric side lamps on front mudguards.
                        Two headlamps on stalks on dumb irons.
                        One tail lamp.
                        One dash lamp.
Self starter: 12 volt Lucas dynamotor type A 900.
Electrics: Lucas throughout.

PRINCIPAL DIMENSIONS
Wheelbase: 9' 3"
Track: 4' 0"
Weights (cwt.):

Chassis	2 str.	4 str.	cabriolet	sports
14	19¼	21½	22¼	19¼

PRICES—The F-type "Silent" Six (1921 to 1926)

	Chassis	2 str.	4 str.	cabriolet
1923	£375	£475	£500	£575
1924	£325	£440	£460	£525

The 15.9 h.p. Oxford

ENGINE
Makers: Morris Engines Ltd., Gosford Street, Coventry.
Cylinders: 4 in line, cast en bloc with detachable head.
Crankshaft: Three bronze backed white metal main bearings.
Bore and stroke: 80 mm. × 125 mm. (3.15" × 4.92").
R.A.C. rating: 15.9 h.p.
Cubic capacity: 2513 cc. (153.362 cu.in.)
Pistons: Aluminium alloy with duralumin rods.
Ignition: Lucas magneto, on nearside of engine. K.L.G. sparking plugs. Ignition control on steering column.
Firing order: 1, 3, 4, 2
Auxiliary drives: Camshaft —By spiral gear from crankshaft.
                        Ignition —By Simms vernier coupling from rear of dynamo.
                        Tyre pump—By spiral gear from camshaft.
                        Dynamo —By spiral gear from camshaft.
Exhaust: Ribbed manifold with rear outlet.
Lubrication: The two camshaft bearings, mains and big-ends fed from plunger type pump driven from single lobe on camshaft.

Cooling:	Thermo-syphon assisted by a four-bladed fan. Calormeter.
Carburettor:	S.U. with Autovac.

CLUTCH AND GEARBOX

Clutch:	Single dry plate.
Gearbox:	Four forward speeds and reverse.
Gear change:	Central ball change.
Gearbox ratios:	Top—direct—1 : 1
	3rd —1.7 : 1
	2nd —2.4 : 1
	Bottom —3.5 : 1
	Reverse —4.45 : 1

TRANSMISSION

Universal joint:	Bronze centre piece with steel spiders. Totally enclosed in a spherical housing on the gearbox.
Propeller shaft:	Enclosed by torque tube.

REAR AXLE

Construction:	¾ floating. Overhead worm drive. Ratio 4.5 : 1

CHASSIS

Front axle:	Reversed Elliott.
Front springs:	Half elliptic.
Rear springs:	Half elliptic.
Brakes:	Internal expanding in 12″ diameter drums. Brake rods fitted above both axles.
Wheels:	21″ × 4″ detachable steel artillery. 5 stud.
Tyres:	31″ × 5.25″ Dunlop Reinforced Cord Balloon.
Shock absorbers:	Four Smiths.

ACCESSORIES

Horn:	Lucas bulb and electric.
Lamps:	5 Lucas lamps with Barker dipping headlamps.
Self starter:	Lucas with Bendix drive.
Dynamo:	Lucas on near-side of engine.
Tyre pump:	Maxwell. Driven forward of timing gear cover.
Instruments:	Clock, ammeter, oil pressure gauge and 0-60 m.p.h. speedometer.
Battery:	12 volt. In cradle inside the frame.
Radiator thermometer:	1927 and 1928—Wilmot Calormeter. 1929—Wilmot Calormeter with wings.

COACHWORK

Body styles:	5 seater tourer. Saloon. Fabric saloon for 1929 season only.

Colours: 5 str.—1927 and 1928—Blue, maroon, grey or brown.

                                    1929—wine-maroon cellulose duotone with claret antique leather, blue-black cellulose doutone with blue antique leather or deep maroon-bronze cellulose duotone with brown antique leather.

Saloon—1927 and 1928—Blue, maroon, grey or brown.

                                    1929—wine-maroon cellulose duotone, stone-brown cellulose duotone or deep maroon-bronze cellulose duotone.

All with brown furniture hide.

Fabric saloon—Body covered in brown fabric with upholstery in natural grain furniture hide.

Seats: 5 str.—Front: semi-bucket separately adjustable.

Saloon—Front: bench type adjustable.

Body fittings: 5 str—Nickel plated automatic windscreen wiper. Rectangular outside mirror.

Saloon and fabric saloon—Nickel plated automatic windscreen wiper.

Inside and outside mirrors.

Roof light.

Smoker's companion.

Roller blinds to rear and all side windows.

Roof parcel net.

Robe rail on back of front seat.

Roof ventilator.

Polished mahogany panelling.

PRINCIPAL DIMENSIONS

Wheelbase:	9' 6"
Track:	4' 8"
Overall length:	14' 11"
Overall width:	5' 10"
Overall height:	6' 2"
Ground clearance:	10"

Weight complete: 5 seater tourer—26¾ cwt.
                    Saloon   —28 cwt.
                    Fabric saloon —28 cwt.
Petrol: Tank at the rear. 10 gallon capacity.
                    One gallon reserve tap. Gauge on the tank.

PRICES—The 15.9 h.p. Oxford

	1927	1928	1929
Chassis	£245	£225	£210
5 seater	£325	£315	£295*
Saloon	£375	£345	£310*
Fabric saloon	—	—	£320*

*with Triplex glass £5, £15 and £10 extra respectively.

PRICES—Morris-Leon-Bollée

Year	Series	Maker's h.p.	Engine	Chassis (fr.)	Complete (fr.)
1926	M	10	72 × 120 × 4	28,500	
	MLB	12	80 × 120 × 4		
1927	M	10	72 × 120 × 4	29,000	
	MLB	12	80 × 120 × 4	34,000	
1928	MLB	12	80 × 120 × 4	26,900	33,900
	MLB "Luxe"	12	80 × 120 × 4	30,000	
	8D	18	70 × 100 × 8	71,300	
1929	MLB	12	80 × 120 × 4		from 37,500
	MLB "Luxe"	12	80 × 120 × 4	30,000	42,500
	15CV	15	74 × 103 × 6	35,000	47,500
	8R1	18	70 × 100 × 8	71,300	on order
	8R3	18	70 × 100 × 8	77,000	on order
1930	MLB "Luxe"	12	80 × 120 × 4	30,000	from 42,500
	T3	15	74 × 103 × 6	42,500	from 55,000
	R3	18	70 × 100 × 8	74,000	on order
	R4	28	70 × 100 × 8	80,000	on order
	T1	12	80 × 120 × 4	33,000	on order

Manufacturer: Sociéte Française des Automobiles Morris-Leon-Bollée,
                              Les Sablons, Le Mans (Sarthe).

FLATNOSE COWLEY PRICES

	1927	1928	1929	1930	1931	1932	1933	1934
Cowley 11·9 h.p.			EXTRA FOR TRIPLEX					
Chassis RWB for 8cwt van	£122-10-0							
,, ,, ,,	£130	£130						
2 str. RWB*	£148-10-0	£142-10-0†	£160 + £2-10-0†	£162-10-0	£160	£165	£165	£140
,, ,,	£160							
4 str. RWB*	£158-10-0	£152-10-0†			£170			
,, ,,								
¾ coupé fixed head	£172-10-0	£170	£175 + £3-10-0	£180	£180	£190	£190	
,, folding ,,	£182-10-0	£175	£180 + £5	£185	£185			
,, sliding ,,								
Sports coupé sliding head			£190 + £7-10-0	£195	£190	£215	£215	£195
Special ,, ,,	£195			£200				
Saloon 2 door		£177-10-0				£179-10-0	£179-10-0	£199-10-0
4 ,, fixed head		£185			£185	£185	£185	
4 ,, folding ,,								
4 ,, sliding ,,								
Comm. Trav. car RWB	£165	£167-10-0	£167-10-0	£210	£199	£195		
,, ,, saloon	£175							
8cwt. van RWB	£160	£165	£165	£165	£160	£160	£160	
,, ,,	£172-10-0							
					wire wheels £3-10-0 extra			
Cowley 13·9 h.p.			EXPORT ONLY 8" wider track. 4 str. and 4 door saloon					
2 str.						£165		
Saloon 4 door fixed head						£179-10-0		
4 ,, sliding ,,						£185		
Coupé sliding head						£190		
Sports coupé sliding head						£215		
Comm. Trav. car						£195		
8/10 cwt. van						£160	£160	£160

* No speedo, clock, gaiters, wiper, calormeter, driving mirror, shock absorbers & combined side and headlamps

†Includes handwiper

FLATNOSE OXFORD PRICES

	BODY AND UPHOLSTERY	1927	1928	1929	EXTRA FOR TRIPLEX
Oxford 14 h.p.	Chassis (open cars)	£156-10-0			
	,, (closed cars) (stiffer springs)	£161-10-0			
	2 str. (leather)	£220	£210	£200	+ £5
	4/5 str. 4 door (leather)	£240	£225	£215	+ £5
	¾ coupé (cloth)			£225	+ £10
	,, ,, (leather) folding head	£245	£230	£230	+ £10
	Saloon (moquette)	£265			
	,, (leather)		£250		
	Saloon de luxe (leather)		£275	£265	+ £12-10-0
	,, steel body (cloth)			£240	+ £12-10-0
	,, ,, ,, (leather)		£250	£247-10-0	+ £10
	Fabric saloon (leather)			£255	+ £10
	Cabriolet (leather)	£295			
	Saloon landaulet (brown furniture hide)	£325			
	Traveller's brougham		£285	£245	
Oxford 11·9 h.p.	4/5 str. 4 door (karhyde leather)		£205		
	Saloon 4 door (,, ,,)		£215		

Appendix 3

Production Figures and Miscellaneous Data

Page   Contents

White & Poppe Engined Oxfords

Standard Models   *De Luxe Models*

	1913	1914	1915
JAN	—	4	15
FEB	—	8	2
MAR	1	12	22
APR	9	8	2
MAY	40	13	3
JUN	50	2	2
JUL	55	5	0
AUG	48	0	0
SEP	51	1	3
OCT	40	11	9
NOV	31	4	3
DEC	27	12	—
	352	82	61

	1913	1914	1915	1916	1917
JAN	—	74	30	2	—
FEB	—	94	13	4	—
MAR	—	113	19	—	1
APR	—	97	10	—	—
MAY	—	114	5	4	—
JUN	—	130	3	2	—
JUL	1	89	5	—	—
AUG	—	9	1	—	—
SEP	—	11	7	1	—
OCT	1	22	3	—	—
NOV	5	29	2	—	—
DEC	34	45	0	—	—
	41	827	98	13	1

Notes: Total Standard Models: 495
           Total De Luxe Models: 980
           Standard Model Chassis Numbers range from 101 to 593
           De Luxe Model Chassis Numbers range from 1001 to 2000
           Engine Numbers range from 5769 to 8278
           32 known survivors

Continental Engined Cowleys

	1915	1916	1917	1918	1919	1920
JAN	—	73	0	20	25	1
FEB	—	70	0	17	19	—
MAR	—	46	6	34	54	—
APR	—	32	7	13	51	—
MAY	—	22	3	13	49	—
JUN	—	63	7	13	36	—
JUL	—	99	12	10	33	—
AUG	—	94	19	11	4	—
SEP	12	119	27	16	4	—
OCT	26	33	19	16	4	—
NOV	62	24	16	23	2	—
DEC	61	9	9	12	0	—
	161	684	125	198	281	1

Notes: Total: 1450
Chassis Numbers range from 3001 to 4485
Engine Numbers range from 10001 to 11999
5 known survivors

F-type Oxford "Silent" Six

	1921	1922	1923	1924	1925	1926
JAN	—	—	—	6	—	—
FEB	—	—	1	8	—	—
MAR	—	—	1	2	—	—
APR	—	—	—	3	—	—
MAY	—	—	2	6	2	—
JUN	—	—	1	2	—	1
JUL	—	—	—	3	1	—
AUG	—	—	—	—	—	—
SEP	—	—	2	—	—	—
OCT	1	—	1	—	—	—
NOV	—	1	2	—	—	—
DEC	—	—	4	—	—	—
	1	1	14	30	3	1

Notes: Total : 50
Prototype has Chassis number 9641 Engine Number 16462
Other Chassis Numbers range from F101 to F149
Other Engine Numbers range from 101 to 188
1 known survivor

Sports Cowleys

	1921	1922
JAN	—	3
FEB	—	—
MAR	1	5
APR	1	4
MAY	14	4
JUN	20	6
JUL	9	4
AUG	10	5
SEP	7	4
OCT	1	1
NOV	4	—
DEC	4	—
	71	36

Notes: Total 107
Chassis Numbers range from 7398 to 15006
Engine Numbers range from 12191 to 22821
1 known survivor

M.G. PRODUCTION FIGURES

1925 season			
	Built in 1924	Built in 1925	Total
4 str.	3	90	93
2 str.	3	33	36
salonette	0	6	6
	6	129	135

1926 season			
	Built in 1925	Built in 1926	Total
4 str.	14	107	121
2 str.	5	60	65
salonette	3	12	15
	22	179	201

	1925 & 1926 Total
4 str.	214
2 str.	101
salonette	21
	336

Notes: Two or three 1924 season 11.9 h.p. and 13.9 h.p. M.Gs were
built early in 1924

"Empire Oxford"

	1926	1927	1928	1929
JAN	—	7	68	55
FEB	—	135	35	9
MAR	—	160	90	11
APR	—	203	35	8
MAY	—	123	30	22
JUN	—	120	12	30
JUL	—	70	17	7
AUG	—	16	6	—
SEP	—	91	1	—
OCT	—	126	11	—
NOV	—	57	73	—
DEC	1	60	53	—
	1	1168	431	142

Notes: Total: 1742
Chassis Numbers range from EO.101 to EO.1841
Engine Numbers range from 1848 to 16774
4 known survivors

BULLNOSE PRODUCTION FIGURES   (*Based on dates despatched from the works*)

	1913	1914	1915	1916	1917	1918	1919	1920	1921	1922	1923	1924	1925	1926
JAN	—	78	45	75	0	20	25	65	68	263	1398	1662	4373	4091
FEB	—	102	15	74	0	17	19	78	244	508	1433	2597	3617	3416
MAR	1	125	41	46	7	34	54	77	377	802	1860	3520	4702	5774
APR	9	105	12	32	7	13	51	125	376	216	1737	3360	5191	4830
MAY	40	127	8	26	3	13	49	192	359	234	2083	2772	5595	3542
JUN	50	132	5	65	7	13	36	160	341	323	2097	2221	4853	4897
JUL	56	94	5	99	12	10	34	308	243	801	1831	2315	5879	4612
AUG	48	8	1	94	19	11	5	163	197	871	636	989	2197	767
SEP	51	12	22	120	27	16	5	244	239	521	1762	3103	5143	77
OCT	41	33	38	33	19	16	10	288	191	332	1878	3657	5867	118
NOV	36	33	67	24	16	0 23	35	131	234	887	1975	3820	3838	44
DEC	61	57	61	9	9	12	37	102	208	1179	1334	2923	2896	15
	393	907	320	697	126	198	360	1932	3077	6937	20024	32939	54151	32183

NOTES: Total: 154244

Chassis Nos. 594–1000 not used

Chassis Nos. 2001–3000 not used

First Chassis No. 101

Last Chassis No. 156424

The above production figures include chassis F101 to F149

Dotted lines enclose war production

The above figures are for Bullnose models only and exclude flat radiator models produced in 1926

August production low due to works holiday

ENGINES MANUFACTURED BY WHITE AND POPPE LTD. *Between 27.8.07 (No. 2428) and 28.4.27 (No. 20850)*

Engine	1907	1908	1909	1910	1911	1912	1913	1914	1915	1916	1917	1918	1919	1920	1921	1922	1923	1924	1925	1926	1927
80 × 85 × 1		3	1																		
80 × 90 × 1	2	13	3	11	4	2															
85 × 85 × 1			250	249	27																
100 × 110 × 1		3																			
80 × 90 × 2	19	7	16	8																	
80 × 90 × 3	3	10	12	1																	
60 × 90 × 4							528	394	8												
65 × 90 × 4														5	2						
80 × 90 × 4	62	80	27	19										2	1						
80 × 130 × 4			43	388	114		58	29	11					1	10	1					
80 × 142 × 4					1	1															
80 × 149 × 4					2	2															
85 × 110 × 4																					
85 × 120 × 4	6	140		3	3																
90 × 110 × 4		57	251	146		13	2										4	26	338	1102	468
90 × 130 × 4	1		39	252		195	114	56	2	1					11	56					
100 × 110 × 4	1															26	3				
100 × 130 × 4		25	10	2						3											
100 × 150 × 4							19	18	14												
105 × 150 × 4																					
110 × 130 × 4	5	26	51	31		112	126	64		1				98	108	214	261	424	412	252	96
110 × 150 × 4							1	79	350	45		18		48			1	1	7		
115 × 150 × 4								44		846	1265	1322	1114	927	90	142	176	570	472	86	4
120 × 130 × 4	29	27	8	13	29	33	32	38													
127 × 130 × 4	27	5	22	25	34	34	47	22						1	3	18	13			1	
127 × 150 × 4							1	594	248												1

Engine	1907	1908	1909	1910	1911	1912	1913	1914	1915	1916	1917	1918	1919	1920	1921	1922	1923	1924	1925	1926	1927
127 × 180 × 4					39	46	38	2	40	21	17	30	22	47	15	30	29	32	20		6
80 × 90 × 6		6	1																		
127 × 130 × 6				2	10																
127 × 150 × 6					6	11	18	3	4	4	2	2									
140 × 150 × 6					1	6	4														
EXPERIMENTAL TWO STROKE ENGINES															1	3					

Year	1923	1924	1925
Morris production	20024	32939	54151
*Total U.K. private car production	71396	116600	132000
Morris as a %age of the total	28.1	28.2	41

* From S.M.M.T.

Note: Total British motor vehicle production (private and commercial) for 1913 was 34000.

Total Morris production for 1913 was 393 or 1.15% of the total.

11·9 h.p. ENGINE

ENGINE NO.	PISTON DETAILS	CONNECTING ROD DETAILS	GUDGEON PIN DETAILS
12001 (16 Sep 1919) to 66930 (Sep 1924)	CAST IRON. 3 and 4 ring pattern. 18½ oz.	STEEL. Clamp little end.	16 mm. fixed.
66931 (Sep 1924) to 73100 (3 Nov 1924)	ALUMINIUM. Morris taper. 2 ring. Top thin section with special spring steel ring underneath. Second ring of ordinary pattern 9½ oz.	AS ABOVE	AS ABOVE
73101 (31 Oct 1924) to 120934 (26 Aug 1925)	AS ABOVE	STEEL. Little end of solid section, bored and phospher bronze bushed.	20 mm. fully floating Cave-Baker fixing device.
120935 (Aug 1925) to 150049 (8 Feb 1926)	AS ABOVE	AS ABOVE	Cave-Baker fixing device superceded. Brass rubbing pieces fitted to ends.
150050 (2 Mar 1926) to 164807 (23 Apr 1926)	As above but gudgeon pin bosses have central support and are widened as made possible by the new type of con-rod. 10 oz.	STEEL. Clamp little end to take 20 mm. fully floating gudgeon pin. Extra oil hole drilled at base of H-section and above big-end. Improved method of fitting brass liners into con-rod end cap, and the sandwiching of the thin brass foil adjusting shims between 2-17g. steel shims on either side.	AS ABOVE
164808 (Apr 1926) to 196138 (Jan 1927)	AS ABOVE	AS ABOVE but less sharply recessed above big end bolt head to give added strength.	AS ABOVE

13·9 h.p. ENGINE

ENGINE NO.	PISTON DETAILS	CONNECTING ROD DETAILS	GUDGEON PIN DETAILS
23182 (1 Jan 1923) to 23591 (13 Feb 1923)	CAST IRON 3 rings 20½ oz.	STEEL. Clamp little end. 16 mm. pin.	16 mm. fixed.
41331 (10 Oct 1923) to 67420 (Sep 1924)	ALUMINIUM. Split skirt. Aerolite, 3 rings at the top. 1 ring inside the skirt. 8½ oz.	DURALUMIN. (a) 16 mm. pin.	16 mm. fully floating. Aluminium rubbing pieces fitted to ends.
(b) 67421 (Sep 1924) to 78481 (15 Dec 1924)	As above but rectangular recesses about gudgeon pin holes to accommodate Cave-Baker device. 2 rings.	AS ABOVE	As above but aluminium rubbing pieces dropped and Cave-Baker gudgeon pin fixing device substituted.
78482 (19 Dec 1924) to 120934 (26 Aug 1925)	ALUMINIUM. Morris taper. 2 rings. Top ring thin section, with special spring steel ring underneath. Second ring of ordinary pattern 10 oz.	As above but 20 mm. pin.	Diameter increased to 20 mm. Cave-Baker gudgeon pin fixing device modified to suit.
120935 (Aug 1925) to 192961 (Jan 1927)	AS ABOVE	AS ABOVE	Cave-Baker device dropped and brass rubbing pieces inserted in ends of gudgeon pin.

NOTES: (a) An aluminium alloy containing as its main constituents copper and magnesium, but also having important though small proportions of silicon and manganese. The total proportion of alloying elements is about 6%.

(b) Except the following which have Morris taper pistons: 74416, 76339, 76341, 76380, 76381 and 76387.

CARBURETTORS

SEASON	1913 & 1914	1915 & 1916	1917 & 1918	1919, 1920 & 1921	1922	1923	1924	Early 1925	Late 1925 & 1926
COWLEY	—	Zenith	Zenith	Zenith	SU sloper Type G2 M4 or No 1 needle	Smith single jet model 26 H.K.M.C. jet 110	Smith single jet 130 fitted at works fit 110 from tool kit after 500 miles model 26 H.K.M.C. jet 110	Smith 4MO 5-jet well—17 or 20 1—25 or 20 or 22 2—22 or 27 3—15 4—10	Smith straight-through 5-jet slow running—15 1—17—16* 2—20—20 3—17—15 4—10—10
OXFORD	W & P No 25	W & P No 25	—	Zenith	SU sloper Type G2 M4 or No 1 needle	Smith HSVO 5-jet well—17 or 20 1—25 or 22 2—22 or 27 3—15 or 17 4—10	Smith 4MO 5-jet well—17 or 20 1—25 or 22 2—22 or 27 3—15 or 17 4—10	Smith straight-through 5-jet Slow running—15 1—17 2—20 3—17 4—10	Smith straight-through 5-jet Slow running—15 1—17—16* 2—20—21 3—17—15 4—10—12
M.G.	—	—	—	—	—	—	SU sloper	Solex type MHD 30 mm. choke—23 main jet—115 mc no pilot jet	Solex type MHD 30 mm. choke—23 main jet—115 mc no pilot jet

* This weaker jet setting, which gives better fuel consumption, depends on the closing of the extra air valve hole to No 1 choke.
This hole is the one nearest to the float and is only present on the earlier Smith 5-jet carburettors.

RETAIL PRICES: SU — £6-0-0
SMITH 4MO — £4-4-0
SMITH SINGLE JET — £3-3-0
SMITH STRAIGHT-THROUGH — £3-10-0

Period Addresses of Works: White & Poppe Ltd., Lockhurst Lane, Foleshill, Coventry.
Zenith Carburettor Company Ltd., 40–44 Newman St. London W.1.
The SU Carburettor Company Ltd., Shipton Works, Prince of Wales Rd, Kentish Town, London N.W.5.
S. Smith & Sons (M.A.) Ltd., Cricklewood Works, London N.W.2.

LUCAS DYNAMOTORS

TYPE	MOUNTING	USED ON	NON-DRIVE ENDSHIELD	CONNECTIONS	BRUSH ADJUSTMENT	STALLED TORQUE lb. ft.	MAXIMUM OUTPUT AMPS (COLD)	ROTOR SLOTS	MAIN POLES	COMMENCES TO CHARGE AT (RPM)
A400	Above gearbox	1919 and 1920 Oxfords	Pressed steel cover	Leads brought out through ebonite plate on frame	Only small brush adjustable	27	9–12	parallel with rotor	skewed	850 to 1000
A400	Nearside of gearbox	1921 & 1922 Oxfords and Cowleys	Ditto	Ditto	Ditto	Ditto	Ditto	Ditto	Ditto	Ditto
A900	Ditto	1923 & 1924 Oxfords and Cowleys	Ditto	Ditto	Ditto	18	8–9	Ditto	Ditto	1500 to 1550
A900C	Ditto	1925 Oxfords and Cowleys	Cast steel	Ebonite terminal strip on frame	Ditto	Ditto	Ditto	skewed	parallel with frame	Ditto
A900T	Ditto	1926 Oxfords and Cowleys	Pressed steel	Ditto	All brushes adjustable	Ditto	Ditto	Ditto	Ditto	Ditto
A900R	Ditto	1927 & 1928 Oxfords and Cowleys	Cast steel	All terminals separate. Negative insulated.	Only small brush adjustable	Ditto	Ditto	Ditto	Ditto	Ditto
A900R	Ditto	1929 & 1930 Oxfords and Cowleys	Ditto	All terminals separate. Negative NOT insulated.	Ditto	Ditto	Ditto	Ditto	Ditto	Ditto

NOTES: (a) In 1924 the A400 cost £20 retail and the A900 cost £13-7-6d. retail.
(b) Rotor slots are skewed to cut down magnetic noise.
(c) Charging rate is reduced when the small brush is moved clockwise looking at the non-drive end.

WHITE AND POPPE ENGINES

SIZE	RAC h.p.	LUBN.	OIL CAPACITY	COOLING	CYLDRS.	VALVES	TYPE OF BOSCH MAG.	CARB. TYPE	CRANK-CASE	REMARKS
80 × 85 × 1	3·97	Splash	½ pt.	Air	Indivl.	T	HT Coil			Motor cycle engine. Peculiar detachable valve seats.
80 × 90 × 1	3·97	"	¾ pt.	Thermo Syphon	"	T			Cast Iron	For marine or stationary use. Marine version cooled by Albany pump. Used by Ariel and Premier.
85 × 85 × 1 / 100 × 110 × 1	4·5 / 6·5	"	½ pt.	Air	"	T / L				For marine and stationary use.
80 × 90 × 2	7·94	Splash	1 pt.	Thermo Syphon	Indivl.	T	D2		Alum.	Used by Clyde, Fairfax, Horley, Singer and Swift.
80 × 90 × 3	11·9	Splash	1½ pt.	Thermo Syphon	Indivl.	T	DR3		Alum.	Used by Clyde, Horbick, Singer and Swift.
60 × 90 × 4	8·92	Splash		Thermo Syphon	En bloc	T			Alum.	Only W & P engine built in unit with gear-box. Used exclusively by Morris.
60 × 100 × 4	8·92			Thermo Syphon	"				"	Long stroke version of 60 × 90 × 4 for proposed 4 seater Oxford.
69 × 100 × 4	11·9	Pump		"	"	L				Never left the drawing board. Designed for the Cowley.
80 × 90 × 4 / 80 × 120 × 4	15·87 / 15·87	Splash / Pump	2 pt.	"	Indivl. / En bloc	T / See Remarks	DR4		"	Inclined ohv operated by single camshaft in crankcase. Never made. For proposed post war W & P car.
80 × 130 × 4	15·87			"	In pairs	L		No. 25	"	See 100 × 130 × 4 remarks. Designed to replace the 80 × 90 × 4.
80 × 149 × 4	15·87			"	"	See Remarks			"	Overhead inlet. 2 side exhaust. 3 built for 1912 Coupe de l'Auto Singers. Development of 80 × 130 × 4.
85 × 110 × 4 / 90 × 110 × 4 / 90 × 130 × 4	17·9 / 20·89 / 20·89			"	" / " / "	T / T / L	DU4	No. 25 / No. 25	" / "	Built up crankcase. Used by Dennis. Used by Dennis, Singer and Withers. See 100 × 130 × 4 remarks. Used by Dennis and Singer.
100 × 110 × 4	24·8	1908 Splash Post '08 Pump	1908 3 pt.	Pump	Indivl.	L	DR4		"	Used by Singer.
100 × 130 × 4	24·8	Pump		Thermo Syphon	In pairs	L		No. 30	"	Only dimensional differences from 80 × 130 × 4 and 90 × 130 × 4.
100 × 150 × 4 / 110 × 130 × 4	24·8 / 30·01	"		Pump	indivl.	L / T	D4		"	Used by Singer and Dennis. Used by Dennis and Withers. Claimed to produce 1½ b.h.p. extra and cost 1/− less for 1911 season. Crankshaft machined from the solid.
110 × 150 × 4	30·01			"	In pairs	T			"	To subsidy specification, i.e. magneto, governor, big-end inspection plates, etc.
120 × 130 × 4	35·71	"		"	Indivl.	T	D4		"	Used by Dennis and Withers. Claimed to produce 1 b.h.p. extra and cost 1/− less for 1911 season. Crankshaft machined from the solid.
127 × 130 × 4 / 127 × 150 × 4	39·92 / 39·92	"		"	"	T / T			" / "	Used by Dennis.
80 × 90 × 6	23·81	Splash	3 pt.	Thermo Syphon	Indivl.	T	DR6		Alum.	Used by Calthorpe, Climax, Heron, Horbick and West.
127 × 130 × 6 / 127 × 150 × 6	59·92 / 59·92	Pump		Pump	Indivl.	T / T	DR6		"	Used by Dennis. Only dimensional differences from 140 × 150 × 6.
140 × 150 × 6	72·9	"		"	"	T	DR6		"	Crankshaft forged from solid.

WHITE AND POPPE ENGINES

SIZE	B.H.P. AT NORMAL RPM (SEE NOTE 1)	PRICE WITH MAGNETO (SEE NOTE 2)
80 × 85 × 1	4¼ @ 1660	?
80 × 90 × 1	?	£33-4-0†
85 × 85 × 1	—	?
100 × 110 × 1	8 @ 680	?
80 × 90 × 2	9 @ 1660	£68-18-0*
80 × 90 × 3	13¼ @ 1660	£87-3-0*
60 × 90 × 4	16·4 @ 2400	Approx. £50
60 × 100 × 4	—	—
69 × 100 × 4	18 @ 1660	£103-7-0*
80 × 90 × 4	23·5 @ 1150	£130-0-0†
80 × 120 × 4	21 @ 1360	£119-14-0*
80 × 130 × 4	27¼ @ 1360	£130-0-0†
80 × 149 × 4	27½ @ 1150	£140-0-0†
85 × 110 × 4	32 @ 1360	£131-18-0*
90 × 110 × 4	36 @ 1150	£150-0-0*
100 × 130 × 4	—	?
100 × 130 × 4	40 @ 1150	£198-1-0*
100 × 150 × 4	44 @ 1100	£198-1-0*
110 × 130 × 4	50 @ 1150	?
110 × 150 × 4	59 @ 1180	?
120 × 130 × 4	74 @ 1180	
127 × 130 × 4		
127 × 150 × 4		
80 × 90 × 6	27 @ 1660	£152-5-0*
127 × 130 × 6	95 @ 1180	Approx. £500
127 × 150 × 6	108 @ 1000	£500-0-0†
140 × 150 × 6		

NOTES

(1) B.H.P. figures are quoted at normal rpm, *not* maximum.

(2) Prices marked thus * are those for 1909 and † for 1911 season.

(3) All W & P engines with magneto ignition had Bosch magnetos.

(4) All W & P engines had W & P carburettors as standard.

(5) All W & P engines had white metal main and big-end bearings other than the 80 × 90 × 1, 90 × 110 × 4 and 100 × 110 × 4 which had phosphor bronze ones.

(6) Under the heading "oil capacity" the amount quoted is the minimum quantity of oil which must be present in the crankcase.

W & P CARBURETTORS—TABLE OF SIZES

FOR DIFFERENT ENGINES: will take up to bore shown below.

No.	1 cyl.	2 cyl.	3 cyl.	4 cyl.	6 cyl.	8 cyl.	PRICE
25	79	79	79	79	65	56	£6-0-0
30	95	95	95	95	77	67	£6-15-0
40	127	127	127	127	103	89	£7-0-0
50	158	158	158	158	129	112	—

BULLNOSE CHASSIS NUMBERS

	1913	1914	1915	1916	1917	1918	1919	1920	1921	1922	1923	1924	1925	1926
JAN	—	1150	1918	3260	—	4032	4205	5161	7197	10461	18983	38976	75609	129464
FEB	—	1218	1933	3312	—	4044	4243	5267	7498	11128	20448	41997	79511	132820
MAR	101	1393	1987	3366	3881	4058	4346	5384	7837	11850	22328	45503	84120	138485
APR	112	1449	2000	3385	4081	4074	4395	5449	8212	11886	24156	49359	89018	143717
MAY	186	1600	3003	3418	3937	4083	4474	5649	8560	12161	26073	51731	94355	146966
JUN	204	1717	1998	3553	3925	4101	4485	5838	8905	12617	28016	54066	99446	151975
JUL	255	1777	1994	3649	3928	4121	5002	6180	9102	13442	30028	57054	105324	156355
AUG	301	1765	1951	3718	3941	4130	5003	6372	9288	14401	30801	57411	107857	156420
SEP	353	1785	3014	3790	3943	4138	5001	6576	9536	14970	32986	60686	112767	156421
OCT	417	1802	3038	3827	3960	4153	5024	6886	9756	15157	34723	64373	118649	156419
NOV	1007	1835	3112	3842	3971	4181	5073	7067	9939	16219	36861	68325	122435	156424
DEC	1043	1898	3169	3848	3984	4175	5102	7129	10119	17335	38153	70938	125040	152350

NOTE: The chassis numbers quoted are the last despatched in each month.

1927	1928	1929	1930	1931
COWLEY 11·9 h.p. 69·5 × 102 mm. 1548 cc. SV. G3	COWLEY 11·9 h.p. 69·5 × 102 mm. 1548 cc. SV. G3	COWLEY 11·9 h.p. 69·5 × 102 mm. 1548 cc. SV. G3	COWLEY 11·9 h.p. 69·5 × 102 mm. 1548 cc. SV. G3	COWLEY 11·9 h.p. 69·5 × 102 mm. 1548 cc. SV. G3
OXFORD 14/28 h.p. 75 × 102 mm. 1802 cc. SV. G3	OXFORD 14/28 h.p. 75 × 102 mm. 1802 cc. SV. G3	OXFORD 14/28 h.p. 75 × 102 mm. 1802 cc. SV. G3		
OXFORD 15·9 h.p. 80 × 125 mm. 2513 cc. SV. G4	OXFORD 15·9 h.p. 80 × 125 mm. 2513 cc. SV. G4	OXFORD 16/40 h.p. 80 × 125 mm. 2513 cc. SV. G4		
	OXFORD 11·9 h.p. 69·5 × 102 mm. 1548 cc. SV. G3			
		MINOR 8 h.p. 57 × 83 mm. 847 cc. o.h.c. G3	MINOR 8 h.p. 57 × 83 mm. 847 cc. o.h.c. G3	MINOR 8 h.p. 57 × 83 mm. 847 cc. o.h.c. G3
	SIX 17·7 h.p. 69 × 110 mm. 2468 c.c. o.h.c. G3	SIX TYPE JA 17·7 h.p. 69 × 110 mm. 2468 cc. o.h.c. G3	ISIS SIX 17·7 h.p. 69 × 110 mm. 2468 cc. o.h.c. G3	ISIS SIX 17·7 h.p. 69 × 110 mm. 2468 cc. o.h.c. G3
			OXFORD SIX TYPE LA 14·9 h.p. 63·5 × 102 mm. 1938 cc. SV. G3	OXFORD SIX 14·9 h.p. 63·5 × 102 mm. 1938 cc. SV. G3 (Large Isis Wheelbase)
				MAJOR SIX G3 14·9 h.p. 63·5 × 102 mm. 63·5 × 102 mm. 1938 cc. SV. G3 (Small Cowley Wheelbase)
			LIGHT TRANSPORT 5 CWT VAN 8 h.p. 57 × 83 mm. 847 cc. o.h.c. G3	LIGHT TRANSPORT 5 CWT VAN 8 h.p. 57 × 83 mm. 847 cc. o.h.c. G3
			LIGHT TRANSPORT VAN 11·9 h.p. 69·5 × 102 mm. 1550 cc. SV. G3	LIGHT TRANSPORT LIGHT VAN 14/32 h.p. 75 × 102 mm. 1802 cc. SV. G3
			COWLEY COMMERCIAL LIGHT TRANSPORT TRAVELLER'S SALOON 11·9 h.p. 69·5 × 102 mm. 1548 cc. SV. G3	LIGHT TRANSPORT FIRE TENDER 8 h.p. 57 × 83 mm. 847 cc. o.h.c. G3

1932	1933	1934	1935	1936
COWLEY 11·9 h.p. 69·5 × 102 mm. 1548 cc. SV. G3	COWLEY 11·9 h.p. 69·5 × 102 mm. 1548 cc. SV. G4	COWLEY FOUR 11·9 h.p. 69·5 × 102 mm. 1548 cc.SV. G4S	TWELVE FOUR 11·9 h.p. 69·5 × 102 mm. 1548 cc. SV G4S	TWELVE FOUR 11·9 h.p. 69·5 × 102 mm. 1548 cc. SV. G3S
FAMILY EIGHT 8 h.p. 57 × 83 mm. 847 cc. o.h.c. G3				TEN FOUR SERIES II 10 h.p. 63·5 × 102 mm. 1292 cc. SV. G3S
COWLEY 14/32 h.p. 75 × 102 mm. 1802 cc. SV. G3	TEN 10 h.p. 63·5 × 102 mm. 1292 cc. SV. G4	TEN FOUR 10 h.p. 63·5 × 102 mm. 1292 cc. SV. G4S	TEN FOUR 10 h.p. 63·5 × 102 mm. 1292 cc. SV. G4S	
MINOR 8 h.p. 57 × 83 mm. 847 cc. SV. G3	MINOR (2 wheelbases available) 8 h.p. 57 × 83 mm. 847 cc. SV. G4 (G3 on 2 str. optional)	MINOR (2 wheelbases available) 8 h.p. 57 × 83 mm. 847 cc. SV. G4S	EIGHT 8 h.p. 57 × 90 mm. 918 cc. SV. G3S	EIGHT SERIES I 8 h.p. 57 × 90 mm. 918 cc. SV. G3S
ISIS SIX 17·7 h.p. 69 × 110 mm. 2468 cc. o.h.c. G4	ISIS SIX 17·7 h.p. 69 × 110 mm. 2468 cc. o.h.c. G4	ISIS SIX 17·7 h.p. 69 × 110 mm. 2468 cc. o.h.c. G4S	ISIS EIGHTEEN SIX 17·7 h.p. 69 × 110 mm. 2468 cc. o.h.c. G4S + Freewheel & Bendix Clutch	EIGHTEEN SERIES II 17·7 h.p. 69·5 × 102 mm. 2288 cc. SV. G3S
OXFORD SIX 14·9 h.p. 63·5 × 102 mm. 1938 cc. SV. G4	OXFORD SIX 16 h.p. 65·5 × 102 mm. 2062 cc. SV. G4	OXFORD SIX 16 h.p. 65·5 × 102 mm. 2062 cc. SV. G4S	OXFORD SIXTEEN SIX 16 h.p. 65·5 × 102m m. 2062 cc. SV. G4S + Freewheel & Bendix Clutch	SIXTEEN SERIES II 16 h.p. 65·5 × 102 mm. 2062 c.c. SV. G3S
MAJOR SIX 13·9 h.p. 61·25 × 102 mm. 1803 cc. SV. G4	MAJOR SIX 13·9 h.p. 61·25 × 102 mm. 1803 cc. SV. G4	TEN SIX 12 h.p. 57 × 90 mm. 1378 cc. SV. G4S	TEN SIX 12 h.p. 57 × 90 mm. 1378 cc. SV. G4S	TWENTY ONE SIX SERIES II 21 h.p. 75 × 110 mm. 2916 cc. SV. G3S
LIGHT TRANSPORT 5 CWT. VAN 8 h.p. 57 × 83 mm. 847 cc. SV. G3	5 CWT. VAN 8 h.p. 57 × 83 mm. 847 cc. SV. G3	COWLEY SIX 15 h.p. 63·5 × 102 mm. 1938 cc. SV. G4S	FIFTEEN SIX 15 h.p. 63·5 × 102 mm. 1938 cc. SV. G4S	FOURTEEN SIX 14 h.p. 61·5 × 102 mm. 1818 cc. SV. G3S
LIGHT TRANSPORT LIGHT VAN 14/32 h.p. 75 × 102 mm. 1802 cc. SV. G3	LIGHT VAN 14/32 h.p. 75 × 102 mm. 1802 cc. SV. G3		OXFORD TWENTY SIX 20 h.p. 33 × 102 mm. 2561 cc. SV. G4S + Freewheel & Bendix Clutch	
		"25" 25 h.p. 82 × 110 mm. 3485 cc. SV. G4S	TWENTY FIVE 25 h.p. 82 × 110 mm. 3485 cc. SV. G4S + Freewheel & Bendix Clutch	TWENTY FIVE SERIES II 25 h.p. 82 × 110 mm. 3485 e.c. SV. G3S

1937	1938	1939	1940
TWELVE FOUR SERIES II 12 h.p. 69.5 × 102 mm. 1548 cc. SV. G3S (G4S opt. extra)	TWELVE FOUR SERIES III 12 h.p. 69.5 × 102 mm. 1548 cc. o.h.v. G4S	TWELVE FOUR SERIES III 12 h.p. 69.5 × 102 mm. 1548 cc. o.h.v. G4S	TWELVE FOUR SERIES III 12 h.p. 69.5 × 102 mm. 1548 cc. o.h.v. G4S
TEN FOUR SERIES II 10 h.p. 63.5 × 102 mm. 1292 cc. SV. G3S (G4S opt. extra)	TEN FOUR SERIES III 10 h.p. 63.5 × 102 mm. 1292 cc. o.h.v. G4S	TEN FOUR SERIES M 10 h.p. 63.5 × 90 mm. 1140 cc. o.h.v. G4S	TEN FOUR SERIES M 10 h.p. 63.5 × 90 mm. 1140 cc. o.h.v. G4S
EIGHT SERIES I 8 h.p. 57 × 90 mm. 918 cc. SV. G3S	EIGHT SERIES II 8 h.p. 57 × 90 mm. 918 cc. SV. G3S	EIGHT SERIES E 8 h.p. 57 × 90 mm. 918 cc. SV. G4S	EIGHT SERIES E 8 h.p. 57 × 90 mm. 918 cc. SV. G4S
EIGHTEEN SERIES II 17.7 h.p. 69.5 × 102 mm. 2288 cc. SV. G3S (G4S opt. extra)			
SIXTEEN SERIES II 16 h.p. 65.5 × 102 mm. 2062 cc. SV.			
TWENTY ONE SIX SERIES II 21 h.p. 75 × 110 mm. 2916 cc. SV.			
FOURTEEN SIX SERIES II 14 h.p. 61.5 × 102 mm. 1818 cc. SV. G3S (G4S opt. extra)	FOURTEEN SIX SERIES III 14 h.p. 61.5 × 102 mm. 1818 cc. OHV G4S	FOURTEEN SIX SERIES III 14 h.p. 61.5 × 102 mm. 1818 cc. OHV. G4S	FOURTEEN SIX SERIES III 14 h.p. 61.5 × 102 mm. 1818 cc. OHV. G4S
TWENTY FIVE SIX SERIES II 25 h.p. 82 × 110 mm. 3485 cc. SV. G3S	TWENTY FIVE SIX SERIES III 25 h.p. 82 × 110 mm. 3485 cc. OHV. G3S	TWENTY FIVE SIX SERIES III 25 h.p. 82 × 110 mm. 3485 cc. OHV. G3S	TWENTY FIVE SIX SERIES III 25 h.p. 82 × 110 mm. 3485 cc. OHV. G3S

Note: G = Number of gears
      S = Synchromesh

261

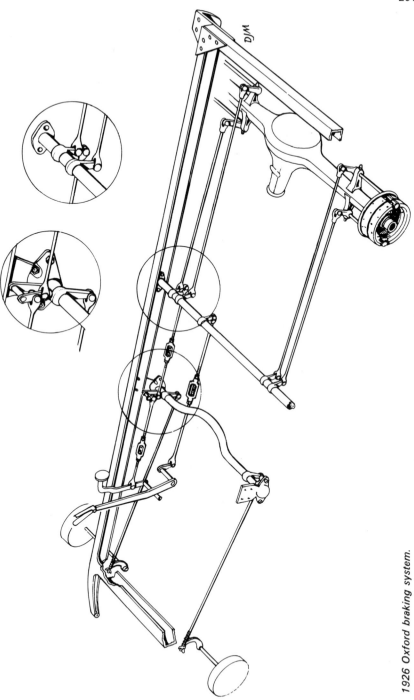

1926 Oxford braking system.

262

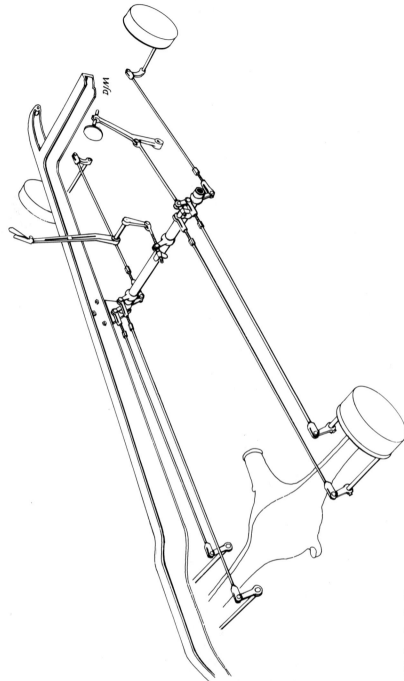

1931 Cowley braking system.

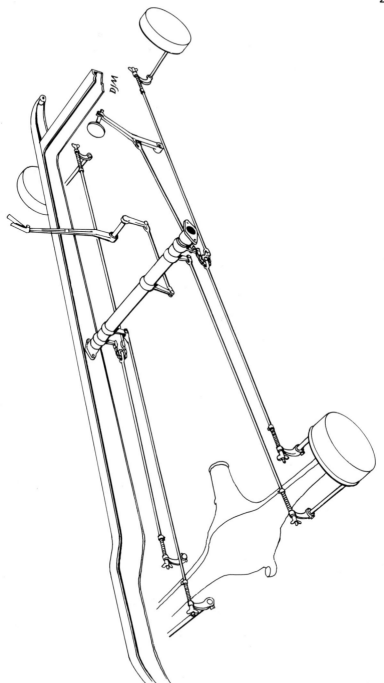

DJM

1929 Cowley braking system.

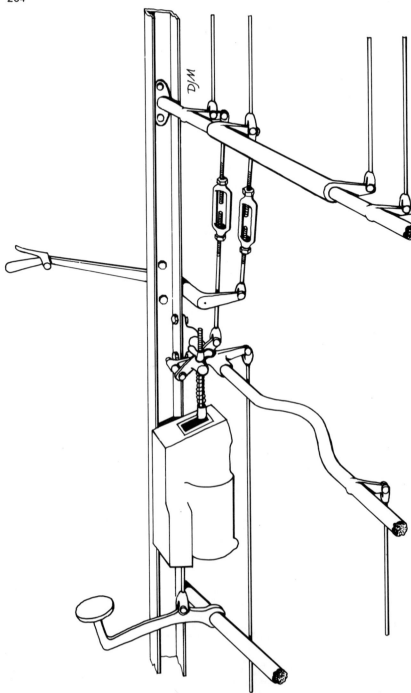

1926 M.G. braking system.

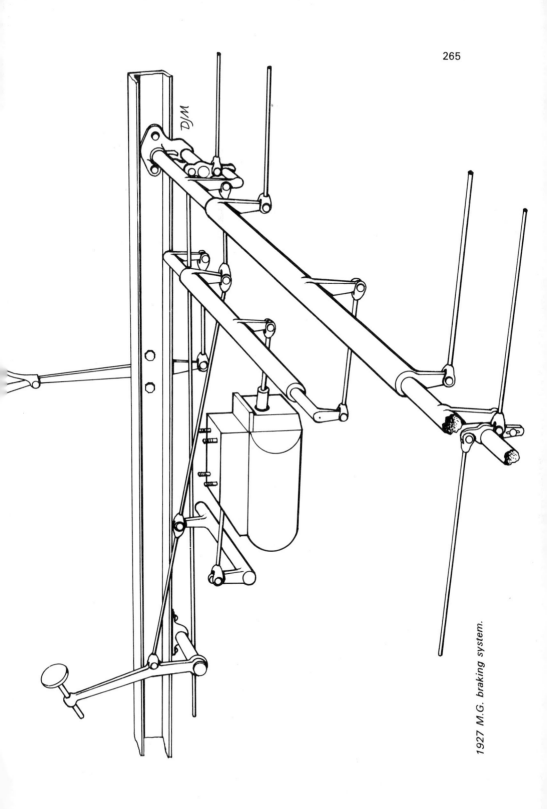

1927 M.G. braking system.

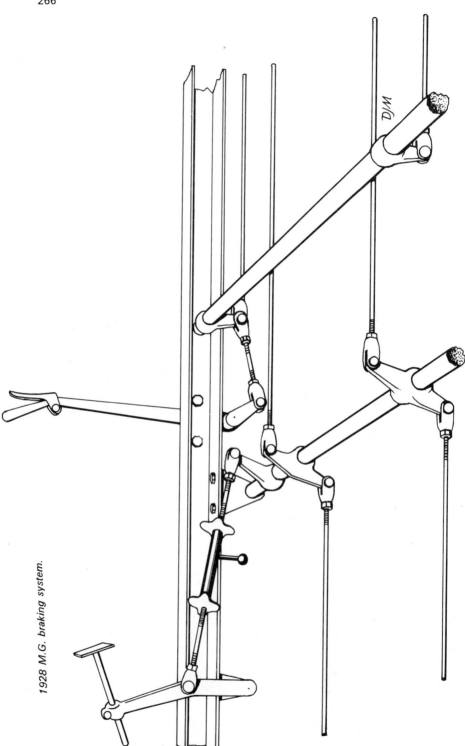

1928 M.G. braking system.

D/M

Index

89, 134, 141; S.U., 143, 151, 181; W & P, 20, 32, 33, 36, 37, 139; Zenith, 43, 89, 113
Carden, 135
Century Motors Co., 104
Chagny, 105
Chalon-sur-Soane, 104
Chandler, 40, 124
Channon, E., 129
Charabancs, 111
Charnock, W. H., 134
Chater-Lea, 15
Chevrolet, 124
Chiesman, C. R. B., 138
Chingford, 56
Christie, Agatha, 167
Chrysler, 150
Chummy bodies, 97, 142, 143
Churchill, Winston, 73, 156
Citroen, 92, 118
Clay Cross, Derbyshire, 65
Clarke, Major A. B. H., 79
Claughton locomotives, 164
Clease, Douglas, 158
Cleveland, 92
Cleveland Varnish Co., 153
Climax, 20, 30
Clutch, cork, 55, 61, 62, 166; Ferodo, 43, 55; maintenance, 193–195; W & P, 22, 24, 36
Clutton, Cecil, 174
Clyde, 20, 30
Clyno, 71, 106, 166
Coatalean, 32
Cockshoot, Joseph, & Co. Ltd, 65
Coffin, Bert, 174
Colmore Depot, 111
Columbia, 40
Continental Automobile Co., 40; engines, 40, 43, 50, 54, 57–62, 162, 165; Motorcars, 40; Motors Company, 39; Motors Manufacturing Company, 38, 39, 40, 41, 50; Motors Corporation, 39, 40
Cooling, 27, 28, 36, 146, 162, 165
Coolridge, President, 40
Cooper, Joseph, 16, 17

Cooper, William, 129, 132
Cooper's Mechanical Joints Limited, 79
"Coppernose Connie", 112
Corbit, 40
Corwen, Wales, 170
Cousins, Cecil, 136
Coventry, 29, 58, 59, 60, 61, 70, 71, 79, 82, 94, 107, 109, 128, 136, 173, 174
Coventry Climax Engines, 71
Coventry Motor Fitments, 58
Cowford, 174, 175
Craig-ne-Baa, I.O.M., 129
Cranham, H. W., 20, 24, 64
Crickmay, J., 142
Cross Street, Oxford, 19
Cubitt, 67, 68
Cuffley 33
Cugenot, 60
Curtis Aircraft Factory, 39
Cyclecar (Wrigley), 109
Cyclecar, The, 24, 25, 76, 109
Cylinder heads, Chesterfield o.h.v., 139; Continental, 42, 54, 61; LAP o.h.v., 139; Pope Ricardo, 139; Whatmough, 162
Czechoslovakia, 106

Daily Mail, 103, 104
Daimler, 59, 68, 104
Daniels, Reginald, 27
Darracq, 75
Darracq, Alexandre, 118
Dartford, 81
Davidson, Norman, 138
Davies, A. L., 58
Davis, 112
Day-Elder, 40
De Dion engines, 30, 76, 176
Defiance, 40
Deiseley, 152
Delage, 122
Delahaye, 122
Delaware, 151
Dennis, 20, 31
Dennis Brothers, 33, 59